T5-DID-063

CHRISTIANITY AND THE CLASSICS

The Acceptance of a Heritage

Wendy E. Helleman

Editor

UNIVERSITY
PRESS OF
AMERICA

Lanham • New York • London

BR
128
.G8
C47
1989

Copyright © 1990 by

University Press of America®, Inc.

4720 Boston Way
Lanham, MD 20706

3 Henrietta Street
London WC2E 8LU England

All rights reserved

Printed in the United States of America

British Cataloging in Publication Information Available

Co-published by arrangement with the
Institute for Christian Studies, Ontario, Canada

Library of Congress Cataloging-in-Publication Data

Christianity and the classics : the acceptance of a heritage /
Wendy E. Helleman, editor.
p.   cm. — (Christian studies today)
Includes bibliographical references.
1. Christianity and other religions—Greek.   2. Christianity and other
religions—Roman.   3. Christian literature—Classical influences.
4. Classical literature—Appreciation.   5. Philosophy, Ancient—Influence.
6. Greece—Religion.   7. Rome—Religion.
I. Helleman, Wendy E., 1945–   .   II. Series. ·
BR128.G8C47   1989   261.5—dc20   89-35897 CIP

ISBN 0–8191–7577–3 (alk. paper)
ISBN 0–8191–7578–1 (pbk. : alk. paper)

The paper used in this publication meets the minimum requirements of American
National Standard for Information Sciences—Permanence of Paper for Printed Library
Materials, ANSI Z39.48–1984.   ∞

CHRISTIANITY AND THE CLASSICS

The Acceptance of a Heritage

Table of Contents

Classical Studies and the German Pietists
by Peter C. Erb

**Christianity and the Classics: A Typology
of Attitudes**
by Albert M. Wolters

Contributors

Jan A. Aertsen, who has been a visiting scholar at the Pontifical Institute of Medieval Studies at the University of Toronto, is professor of philosophy at the Free University of Amsterdam.

Theodore S. de Bruyn, after completing doctoral studies at St. Michael's College of the University of Toronto, now teaches at the Atlantic School of Theology in Halifax, Nova Scotia.

Peter C. Erb is professor of religion and culture at Wilfrid Laurier University, Waterloo, Ontario.

Wendy E. Helleman teaches classical languages at Scarborough College of the University of Toronto, after having taught Greek and church history at Asian Theological Seminary and at Alliance Biblical Seminary, both in the Philippines.

William V. Rowe now teaches the history of philosophy at the Institute for Christian Studies in Toronto, after having taught philosophy at The King's College in Edmonton, Alberta.

Donald Sinnema, after completing doctoral studies at St. Michael's College of the University of Toronto, now teaches biblical studies and church history at Trinity Christian College, Palos Heights, Illinois.

Beert Verstraete is professor of classics at Acadia University, Wolfville, Nova Scotia.

Arvin Vos is professor of philosophy at Western Kentucky University, Bowling Green, Kentucky.

Albert M. Wolters teaches biblical studies and classical languages at Redeemer College, Ancaster, Ontario, after having taught the history of philosophy at the Institute for Christian Studies, Toronto.

Introduction

Wendy E. Helleman

Since the Enlightenment and the Romantic Neo-Hellenist revival of interest in classical antiquity, Christianity and the classics have often been regarded as polar opposites, representing respectively authority, revelation, and religion over against reason, enlightenment, and philosophy. The marriage of the two in late antiquity is regarded as a grave error, Clement of Alexandria is accused of compromise, and Tertullian is praised for his realization of the ultimate incompatibility of the partners.[1] Christianity, as a factor in the Roman Empire, would be of little interest for a study of the classics; from the perspective of a study of the origins and early theological writings of Christianity, acquaintance with the classical languages and literature would be restricted to the minimal knowledge of Greek necessary for understanding the New Testament.

Much has changed during the intervening centuries. Intensive study of the church fathers has revealed that even early church leaders like Irenaeus were ready enough to use the rhetorical figures of their education in the pagan schools as they developed arguments against the heretics. And Tertullian was not nearly so antagonistic to the culture of his day as once was supposed; his borrowing from the Stoics in psychology and use of the methods and terminology of legal argumentation in his writings are telling witness of the profound influence of the classical culture on his views.[2]

Within the study of the classics, the Romantic idealization of the "noble simplicity and serene greatness"[3] of ancient Greece inspired classical scholarship which eventually led to the undertaking of massive projects in the study of poetry and prose, history, religion, and philosophy; such studies would draw not only on the available texts but also on the evidence of coins, art works, inscriptions, and papyri to contribute towards the understanding of the text and to present a more unified picture of the ancient world than had been available.[4] The evidence of archaeology has done much to break down the supposed isolation of Greek culture from its "barbaric" neighbors.

The historical understanding of antiquity, *Altertumswissenschaft*, associated especially with names like Mommsen and Wilamowitz took a new interest in periods not previously regarded as significant components of classical antiquity, periods such as the Hellenistic or the late Roman Empire.[5] The older idealistic view of the Greeks as an enlightened people, guided by reason in all their affairs, was to be replaced by a more realistic appraisal of antiquity.[6] In his critique of the older classicism, Nietzsche did not hesitate to point out those aspects of Greek literature or religion which did not agree with a portrayal of their culture as rational; but he also criticized historically-oriented studies as a materialistic accumulation of facts in a desire to compete with achievements in the natural sciences, an overemphasis on technique at the expense of a sober evaluation of the data accumulated.[7]

Positivism and historicism are no longer strong motivating factors in classical studies; Jaeger tried to revive humanism; Marxist dialectical materialism has influenced some scholars.[8] Of greater interest for the present study is the revival in post-war years of a religious interpretation of history, associated with names like K. Löwith, H. Butterfield, or C. Dawson.[9] Renewed interest in the Christian Middle Ages also meant a new look at its roots in late antiquity; where the earlier work of *Altertumswissenschaft* had helped to incorporate the Hellenistic period, the study of late antiquity as a prelude to the medieval period was to contribute toward an integration of the study of early Christianity with that of the Roman Empire.[10]

With the present study we hope to make a contribution to this discussion by investigating the interaction of Christianity and the classics in various periods of the history of our Western civilization, beginning with representative attitudes from the late Roman Empire and ending with Hegel.

A. Purpose and Scope of this Study

The papers included in the present study had their origin in a conference held in June 1984 at the Institute for Christian Studies in Toronto. The speakers at that conference had been asked to address themselves to a number of questions considered essential for clarifying the way in which Christians of the different periods of European history had justified their use of the literary and other cultural remains of the Greco-Roman past, materials which as such were recognized as being of pagan origin. Could (or should) this cultural heritage be successfully integrated with a Christian position?

Our primary aim was to look for *motifs* in the reception of the classical heritage by noteworthy individual Christians or identifiably Christian scholarly circles such as the Pietists. Because of the time span under consideration, it was useful for each of the contributors to locate these writers within their respective historical context and also to identify clearly the nature of the classical heritage which was of interest at that time; although Aristotle exemplified classical antiquity for the scholastics, humanism looked to men like Cicero or Seneca to provide models of classical literature. A certain diversity in approach to the subject was inevitable since we are dealing with a variety of periods and historic positions; uniformity has been maintained by focusing on the motifs which can be found in the writings of Christian scholars and have been specifically grouped in a typology in the final paper.

The search for motifs has also determined the selection of representative groups or individuals to be investigated. Philosophical positions receive considerable attention since in late antiquity Christians were especially challenged by the philosophical schools and, in reflecting on their use of classical authors, often used philosophical arguments based on the Platonists; the positions of both Basil and Augustine were to be echoed many times in subsequent centuries. To keep the scope of this study within manageable limits, we have chosen to start with the Christian church fathers rather than with the roots of their attitudes in the relationship of Hellenistic Judaism to Greek culture.[11] We have not attempted to include Byzantine classicism[12] or manifestations of it among later Greek and Russian Orthodox scholars, nor have we dealt with parallel relationships between Islamic Arabic or Syrian scholarship and the classics.[13] We have been highly selective even within the assigned scope of European scholarship, passing over many interesting medieval thinkers or groups of writers like the Cambridge Platonists. In short we have made no attempt to be exhaustive; nor is this study to be characterized as primarily historical, even though a sketch of the history of classical scholarship in Europe is useful and valid and may well prove to be crucial for a new evaluation of the role of the classics in European education and culture. In the search for motifs we have aimed primarily at giving a clear restatement of the traditional positions in order to examine the material from a new perspective and to provide the basis for a reevaluation of these motifs.

B. Method: Various Approaches
The subject of the relationship of Christianity and the classics can be approached in a variety of different ways. One may take the classical writers as the point of departure or start with Christianity; one may focus on the relationship as one of inevitable tension or regard it as a form of synthesis; one may regard Christianity and the classics as primarily religious phenomena, or deal with them as cultural manifestations.

1. Point of departure
In their attempt to recover a vision of the pristine golden age of Greece, the world of "beautiful harmony"[14] the neo-Hellenists emphasized the recovery of art work and literary texts in their original form, removing evidence of tampering or distortion due to the moralizing approach of Christian scholars. Taking the classics as point of departure in this way, one could conclude that orientalizing thought has muddied the waters;[15] only that which meets the test of "reason" could be included in the canon of classical texts.

Our search for motifs in the relationship of Christianity and the classics, however, means that we begin with the perspective of the Christians on this relationship. Inasmuch as classical works were recognized to have a pagan origin they might be looked upon as a threat, a dangerous element, the fruits of an idolatrous culture, luring one back to the worship of false gods and demons.[16] There were others, however, who regarded classical culture positively, not only from an apologetic perspective but also as the means of becoming educated and of placing such an education in the service of the Christian church, the worship of the true God.[17]

2. Tension or synthesis?

Those who regarded the classical authors as primarily dangerous for Christians would at all costs avoid overt contact as a contamination. At best the Christian should assume the responsibility of purging the alien elements, the most blatantly pagan aspects of the literature. It is of interest to note, however, that even those Christians like Tertullian who were most staunch in asserting a position of antithesis from the perspective of history are found to have assimilated much more of the culture of their time than they might have been willing to acknowledge.

By no means all Christians have regarded the classics with such a negative attitude; there are many examples of Christians who have taken a more positive approach, accepting the classical writers with more or less critical investigation of their claims. In the discussions which form the basis for the present study, we have come to the conclusion that neither a wholesale rejection nor an uncritical acceptance of the classical heritage present truly viable options for the Christian today. But does this mean that the only alternative is to recognize a *synthesis* of Christianity and the classics? Are we to regard the relationship as one of accommodation or compromise? If so, is it still possible to acknowledge the relative integrity of the classical text on the one hand and of the Christian perspective on life on the other?

To begin with, synthesis usually refers to the juxtaposition or union of at least two component parts in the formation of a new entity, a new whole in which the components can no longer be recognized as such; in chemistry simple elements or compounds combine to form a more complex compound, and in logic simple principles of reasoning are combined to lead to a conclusion or application. If a stable bridge or union is to occur in the formation of the new synthesis, a degree of equality or commensurability in the two factors is important.

Can we apply this model for the relationship of Christianity and the classics? Are the component elements in fact comparable or equal? It is significant in this regard that Hegel when he spoke of a synthesis of Christianity and classical views regarded Greek religion as the clearest representation of its culture; the synthesis involved two religions as component elements.[18] We need to ask ourselves whether the relationship between Christianity and the classics as understood in this study is in fact a relationship between

Christian and classical (pagan) religion or between Christian and classical (pagan) culture. In either case a clear choice can be made between the one or the other; if we opt for both, it is inevitably a matter of compromise and accommodation of the one factor with the other.

3. Religion and culture

Beginning with Christianity, we must ask ourselves whether we are dealing primarily with a religion or a culture. When we look at the views of various Christian writers, we are obviously not dealing with a church or denomination as the manifestation of Christianity. Christianity has had a long history, and we do at times identify European or North American culture as "Christian." Nonetheless, it soon becomes clear that Christianity as such cannot be identified with any one particular cultural manifestation. In fact, in the course of history it has been inculturated in many different ways, and has shown an enormous capacity of adaptation as an influential factor in many different countries around the globe.

Christianity stands or falls with the allegiance to Christ and the testimony of him given in the Scriptures. The question, Who is the Christ? lies at the heart of Christianity; other equally basic questions, Who am I? Who is God? How do I relate to God, to my fellow humans, to the world around me? are implicit in that first vital question. These are clearly religious questions and Christianity is primarily to be regarded as a religion. The effects of taking such a religious position are as broad as life itself and will inevitably affect a perspective on life or worldview, as well as having implications for cultural activities, societal relationships, or political structures and for scholarship or philosophical discussions. However, at its core, Christianity is a religion; it means taking a religious position, which results in a religious perspective or worldview.

When we turn to the classics, it is not so clear that we are dealing primarily with a religion or a religious perspective, even though such a religious position may be assumed to play a role for many of the artifacts or literary texts which remain from classical antiquity; the precise religious character of the altar of *Victoria* was much more apparent to Symmachus and the Roman senators of the late fourth century than it would be to us were we to discover it among the buried treasures of Italy today.[19] In studying the classics and classical antiquity, we are primarily concerned with the cultural remains which can be rather precisely dated in history and traced to a particular geographic area around the Mediterranean sea. In the attempt to understand classical antiquity as we move beyond the text to look at the sculpture or paintings, coinage, inscriptions, as well as architectural monuments, we are dealing with cultural artifacts, all of a more or less refined and polished nature according to the use for which they were created. Unlike the objects in the study of nature, whether in biology or even psychology, in the classics we are dealing with cultural forms that are the result of human shaping, refining, the development of skills, whether in language and its expression or in other forms of communication, in the plastic arts, music, or scholarly activities.[20]

There is more to the classics than the investigation of cultural artifacts and literary texts as such; implicit in the reference to Greco-Roman antiquity as "classical" is a specific theory of culture and education. The term *classicus* was introduced in late antiquity to indicate those authors whose works might be regarded as models on the basis of a grammatical criterion for speech or writing; as such it was borrowed from the division of citizens in various ranks, the *classici* as those of the first or highest rank, those who paid taxes, over against the *proletarius* who made no such contribution.[21] A selection of model authors was in turn based on a determination of genres, epic poetry, tragedy or comedy, and the classification of authors according to the genres. The philologists of Alexandria began this work of classification.[22] Only a few authors, like Aeschylus, Sophocles or Euripides, and only their very best works would be received into the canon or catalogue, whether for tragedy, epic, or historical writing. The standards set by these early Alexandrian scholars have had an enormous impact in limiting the texts of the ancient writers which are available to us and have formed the core of the classical tradition as it has been handed on from one generation to the next.

Even in Greco-Roman antiquity it was common to give preference to the older, more ancient writers, the sages, rather than to the new, the more recent and even contemporary authors, especially when looking for models or classics.[23] To be labeled as *novi* would have a pejorative connotation, in a way which may seem strange to us. But for writers to be acknowledged and incorporated in the canon, their works had to be tested by time and proven to be of enduring worth. Such cultural values are especially significant for education, the process by which we pass on the accumulated wisdom and experience of the past and prepare students to take an active and productive part in society whether in the professions, trades, or the arts. Models are important for setting standards and clearly realizable goals, for inspiring the students, and for stimulating excellence in their work.

An education based on the classics as models thus came to be identified with a tendency to look backward to an earlier period, a time of exemplary achievements and worthy accomplishments in art or literature. Even later among the humanists and Romantic Neo-Hellenists we find this tendency to look backwards for models. Erasmus looked back to classical civilization as a golden age, a time of great cultural achievements.[24] Similarly Oetinger considered classical antiquity as part of that golden age at the beginning of time when the revelation of God in nature was as reliable as that of the Scriptures; consequently, the testimony of classical authors, whether or not they were pagans, should be considered closely for the interpretation of God's Word, especially because it too used the Greek language.[25] As a theory of culture, thus, the classics look to the past rather than to the present or future for its utopia or golden age.

Even in antiquity one could challenge or reject the role of the classic models and appeal to the *neoterici;*[26] in the Middle Ages the classical view was rarely challenged. But from the twelfth century such a view was regularly opposed by a view which recognized the need to move on, to progress in the development of national languages and their literature, to go further than the ancients in science, in medicine and biological or zoological analysis, in astronomy and cosmology. In time the inadequacy of the positions and theories of the ancients as a source of knowledge in these areas came to be recognized. Gradually, the entire cultural attitude of looking to the past for models came to be challenged. In our own time with its ongoing changes and continual development in industry and technology, at a pace with which only a few can keep up, we are overwhelmed by the urge to press on, to look to the future, or at best to keep up with the present. We tend to regard looking backward in history as a luxury which we can ill afford.

In the study of the relationship of Christianity and the classics it is important to recognize that with the classics we are primarily concerning ourselves with cultural achievements and a theory of culture and education, whereas we regard Christianity primarily as a religion and a religious worldview. Christianity has certainly influenced European culture, and classical texts also give evidence of a religious perspective. But if we are to regard interaction of Christianity and the classics as a synthesis, we will need to discern carefully the specific religious or cultural aspects which are juxtaposed, accommodated, and even compromised. To the extent that we recognized the primary religious character of Christianity and the nature of the classics to be primarily cultural, we may need to modify our use of the term "synthesis" since the relative integrity of the two poles in the relationship is inevitably lost or threatened in a synthesis.

Classical culture has influenced the Christian church, especially in the direction of favoring an intellectualistic interpretation of religion, emphasizing dogmatic formulations as well as the need for an educated clergy. Christian influence on the reading of classical texts has generally been detected in the moralizing emphasis in reading the text. Where the classics look back to a golden era in Greco-Roman antiquity, Christianity is also anchored in the decisive events of the first century of our era, the life, death, and resurrection of Jesus Christ.

The nature of the synthesis worked out during the centuries covered by this study will receive greater elaboration in each of the particular papers which follow. It should be noted, however, that within Christianity there has also been an anti-intellectual reaction, having its source in part with the monastic movement which felt threatened by pagan cultural values perceived to be invading the church, in part with mysticism and pietism which emphasized the primacy of the experience of renewal in the Christian life over against a conceptualization, an abstract statement of the faith.[27] Within the classics close study of classical antiquity, historical research, and the evidence of archaeological remains have contributed to break down the idealized picture of the harmony, serenity, and beauty of life in the ancient *polis*. The classics no longer dominate education or have an unquestioned role in providing models at the preparatory level. In fact, they share with Christianity a degree of irrelevance in the mainstream of our modern world.

C. Historical Survey

In our historical survey of the way in which the classics were appropriated by Christians as a heritage which they could not ignore, we have begun with the early period of the development of Christianity within the Roman Empire, a period when the fabric of life was still closely interwoven with that of the Greco-Roman environment. The early leaders in the Christian church formulated a number of positions on the relationship between the pagan culture of which they were still a part and product and the new life in Christ as they understood it. Two Christian thinkers, Basil and Augustine, addressed themselves specifically to the revival in the pagan classical tradition of the fourth century A.D.

Basil considered the reading of the pagan authors useful for Christian students if they could recognize in these a portrayal of *arete* (excellence, truth, virtue); this element would help them in their education, defined by Basil as the cultivation of the soul to prepare it for pilgrimage on the road to eternal life. In "Basil's *Ad Adolescentes:* Guidelines for Reading the Classics," W. Helleman shows how Basil's formulation of a qualified acceptance of the study of the pagan authors as a *praeparatio evangelica* paved the way for continued acceptance by Christians of the traditional education in the liberal arts, provided these studies were regarded as giving the students the tools, whether moral or literary, for further study of biblical truth.

Like Basil, Augustine was much influenced by the Platonists and regarded human salvation in terms of a pilgrimage from the present to the eternal life. In "Jerusalem versus Rome: The Religious and Philosophical Context of Augustine's Assessment of the Roman Empire in the *City of God*," T. de Bruyn shows how the distinction between time and eternity, temporal and eternal immutable being, borrowed from Plotinus, becomes a crucial factor in the distinction between the two cities, the earthly and the heavenly. Nonetheless, Augustine is much more radical in his critique of the religion of the Romans, rejecting their polytheism and demonology, and modifies the Platonist view of the soul by asserting that souls too are created and are unable to order the passions of the body without the help of the Mediator. The Neoplatonic view of reality must fit the biblical view of history. The achievement of the empire, the establishment of peace, and even the virtuous deeds of some of its great leaders have only a relative, temporal value.

With his view of the two cities representing two opposing directions, whether in love to god or for human glory, Augustine effectively undermines the political and religious assumptions of the Roman aristocracy; a society which is directed to temporal gains will find that the object of its love cannot sustain it and is bound to perish.

Christian thinkers of the medieval period were further removed from the pagan classical authors. Aquinas responded to the rediscovery of Aristotle in the thirteenth century by making extensive use of his writings in physics, psychology, or metaphysics in the service of a defence of the faith, or of theology. In "As the Philosopher Says: Thomas Aquinas and the Classical Heritage," A. Vos shows how Aquinas appealed to Aristotle to affirm the basic goodness of the natural world, repudiating the Augustinian-Platonic denigration of this world, the temporal order. In philosophy Aquinas recognized the operation of the natural light of reason, for in philosophical investigations one must weigh the evidence, not accepting all on authority alone. But for the basic human desire to know and to return to God, human intellect is as such insufficient and needs the help of supernatural revelation, theology. Philosophy is thus allowed a position of service, as the handmaiden of theology, in much the same way that Basil outlined a preparatory role of the pagan classical authors for the understanding of Christian truth.

In response, J. Aertsen points out that the Platonists do find a place in Aquinas's thinking, alongside Aristotle. This is particularly evident in the motif of the circular movement of all reality from God and returning to him. Aquinas explains the Aristotelian statement, "All men by nature desire to know," by saying that human perfection consists in being united to the source; it is only by the intellect that the knower can be assimilated to the known. Grace enters at this point, not to destroy, but to perfect the natural order where it is inevitably limited in its understanding of God and to lead human beings to their ultimate destinies. Aertsen thus reinforces the assessment of Aquinas's acceptance of the pagan classical tradition in philosophy in terms of the motif of the natural order being perfected by grace.

Many works of classical authors were recovered during the Renaissance. In Erasmus we find an eloquent defender of the role of pagan classical authors, not only in education but also in the cause of the gospel and for renewal in the church and society. His approach to the authors cannot be easily typified, for as B. Verstraete shows in his "Erasmus's Christian Humanist Appreciation and Use of the Classics" the earlier uncritical classicism was modified after the journey to Italy. In early writings like the *Adagia*, classical authors are regarded as providing models for Latin composition and style and treated as a treasure of human knowledge. In the *Antibarbari* he presents the classics as the products of a culture which played a crucial role in God's plan for humankind and defends use of such a heritage by appealing to the biblical motif of the Israelites spoiling the Egyptians. In later works Erasmus shows how useful a training in the classical authors can be for studying the Scriptures, avoiding the excesses of allegorizing interpretation and contributing to sound preaching. If we find in Erasmus's writings echoes of the *praeparatio evangelica* theme, his advocacy of the philological-rhetorical method of exegesis greatly enriched the way the classical heritage could be used in serving the *philosophia Christi* and was to bear rich fruits in the biblical commentaries of John Calvin.

In "Calvin: The Theology of a Christian Humanist," A. Vos shows how the literary education typical of Renaissance humanism, with its focus on the classical texts, influenced Calvin in his approach to the Scriptures and in his interest for writers like Cicero and Seneca, or in the church fathers, rather than Aristotle or the Schoolmen. His commentaries demonstrate a remarkable historical sensitivity; he was able to penetrate the meaning of the text in its original setting quite unlike any medieval commentator before him. Concentrating on exegetical work he was able to revitalize the interpretation of the Scriptures; his rejection of the traditional role of philosophy as the handmaiden of theology, however, hampered him in giving a systematic theological presentation of his teachings. He never did revise the *Institutes*, which started as a simple handbook for faith, into the format of the theological dissertations of the time.

What then of the attitude of orthodox Calvinist theologians to the pagan classical authors? In "Aristotle and Early Reformed Orthodoxy: Moments of Accommodation and Antithesis," D. Sinnema focuses attention on a number of Calvinistic scholars of the late sixteenth century. From lecture lists and representations of the 1575 procession inaugurating the University of Leiden we know that biblical figures appeared alongside pagan authors. Aristotle soon came to dominate the arts faculty. Ursinus argued at length against Ramus's simplification of Aristotelian logic, and Beza similarly defended the use of logic as a tool in the service of theology, not to influence theological content but to provide a method for the orderly teaching of theology. Zanchi's argument for the superiority of Aristotle, in his preface for an edition of Aristotle's *Physics*, is also clearly reminiscent of earlier scholastic positions. Daneau's attempt to base the study of physics on the book of Genesis in a biblicistic rejection of Aristotle as the source of knowledge was not an unqualified improvement. Most Calvinist theologians thus were ready to make judicious use of the pagan authors, especially Aristotle, be it in purified form, justifying this use by indicating that all truth has its source in God or that the pagans had received their wisdom from Moses by way of the Egyptians.

The attitude of the Pietists is of interest not only because they gave the study of Greek and Latin a central place in the education of pastors at the University of Halle or for the groundbreaking work of Bengel in biblical textual criticism. As P. Erb points out in "Classical studies and the German Pietists," it was Oetinger's positive view of classical antiquity, its proximity to the primitive golden age, which was to influence Goethe and the Romantic poets in their glorification of Greco-Roman antiquity. Among earlier Pietists we find some polemical references to Aristotle, and a moralizing reading of the text prevails. With Oetinger classical philology is given a very important role for biblical exegesis. Since God has revealed himself in nature or the world, theology must be open to that revelation. In earlier time God's self-revelation was much clearer in nature, and therefore the organ of the soul by which such knowledge is acquired, the *sensus communis*, gave a more reliable witness to God in earlier cultures, especially that of the classical period. It is significant for Oetinger that it was the Greek language which became the vehicle for God's Word in the New Testament. With his appreciation of Greek culture, Oetinger clearly anticipated the Neo-Hellenist use of classical antiquity to criticize their own time.

Hegel's attitude to classical antiquity, especially that of Greece, shows traces of the idealization characteristic of Romantic Neo-Hellenists. Hegel is of interest to us because he went beyond such idealization to reflect on the relationship of classical views to Christianity. As W. Rowe shows in "Hegel on Greek and Revealed Religion," Hegel regarded the Greek and Christian religions as important moments in the phenomenology or pedagogy of Spirit, but both of these were in turn relativized with respect to the concept, or absolute knowing. Religion falls short of scientific knowing because it is rooted in representation, for the Greeks in art or drama, for Christians in the incarnation of God in Christ. The Greeks had only an implicit identity with Spirit, mediated through art, which as such cannot resolve the conflict of unhappy self-consciousness as portrayed in tragedy. Christianity as revealed religion allows more clearly for the identification of the finite consciousness with its object, Spirit, or absolute knowing. Revelation is in fact the union of humankind with God as he makes himself known in our believing knowledge of him, the subject-object distinction falling away. For Hegel the Greek and Christian religions were not ultimately in conflict but were united in a new synthesis which was necessary in the pedagogy of Spirit. Just as non-A includes A, so also Christianity by negating Greek religion had incorporated the latter within itself, yet needs to overcome that Greek element in its own content in order to pass from religion to thought, or to absolute knowing. Hegel's position on the relationship of Greek and Christian religion was to be very influential for further study in both early Christianity and classical antiquity. Reinforcing the Romantic view of Greek culture as a model in its own right, Hegel also set the agenda for Christian theology, namely, to purge itself of alien Greek elements which it had incorporated since the time of the Greek and Latin church fathers.

The final paper "Christianity and the Classics: A Typology of Attitudes" by A. Wolters, summarizes much of the discussion of earlier papers, pulling together the various strands of the presentations. Wolters restates the basic problematic of our study in terms of the relationship between the new life in Christ over against the old life which does not acknowledge him as Lord and Savior. Using Niebuhr's typology of the relationship of Christ and culture, or grace and nature, five basic relationships are delineated: (1) antithesis, (2) grace perfects nature, (3) grace parallels nature, (4) grace restores nature, and (5) grace is equated with nature. For each of these types one can give examples from the classical or biblical scholars, but the two positions most clearly represented among

Christians are the second and the fourth. Already with Basil's *praeparatio evangelica* motif we have an example of the Greek authors taking an inferior, subordinate role with respect to biblical truth. With Aquinas this position receives its classic statement; for him the inadequacies of the natural order find their fulfillment through grace. Although Erasmus subscribed to the *praeparatio evangelica* motif, he also showed a tendency to accept the fourth motif, that of grace restoring nature. This position was already found in Augustine, characterized by the use of the story of the Israelites spoiling the Egyptians, taking their gold and silver, not to be ensnared by these but to convert them for the service of God.

The latter, the *spoliatio* motif, is also favored by Wolters himself, for it allows Christian acceptance of the classical authors, affirming that which is creationally valid and acceptable, yet without ignoring that which has been perverted due to human sinfulness. One must distinguish between the authors' legitimate response to creational structures and the misdirected or spiritually distorted use of valid insights in the classics.

D. Conclusion

In accordance with this view of a Christian approach to classical scholarship, there are basically two functions which the scholar as Christian performs in dealing with the cultural remains of antiquity, to convert or restore them to the service and worship of the true God: the *appreciative* and the discerning or *critical*.

In the appreciative role one must first of all recognize the genres and the structures, whether of poetry, art, or architecture.[28] Factors related to the transmission of the text, editing, historic interpretation or translation are also to be taken into account. It is important to begin with a sincere desire to understand the text and give an interpretation which is both accurate and true to the author and context in which a work was written, to let the text speak for itself, as it were, insofar as that is possible.

Such a process requires careful discernment and is not without its own difficulties since we do not approach the classical texts without our own preconceptions.[29] We inevitably work with our own questions or approach the text with the desire to confirm or enrich our own particular view of a period or personality. Our own cultural context will also determine the motivation or hermeneutical point of departure with which we take up the work of interpretation. Aware of the danger of imposing an interpretation, one must use the data at one's disposal, especially the knowledge accumulated from years of intensive study, whether in history, archaeology, or other disciplines, to arrive at an understanding of the text which allows it to be integrated with what we already know of classical antiquity and present a unified picture of the past.

It is at this level that we may recognize the cultural achievements of classical antiquity, whether in logic or philosophy, in poetry or history, as gifts of God, to be accepted thankfully and used judiciously. Because we all share in the same creation and in the goodness of the Creator, we need not resort to explaining the achievements of the ancients as an anticipation or preparation for scriptural truth, direct inspiration by God himself, or as a borrowing from the Jews whether through Moses, Solomon, or some other linking figure. We can affirm that which is creationally valid, and in accordance with the intent of the Creator.

However, our world is not only created, it is also fallen and under the spell of sin. We all deal with its consequences, and the misdirected use of the creation, the perversion of our God-given talents and abilities. Thus the second important role of Christians in their use of classical texts is that of critical discernment. If, like the spoils from the Egyptians, the classical heritage is to be restored to its proper function, to be put in the service and worship of the only true God, we must not only recognize but also reject those elements which are in opposition to his demands, give evidence of the distortion of sin, and are in conflict with his Word.

Christians have long been busy with such a recognition of the results of sin. Basil realized that the orators were skilled in the art of lying; Augustine ridiculed the immoralities of the pagan cults; and Aquinas argued that Aristotle's position on the unicity of the intellect was in conflict with the principles of philosophy as well as being contrary to the testimony of faith.

To the extent that we are dealing with literary texts, whether in poetry or prose, which have long been regarded as classical models, our very interest in these is motivated by a degree of perfection displayed in them. Nonetheless a critical approach demands that we discern the spirit of the classical text at hand, that we note the purpose and even the religious context for which it was created. Because of the span of time which separates us from the original context, the religious orientation of the literature may not always be apparent. Although we recognize the classical heritage to be primarily cultural in nature, a true understanding of literature, such as Greek tragedy, demands that we also pay attention to the religious festivals in which they had their origin. If we are to revitalize the reading of the classical texts, it is important to recognize fully their religious roots, the spiritual forces which motivated their creation. A critical reading cannot be content with ignoring or isolating the religious factor as a separable element, with simply glossing over references to the pagan gods as evidence of a spiritually immature view of deity, or with eliminating the offensive passage from the text.

A Christian approach to classical literature will also go beyond the "moral reading of the text." Without disregarding evidence of immoral behavior, we must also consider that the effects of sin go far beyond what we consider as immorality. From its very beginning Christianity was concerned with the healing of incurable diseases, with the oppression of the poor and helpless, and with the position of women in the family or in society. These issues are still of interest and may provide an indicator for the type of questions with which we can approach the classical texts today.

Because we not only recognize the inevitable distortions resulting from sin but also affirm the goodness inherent in the classical tradition, we can still learn from this cultural heritage. Not only do we find there the roots of our own culture; the very distance by which we are removed from it allows us to see more clearly the consequences of positions taken; some like the worship of the Olympic gods have already run their course, but others like mysticism in religion or philosophy are still influential.

As for the relationship between Christianity and the classics, it is not enough to recognize the classical texts as models since our time looks for models elsewhere, much closer to the present or even in the future. Nor is it enough to recognize the historic significance of the cultural heritage since that might only assure the remains a location of prominence in our museums. As in our evaluation of the classical texts as such, so also in our analysis of the early period of interaction between Christianity and the classical culture, it is the distance separating us from the Christian writers which allows us to understand more fully not only what they were saying, whether in acceptance or rejection of their cultural environment, but also the nature of the synthesis which took place. The continuity of the tradition allows us to still identify with the positions taken in the past.

The Enlightenment and Neo-Hellenist position only recognized an element of tension between Christianity and the classics; this is indeed a factor inasmuch as we understand the relationship as one between "Christian" religion and "pagan" culture. However, the nature of the Christian religion is such that it inevitably involves its adherents in an interaction with the culture of its own time. It addresses itself to contemporary issues affecting the individual or societal groups, discerning and even judging the spirit of that culture: whether it recognizes the true God or seeks to glory in itself, in the false gods and idols it has chosen. As Christians in our own time we struggle with issues like nuclear warfare, refugees, or AIDS; in antiquity Christians recognized elements of inconsistency in polytheistic religion, immorality in the worship of the gods, and injustice in the treatment of peoples in the empire.

These Christians were not only observers of the culture of their time; they were also active participants in it. Understanding of one's own immediate cultural context is never a purely objective matter. Inevitably there were substantial aspects of the culture and worldviews of Greco-Roman antiquity which influenced early Christians. Nor was the degree of assimilation to popularly accepted views, as to that of a hierarchy of reality or being,[30] always fully obvious to Christians. It is important to distinguish an overt rejection or accommodation to positions of non-Christians from a more unconscious assimilation or acceptance of a position which may enjoy prevalence in a particular culture or time in history. Here also the distance of time and the perspective of history gives us an advantage of clearer insight into the nature of the interaction, partnership, or synthesis. From the perspective of history it may well become evident that we too in our own time have taken positions which in subsequent years will more clearly be seen as inherently incompatible with a biblical Christian position.

Only when the poles in the relationship between Christianity and the classics are both cultural and we study Christianity in its specifically cultural manifestation, as for example in one of the countries of medieval Europe, or both religious and we look at the cultural remains of Greco-Roman civilization in their specific religious orientation do we have the basis for regarding the interaction between these as a true synthesis. When the issues are drawn so clearly, the only valid Christian response is one of reject-ing that which is pagan. However, as we have seen, there is no one specifically Christian culture which may be taken as normative for others; Christianity has historically been inculturated in many countries in different ways. Nor has the attitude of total rejection been historically successful or consistently tenable.

It is the fourth motif, therefore, by sketching the relationship between Christianity and the classics as that between a religious position and the culture of Greco-Roman antiquity, using the model of Christ restoring culture, which allows for the relative in-tegrity of both the Christian perspective and the classical text. It allows for a positive approach to the classics without compromis-ing the religious discernment of pagan elements and gives us a method by which we can judge the history of classical scholarship as well as the Christian use of the classical heritage.

Notes

1. An interesting discussion of this position is found in W. R. Schoedel and R. L. Wilken, eds., *Early Christian Literature and the Classical Intellectual Tradition: Essays in Honor of R. M. Grant* (Paris, 1979), intro., 10-11.
2. Ibid., 11-13; see also the discussion of Tertullian in Albert M. Wolters, "Chris-tianity and the Classics: A Typology of Attitudes," in this book, 189-203.
3. J. J. Winckelmann's (1717-68) own words; cf. R. Pfeiffer, *A History of Classical Scholarship 1300-1850* (Oxford: Clarendon Press, 1976), 167ff.
4. Ibid., 180ff.
5. Lloyd-Jones gives an interesting sketch of *Altertumswissenschaft* in his introduc-tion to the translation of U. von Wilamowitz-Moellendorff, *History of Classical Scholarship* (London: Duckworth, 1982), intro., ix-xvii (hereafter cited as *History*). Pfeiffer's judgment of Theodor Mommsen (1817-1903) is that he did more than anyone to further the forces of historicism and realism; op. cit., n.3, 190.
6. Lloyd-Jones, *History* xi.
7. Lloyd-Jones, *Blood for the Ghosts* (London: Duckworth, 1982) 165ff., esp. 174-77.
8. A. Momigliano, "Historicism in Contemporary Thought," in *Studies in Historiog-raphy* (London: Weidenfeld & Nicolson, 1966), 221-38, esp. 224, 228-29, and n.45; cf. Lloyd-Jones, *History*, xxx. On W. Jaeger (1888-1961) see Lloyd-Jones, *History*, xxvii-xxviii.
9. Momigliano, op. cit., 224, 228.
10. On the work of A. Harnack see W. Jaeger, *Early Christianity and Greek Paedeia* (Oxford, 1961), 105, n. 2. Also J. Geffcken, *The Last Days of Greco-Roman Paganism*, trans. S. MacCormack (orig. 1929; Amsterdam: North-Holland, 1978).
11. K. J. Popma, *Evangelie contra Evangelie, Joden en Grieken in het Nieuwe Testament* (Franeker: T. Wever, 1941); also his *Eerst de Jood, Maar ook de Griek* (Franeker: T. Wever, 1950).
12. P. le Merle, *Le Premier Humanisme Byzantin* (Paris, 1971).

13. R. Walzer, "Early Islamic Philosophy," in *The Cambridge History of Later Greek and Early Medieval Philosophy*, ed. A. H. Armstrong (Cambridge, 1967), 643ff.

14. See William Rowe, "Hegel on Greek and Revealed Religion," chap. 10 in this book, 161-188.

15. Cf. Albert M. Wolters, "A Survey of Modern Scholarly Opinion on Plotinus and Indian Thought," in *Neoplatonism and Indian Thought*, ed. R. Baine Harris (Norfolk: International Society for Neoplatonic Studies, 1982) 295.

16. On Basil's attitude to an anti-intellectualist fear of pagan writings, see Wendy E. Helleman, "Basil's *Ad Adolescentes: Guidelines for Reading the Classics*," chap. 2 in this book, 31-51.

17. Ibid.; cf. R. A. Markus, "Paganism, Christianity and the Latin Classics in the Fourth Century," in *Latin Literature of the Fourth Century*, ed. J. W. Binns (London and Boston: Routledge & Kegan Paul, 1974).

18. See William Rowe, "Hegel on Greek and Revealed Religion," chap. 10 in this book, 161-188.

19. Geffcken, op. cit. in n.10, 163-66.

20. Biology may be of interest to the student of antiquity, but it is only inasmuch as writers like Aristotle left their observations in biological treatises; even here we are concerned with an aspect of the culture of the ancients.

21. Aulus Gellius, *Noctes Atticae* 19.8.15; on this see E. R. Curtius, *European Literature and the Latin Middle Ages*, trans. W. R. Trask (New York: Harper & Row, 1963) 249-50.

22. Curtius, op. cit., 248-51; also K. Quinn, *Texts and Contexts* (London: Routledge & Kegan Paul, 1979), 7-14.

23. Curtius, op. cit., 251ff.; also G. W. Bowersock, "Historical Problems in Late Republican and Augustan Classicism," in *Le Classicisme à Rome, Entretiens Tom. XXV* (Geneva, Vandoeuvres: Fondation Hardt, 1979).

24. See Beert Verstraete, "Erasmus's Christian Humanist Appreciation and Use of the Classics," in this book, 91-107.

25. See Peter Erb, "Classical Studies and the German Pietists," in this book, 149-159.

26. Curtius, op. cit., 251.

27. In the case of Basil such anti-intellectualism was challenged; see Helleman, op. cit. in n.16, 47.

28. To facilitate analysis, in the sequel I will consider literary texts as representative of the cultural remains of classical antiquity; it would be too cumbersome at this point to deal with analogous treatment of artworks, coins, or architecture. They are nonetheless equally important witnesses to the culture of classical antiquity.

29. See Beert Verstraete, "Erasmus's Christian Humanist Appreciation and Use of the Classics," in this book, 91-107.

30. See Theodore S. de Bruyn, "Jerusalem versus Rome: The Religious and Philosophical Context of Augustine's Assessment of the Roman Empire in the *City of God*," in this book, 53-67.

Basil's *Ad Adolescentes*: Guidelines for Reading the Classics

Wendy E. Helleman

A. Introduction

With his recent study of the history of Basil's treatise, L. Schucan[1] has clearly shown the importance of the *Ad Adolescentes* for the classical tradition, particularly in the context of the Christian church and its schools. Christian humanists of the Renaissance appealed to this orthodox church father for support in their use of pagan classical authors.[2] In the nineteenth century the Jesuits, in opposing those who regarded the reading of Homer, Sophocles, or Vergil as a concession to paganizing Neo-Hellenists, also turned to Basil's treatise for a defense of their use of the classical authors.[3]

Since the Renaissance Basil's *Ad Adolescentes* was often read at schools like the Gymnasium as part of the curriculum, to remind students why they were reading the "glorious pagans." Many of the editions, translations, and commentaries date from this period.[4] But at least a century has passed since the treatise enjoyed a degree of popularity. A recent conference dealing with Basil as Christian, humanist, and ascetic[5] gave but scant attention to the *Ad Adolescentes* and patristic scholars like P. de Labriolle,[6] A. Puech,[7] and even H.-I. Marrou[8] refer to the superficiality of the argument, its weaknesses, its justification of the status quo in education.[9]

Nonetheless, the importance of this treatise for the classical tradition alone would justify a reevaluation of Basil's argument. Schucan has shown that many who appealed to Basil as an authority were more eager to use his name than to analyze the arguments presented.[10] Furthermore, there is no unanimity among contemporary scholars in assessing Basil's appreciation or repudiation of the pagan authors like Plato, Plutarch, and others from whom he borrowed substantially. L. V. Jacks concluded that Basil never formally condemned a study of the pagan authors,[11] but E. L. Fortin has shown that Basil clearly recognized the dangers of reading pagan authors and provided a variety of measures to prevent the students being irrevocably poisoned by them.[12]

B. Needed: A Reevaluation of the *Ad Adolescentes*

The primary aim of the present discussion of Basil's treatise is to provide the basis for a new evaluation of his work in the context of the intellectual climate of late Greco-Roman antiquity. With a view to the current attitude of contempt for the treatise and the misconceptions regarding its purpose, it is useful to study closely the argument of the ten chapters if we are to understand clearly his appreciation of the classical authors.

Analysis of the treatise will begin with a summary of the argument of the treatise. A careful look at the argument is necessary if we are to correct a number of erroneous assumptions regarding Basil's purpose for giving advice. Such an analysis is also necessary for an assessment of the place of Basil's treatise in the history of the classical tradition and for determining its portrayal of the relationship of Christianity and the pagan classical authors.[13]

We are particularly interested in understanding how Basil defended use of pagan authors as a *praeparatio evangelica*,[14] anticipating the position on the relationship of pagan classical antiquity and the Christian faith long accepted by Christian humanists. To do justice to Basil's intention in writing the treatise, the present study hopes to show that it must be evaluated as a genuine attempt on his part to deal anew with an educational tradition which in his time was already centuries old and by nature conservative, even more so in a time of social and political change.[15] Basil presented the Christian community with a significant option for relating to the educated classes, the aristocratic elite of late Greco-Roman antiquity, and of being considered worthy of respect by them. He provided the Christian church with an argument for preserving the pagan classical works, making judicious use of them, and protecting them in a time of upheaval and invasion. From the earliest years of the Christian Roman Empire, his argument found acceptance in the Byzantine East.[16] Except for indirect acquaintance with Basil through Ambrose, Western Christianity made more extensive use of his argument at a much later date.[17]

C. *Ad Adolescentes*: The Argument
Basil's purpose in writing *Ad Adolescentes* is clearly stated in the introductory chapter: he wished to advise his nephews who are reading the works of famous authors in the pagan schools (1.8-10, 20-22),[18] to indicate to them how they can discover what is useful and distinguish it from what is to be overlooked. They are not to hand over the direction of their thought (*dianoia*) to pagan teachers and authors (1.26-27).

Noteworthy at the introduction of the second chapter is the broad base of the argument: just as goods of this life cannot compare with those of the next, we also are not to value an education which prepares only for this life and for its characteristic goods, such as honor, beauty, or strength (2.1-8). In education we must prepare for that other life which is more precious, just as the soul is more precious than the body or true happiness when compared to the dream (2.9-25).

To describe that other life more fully is beyond Basil's purpose here; the nephews are too young to understand, and the Scriptures teach by mysteries too deep for their minds (2.26-28). They need preliminary exercises to help them prepare for the real contest (2.30-37). The eye must accustom itself to light by looking at reflections before looking at the source (2.46-7); the eye of the soul must similarly prepare itself to apprehend the truth by means of preliminary exercises (*progumnadzometha* [2.30]) or by analogies. Just as dye leaves an indelible mark on the cloth when dyers have given a preliminary treatment before color is introduced, so also an indelible impression will be left on the soul when at an early age it has appropriated the truth in a manner suited to its capacities (2.40-5).

Pagan literature is not without usefulness, since even Moses was taught the wisdom of the Egyptians and Daniel that of the Chaldeans (3.11-17). Christian teaching is compared with that from "outside" (*thurathen* [3.9]) in terms of the striking image of a tree. Just as leaves and branches protect and beautify the fruit, the *arete* or peculiar excellence of the tree, so also pagan authors are assigned the role of protecting and adorning the peculiar excellence or *arete* of the soul, namely, truth (3.4 11).

Basil continues by giving basic rules for the student in reading the poets, prose writers, and orators. Passages which praise virtue and condemn vice are to be valued (4.35-36). Both words and deeds of good people are to be imitated. The young men are not to allow poetic language to mislead them to approve adulterous or drunken behavior, certainly not as portrayed by the pagan gods (4.12-28). The student is to attend to passages which describe behavior suitable for Christians, akin to the truth and useful in their task (4.46-51).

The fifth chapter explains how the student is to recognize virtue, praised by the poets as a possession for eternity. The crucial choice between virtue and vice is clearly portrayed in the story of Heracles; he spurned the charm and beauty of vice (*kakia*) when virtue (*arete*) offered the prize of deification, be it at the end of a long and difficult road (5.61-77). Also for us virtue is the key to that other life, *arete*, here identified as truth, goodness, and the peculiar excellence of human life (5.1-2, 20).

Basil goes on to say that it is not enough to listen to words of wisdom; love of wisdom must be confirmed in deeds, harmonizing practice with theory. Plato already claimed that simply to appear to be just without truly being just was in fact the worst injustice (6.25-6).

In the seventh chapter Basil gives a series of examples of virtue to be imitated: Pericles ignoring insults, Eucleides controlling his anger, and Alexander conquering his lust for the beautiful daughters of Darius (7.5-44). These examples are said to portray behavior similar to that taught in Scripture and are, therefore, worthy of imitation (7.31-2, 44-47). Cleinias's refusal to take an oath, according to Basil, indicates that he may have been familiar with biblical teaching (7.48-53). Imitating such examples gives the youth a good preparation since it paves the way for obedience to the teachings of Scripture.

Basil next returns to the broader question of how to determine what is useful for an education focused on the care of the soul. Like the pilot, we are to make straight for the safe harbor, the goal of life. We know the prize, no mere crown of laurel, and also know how, with the guidance of intellect (*nous*), to steer safely toward that goal (8.17). It should not be difficult to choose preparatory exercises which will set us on course toward the goal of eternal life.

The ninth chapter gives a clear outline of the life of Christian virtue, a life devoted to the care of the soul. The soul is not to be enslaved to the body but through philosophy to free itself from the body, as it were from a prison. Quoting Plato, Basil says that the soul should attend to the body only as much as it will serve it in its pursuit of wisdom, for Paul (Rom. 13:14) also tells us not to attend to the desires of the body (9.61-6). We are instead to concentrate on the purification of the soul (*psuche*) or mind (*nous*) (9.33ff.) so it will be able to behold the truth and come to proper self-knowledge. We are to scorn excess of food, dress, and pleasure of sense, sight, sound, or smell, as well as pleasure of wealth, possession, or flattery. The soul must have complete mastery over the body and its passions, using the body as its instrument rather than being enslaved by it.

Finally, in the tenth chapter, Basil says that even if all such precepts are more clearly taught in Scripture, with pagan authors teaching them only by way of a shadowy sketch of true *arete* (10.1-4), this is not in itself sufficient reason to ignore teachings which are beneficial, whatever their source. Young men must acquire the baggage they need for the journey of life, preparing themselves not only for this life but for eternal life itself (10.11-24).

D. Analysis of the Argument

The above summary is useful in clarifying what Basil means by the preparatory role of an education in the pagan classical authors. It also provides the basis for correcting some of the misconceptions regarding the scope of the argument presented and Basil's purpose in writing the essay.

1. Usefulness of the literature

The relative usefulness of the literature read by the students and the benefit to be derived from it (cf. 1.27) are significant factors for Basil in persuading the young men to take their studies seriously. Subsequent argumentation defines the nature of this usefulness and describes how it is to be discerned in the literature. Various scholars have interpreted such references to usefulness as indicating an eclectic or pragmatic attitude; Basil is apparently accepting the traditional education because he has no viable alternative for it.[19]

I would like to suggest that emphases on usefulness, rather than indicating a pragmatic acceptance, should first of all be regarded as Basil's reply to a negative attitude among Christians in the matter of sending their sons to be educated in the pagan schools. Note the significant reference (first given at 1.13ff. and recalled strategically in the closing words of the treatise) where those in need of Basil's advice are compared to the sick in need of a physician (10.34-42), he ends with the prayer that the students will not become like foolish men who do not even listen to physicians when they come, avoiding men of sound reason.

Christians need not remain uneducated, veritable barbarians in the eyes of fellow citizens, to be true to the faith. Basil does not want the young men to miss the preparatory benefit for their task as Christians, even if the teaching has its source with pagan authors or schools.[20]

It should be noted that in this treatise Basil consciously addressed himself to a Christian audience.[21] The nephews were certainly from Christian homes and the wider audience which Basil would have had in mind in publishing the treatise was also the Christian community of Asia Minor. The pagan intelligentsia had no need of such arguments. Matters of dating and publication as such are beyond the scope of the present article;[22] but even internal evidence indicates that Basil distinguishes clearly between pagan writings as those coming from outside, *thurathen* (3.9), *ta exothen* (10.3), whereas the Scriptures are described as ours, *hemeteroi logoi* (10.1). Such an insider-outsider distinction, which is clearly present in the presentation of the argument and has overtones which might have been offensive to non-Christians, is not always sufficiently recognized by those who regard Basil as a pragmatist, maintaining the status quo in education by his acceptance of the pagan authors.[23]

2. Broad scope of the argument

The broad scope of the argument, beginning as it does with the distinction between our present human life and that other (eternal) life, may also come as a surprise to those who are familiar with Basil as an eclectic or moralist.[24] An education which prepares only for the present life is inadequate, according to Basil, since all of life is itself a preparation for the next (2.1-13). Students are to attend to those literary examples which will help them prepare for that other life.

Even Schucan in his analysis of the argument at this point distinguishes between the supposedly Christian context and the less specifically Christian aspects of Basil's argument.[25] Yet for a reader with only a rudimentary acquaintance with Plato, it is clear that in the body-soul distinction and in the arguments based on that Basil has borrowed extensively from the philosopher.

If, as we have indicated, Basil addressed himself primarily to a Christian audience, is there still a justification for separating those portions of his argument which may be considered universally valid from a supposedly Christian framework within which we find these central claims? Such a distinction becomes even less tenable when one recognizes a clear dependence on Platonic motifs even within this framework. Nor does the fact that, in both the wider framework and the central arguments for assigning the pagan authors a preparatory role in education, Basil uses positions borrowed from Plato allow us to qualify his entire presentation as non-Christian, since it was clearly not understood as such in its own time. We will return to the question of Basil's use of Plato in the next section.

By assigning an important role to the reading of pagan classical authors within the context of an education which prepares one not only for the present but even for the next life, Basil on the one hand provides a wide horizon for application but also a heavy weight of responsibility in the reading of these authors. Study of the poets, historians, and orators may indeed be revitalized when they are questioned with respect to their contributions for those who would prepare for that other life. What should not be forgotten, on the other hand, is that the place assigned to the authors could also have the reverse effect, limiting the students in their understanding of the authors, the aesthetic quality of poetry, or historic importance of significant events since Basil was primarily interested in the portrayal of *arete* in the literature. What does become clear is that Basil neither wholeheartedly endorses the pagan authors, nor does he completely repudiate the contribution they can make when he assigns them their peculiar role in his educational scheme.

3. Basil's use of the Platonists

The difference between this and that other life is described in terms of the difference between body and soul, or dream and reality. Such distinctions were extremely important for Basil and indicate the influence of Platonic motifs on his thought.

The Scriptures teach by means of mysteries (*aporrheton* [2.25,46]) and students, therefore, need a preparatory education suitable for their level of understanding. The soul is to be taught by means of analogies, shadows or reflections, by which the soul's eye may accustom itself before it can look at the source of light (i.e. the truth) itself (2.26ff., 9.33-35). The goal of education is the purification of the soul's eye, the *nous*, which is to guide the soul on the journey to its destination; the shadowlike reflections of the truth which can be found in the pagan authors (10.2-3) may be useful in an education in the same way that drills which soldiers use before a battle or exercises which athletes undergo prepare them for the true contest (2.26-34). Just as bleary eyes cannot look upon the sun, our *nous* cannot truly know itself without repudiation of that which is alien, purifying itself of bodily passions. In this the pagan authors can provide a useful initial exercise.

It is clear that images and arguments derived from Plato were crucial for Basil in assigning a preliminary role for the study of the pagan authors, as they provide the first steps in the care of the soul, its purification, on the journey toward attaining eternal life. Were one to question any of the basic Platonic motifs, especially that of the body-soul distinction as presented, this would have significant implications for Basil's position regarding the use of the pagan authors in education. Are we then to conclude that in this essay Basil reveals himself more a Platonist than a Christian?

Within the scope of the present discussion it is hardly possible to do justice to the larger question of Plato's influence on Basil, but it should be noted that Basil was not an exception among the Greek church fathers in his use of Plato; men like Origen or Basil's own brother Gregory of Nyssa also went far in their use of the philosopher. Plato was not just one of the pagan authors to be read in the schools; in the search for truth, Plato was regarded as an ally. Among those authors in whose writings Basil could discern an anticipation of biblical truth, Plato took first place; consequently, biblical distinctions were often read into such Platonic distinctions as those of mortality and immortality, or body and soul. But the recognition of a shadowy anticipation of biblical truth was clearly the deciding factor in Basil's advice to the young men that they take their studies in the pagan authors seriously.[26] In this regard one would not do justice to Basil were one to consider him as a Platonist first and only secondarily a Christian.[27]

Nor was Basil particularly slavish in his use of Plato. He freely adapted Plato's imagery and the intent of the arguments for his own purposes. For Plato, poets and historians had but a negligible role in education; mathematical sciences (of which Basil makes no mention whatsoever) were much more important in preparing the soul for the abstractions necessary in philosophical thought. A literary education may have been the more valuable for Basil precisely because of the literary character of the Scriptures, the ultimate source of truth. Just as the soldier cannot do battle without proper drill and the athlete must exercise to prepare his body for the real contest, the students of Scripture also must be equipped with the proper tools to understand and explain the sacred writings if they are to be able to defend the truth.

4. *The metaphor of the fruit of the tree as its Arete*

Basil uses an interesting analogy when he compares two types of *paideusis*, Christian and pagan education, in terms of the tree with its branches and leaves protecting the fruit, its *arete* (3.6). Many similar metaphors occur in the treatise and commentators are quick to indicate the literary sources, especially with the rhetorical authors;[28] but Basil clearly uses the metaphors for his own purposes, and they do add much in vividness and clarity to his argumentation. It should be remembered that use of stock illustrations, especially when borrowed from well-known sources, would not have discredited Basil as a plagiarist in his own time. Instead, it marked him as a man of education, well-equipped to advise students accustomed to learned references in the lectures of their pagan teachers.[29] Originality has not always been accorded the honor it receives in contemporary education.

Noteworthy in the analogy of the tree is the reference to the fruit as its peculiar *arete*, to be compared to the truth (*aletheia*) as the *arete* proper to the soul. Leaves which surround, protect, and beautify the fruit represent the wisdom of the pagans (3.4-11). With this image Basil clearly anticipates the designation of literary studies or the liberal arts, which were as such mainly of pagan origin, to the role they were to acquire in the Middle Ages, as the handmaiden of theology or of the truth given in the sacred Scriptures. And indeed, use of pagan authors as a *praeparatio evangelica*, as Basil introduces it here, does not differ substantially from the role assigned to them later, a role subservient to the needs of theological studies.[30]

Since truth or the fruit of the soul is designated as its *arete*, it is not surprising that when Basil elaborates on the meaning of an education defined in terms of the care of the soul, he does so by means of a choice between *arete* and *kakia*, virtue and vice, portrayed most clearly in the story of Heracles's choice (5.60ff.). We enter that other life only by *arete*; in fact, *arete* alone of our possessions cannot be taken away! Clearly, *arete* has taken on a role much more extensive than what we might commonly assign to virtue. *Arete* not only represents the truth, it is also, when contrasted with *kakia* or *poneria*, evil or vice, representative of a broad spectrum of activities which may be designated as "good" or, for a Christian, "obedience to God's laws" since these are transgressed in cases of drunkenness or adultery but above all in idolatry and the acceptance of a multiplicity of gods.[31]

5. Recognition of virtue in pagan authors
The rule which Basil suggests in the reading of the poets, historians, and orators is rather straightforward: pay attention when the author praises virtue and condemns vice (4.34-36). More specifically, students must note those elements which are suitable for Christians, in nature akin to the truth, and useful in their task, that is, the care of the soul (4.45-51).

But how are the young men to recognize in pagan authors the Christian virtue, truth, and goodness which they have not yet studied in the Scriptures, the true source? Is not Basil begging the question when he expects the students to identify *arete* in the pagan authors as a reflection of biblical truth when they have not yet become acquainted with the original and, by his own admission, are not ready for the truth in its original form?

Basil was apparently not unaware of this problem, for in the sixth through ninth chapters he deals at length with examples of virtuous behavior, especially in connection with his reminder that the young men should not only know what virtue is but also be able to show in practice that they have learned their lesson.

Of course Basil could presuppose a certain amount of teaching in the family situation since the boys, if indeed they were his nephews, came from Christian homes, and the parents would have provided a rudimentary instruction in the Christian faith and a life-style appropriate for Christians. Moreover, when Basil finds that biblical teachings have specifically been anticipated in the pagan literature, as in the story of Socrates offering the other cheek (7.23-34), he does not seem surprised but comments that anyone who considers biblical demands too difficult is proven wrong by the example of obedience of someone not even versed in Scripture. From the case of Cleinias, the pupil of Pythagoras, who paid a fine rather than swear an oath, Basil concludes somewhat differently that the coincidence of his action with biblical teachings against the taking of an oath cannot have been a chance occurrence; Cleinias must somehow have heard of the biblical teachings and acted upon it (7.47-53). How Cleinias might have been acquainted with biblical teachings is not made clear; Basil seems to assume that this needs no further explanation. Instead, the occurrence of obedience to biblical laws by those outside the Christian community helps to prove and to reinforce for him the propaedeutic role of a training in the pagan authors and their portrayal of *arete* for the Christian.[32]

6. Basil's tolerance of the pagan authors
In spite of the lofty claims made by Basil on behalf of virtue in the fifth and sixth chapters, where he says that most writers who are considered wise have written in praise of virtue, it is clear from the rest of the treatise that he was by no means unaware that poets and historians were not always praising virtue and that orators too were skilled in the art of lying as they persuaded their audience and tried to gain the praise of others (4.30-31, 9.133ff.). The students are to be on their guard, lest they partake of the poison of unacceptable advice, along with the proverbial honey of pleasing literary arrangement of words (4.1215). The thorns among the roses, the harmful elements, are to be avoided as they seek out what is useful (4.48-51).

Basil's attitude toward the undesirable elements in the pagan literature is not a vehement one. We find no violent repudiation of the errors of the pagans as was characteristic of other church fathers like Jerome.[33] Instead, Basil advises the students on what they are to overlook, or set aside (*paridein* [1.27]), while reading the literature. He speaks of avoiding imitation of wicked deeds, by (figuratively) stopping one's ears, as was said of Odysseus and the Sirens (4.7-11). His attitude is perhaps best summed up in the analogy of the bees who, as they look for honey, alight upon the flowers but take away only what is useful for them, leaving to others the enjoyment of the color, arrangement, or pleasing smell; what is not useful, one should pass over 4.36-48).

This attitude of tolerance is at least in part to be explained by recognizing the context in which Basil is giving advice; unlike Augustine's *De Doctrina Christiana*, the present treatise does not pretend to offer a complete system of Christian education.[34] The students to whom Basil addresses his advice were probably close to finishing their study with the literary teachers, comparable to our secondary education. Normally they would proceed to studies in rhetoric upon completion, or parallel to the grammatical studies.[35] They would not, therefore, be helped by advice to pass over or refrain from reading certain authors or passages required by their teachers; Basil does not attempt to compete with the teachers in that way. Rather, he guides the students in paying attention to those passages which will be of value to them in a way which far transcends any immediate purposes the teachers may have had in assigning them.[36]

7. The Ad Adolescentes *as a protreptic to Christian philosophy*

Absence of an antagonistic attitude on Basil's part may also be explained by taking a broader view of his role with respect to his nephews. Much of the advice focuses on moral conduct, the question of how to discern the truth and to live in accordance with it. As a close relative, Basil was not a disinterested observer and there are many indications in the treatise of a deeper interest in their life and educational achievements. In chapter ten he mentions the further opportunities he hopes will be available to him, to give them clearer teaching based on "our own literature" (*hemeteroi logoi* [10.1]), and more examples for their benefit in later life (10.32-33).

We see Basil in this role as a spiritual mentor, acting as it were on behalf of the parents, guiding the young men in upright, virtuous Christian behavior. In his treatment of moral issues, however, one can hardly avoid the impression of Basil's assuming a further role, that of introducing his students to the first and by far the most important branch of philosophy of the Hellenistic period: ethics. He tells them that the pagans have many useful things to teach them with regard to *arete*. Although Basil is reluctant to elaborate on the deeper spiritual truths of the Scriptures, it is equally clear that he shows little interest in guiding them toward further studies in rhetoric. He is in fact preparing them to continue their education in philosophical studies.

It is of interest, in this connection, that in the exhortation to virtue, found in the passage portraying Heracles's choice, we find a double occurrence of the participle *protrepon* (5.10,19). In his admonition to the students to look beyond the more obvious literary merits of the authors studied and find an anticipation of the truth as it is to be found even there, be it in shadowy form, Basil evidently casts his essay in the traditional role of the encouragement to study philosophy, the protreptic.[37] Basil thus indirectly exhorts the students to the study of philosophy, or more specifically a Christian philosophy, even though it was in many respects to be closely modeled on that of the Platonists.

From this conclusion it is also easier to find an explanation for a rather surprising reference to the supposed difficulties in the understanding of Scripture; Basil says that young men are not ready to understand its deeper meaning (2.26ff.). In a perceptive article dealing with the *Ad Adolescentes*, E. Lamberz suggests that Basil was surely not thinking of rudimentary instruction in the Christian faith, the *catechumenate*, but of the future education of the youths in theology, when he wished to postpone their education in Christian teaching to later years.[38] Lamberz was aware that he anticipated historical developments by several centuries, since a structured education for clergy did not become a reality until much later in the history of the church. For the Greek fathers of this period, however, theology and philosophy were in fact so closely intertwined as to be almost indistinguishable in purpose.[39]

The model for such advanced philosophical and Christian teaching as it was known to Basil was that of the Alexandrian school of Clement and Origen. Basil may not himself have been an original philosophical thinker, certainly not when compared to his younger brother Gregory, but he did align himself consciously with the asceticism of the Alexandrian school, in contrast with many anti-intellectual monastic groups of the Eastern Roman Empire.[40] Many echoes of the works of Clement and Origen have found their way into the argument of the *Ad Adolescentes*; the broad

scope given to an education as a preparation not only for mature
participation in this life but also as a preparation involving all of
this life and looking towards the other, eternal life, was clearly anticipated by Clement in his *Paidagogos*.[41]

Gregory Thaumaturgus forms the connecting link between
Origen and the Cappadocian fathers.[42] In his farewell address to
Origen, as well as in Origen's reply, specific reference is made to
the value of the cycle of studies in the liberal arts and in philosophy
as a preparation for understanding the deeper truth of Scripture.[43]
Basil's grandparents were greatly influenced by Gregory
Thaumaturgus, and Origen's reply found its way into the collection made by Basil and Gregory Nazianzen of favorite passages
from Origen's works, the *Philocalia*.[44]

If indeed, as E. Lamberz suggests, Basil's asceticism was
modeled on that of the Neo-Pythagoreans and later Platonists, and
the ninth chapter of the treatise is to be understood as an appeal to
the young men to prepare themselves for a Christian ascetic or
monastic life,[45] his underlying reasons for writing the treatise and
his attitude toward the pagan authors (with important consequences for the survival of their works in the classical tradition) all come
into clearer focus. For Basil's asceticism was clearly not anti-intellectual; his students are to make full use of scholarly, literary tools
as they prepare themselves for the study of biblical truth. Theory
and practice, especially for the Platonists, were closely connected;
Basil was no exception when he urged people to live in accordance
with their understanding of the *arete* proper to humankind. Unlike
the church fathers who completely rejected the pagan cultural
heritage or were at best deeply skeptical of an education in the
pagan authors, Basil had a closely defined appreciation of an education in the Greek classical authors. They were of value to him
precisely as they contributed, within the context of a Christian
perspective on life, in the preparation for study of the deeper truths
of Scripture. In an education defined in terms of the care of the soul,
they provided examples of the soul being freed from the grip of
bodily passions, purified, so that it could more clearly know both
itself and the truth at its source.

E. Conclusion
Basil's advice to young men studying the pagan authors takes on
a new meaning when approached from the perspective of his con-

tribution to the Christian ascetic or monastic tradition. From a careful examination of the treatise, we have seen that the current misunderstanding of the nature and intent of the work is based on a tendency to lift the argument regarding the use of pagan classical authors out of the context of the historical situation in late antiquity as well as out of the immediate and clearly stated Platonist philosophical position which forms Basil's rationale for giving advice.

Basil's designation of studies in the pagan authors as preparatory, or propaedeutic, is itself rooted in the Platonic distinction between the world of eternal truth and that of shadows and dreams. Aside from his conviction that even nonChristians could anticipate biblical teachings, it is the shadowy reflection of truth to be found in the way pagan authors have portrayed *arete* which justified their usefulness as preparatory exercises for Basil. Designation of these studies as propaedeutic implies that something more important is to follow; given adequate preparation, students would soon be ready to reap the fruits of their labors when they study the truth at its source: the Scriptures.

Designation of a preparatory role for the pagan authors, Homer, Sophocles, or Herodotus, was also based on a prior assumption, common in antiquity, that it was the knowledge of such authors which marked the educated person. Basil did not try to compete with this. In fact, many centuries were to pass before education in Europe was to free itself of the conviction that the knowledge of the classics, whether Greek or Roman, provided a key criterion of wisdom. In the long Christian humanist tradition, as with the monastic groups which regarded judicious use of pagan classical authors as a *praeparatio evangelica*, Basil's orthodox position was often cited.[46]

Such preparatory use of pagan authors would, from one perspective, indicate a high evaluation of the contributions of these writers, especially when seen as an anticipation of Christian truth. On the other hand, such a preparatory use of pagan writers would also tend to limit the range of interest in the literature to that which was useful in the further development of Christian thought or philosophy. On both fronts the *praeparatio evangelica* motif has come under attack. Neo-Hellenists, in their concern for "beauty," wanted to appreciate the Greek authors in their own right, not hemmed in by the extent these classical writers anticipated "Christian truth."[47] Calvinists like Groen van Prinsterer, on the other hand, have attacked the *praeparatio evangelica* motif for giving too much credit to non-Christian writers as anticipating biblical truth outside of an acceptance of the central message of repentance and salvation in Christ alone.[48] Salvation comes only through divine intervention; the shadowy anticipation of virtue in pagan authors is insufficient to appropriate the truth.

In our own time it is perhaps the erosion of a basic assumption which has held the field for many centuries, namely, the knowledge of classical Greek and Latin writers as the mark of an educated person, which has relegated Basil's treatise to the dusty shelves of graduate libraries. This does not, however, justify the current lack of appreciation for the very important role which Basil, especially with his *Ad Adolescentes*, has played in the history of education and of the classical tradition. He can be appreciated even today for his insistence that being educated, even according to the standards of the day, need not be a threat to the faith of the Christian. As a recognizably orthodox church father, Basil is to be given much of the credit for promoting the acceptability of intellectual pursuits within Christian and, more specifically, monastic circles. He did not hesitate in advising students to use the tools of a literary education for the study of Scripture. His value to the classical tradition is thus doubled since we know that it was primarily through the protection of the Christian church and its monasteries that a majority of the manuscripts of the classical authors have been transmitted to us.

Notes

1. L. Schucan, *Das Nachleben von Basilius Magnus "ad adolescentes,"* Ein Beitrag zur Geschichte des Christlichen Humanismus (Geneva, 1973).
2. Ibid., 66ff.
3. Ibid., 244ff.
4. In the introduction to his edition, F. Boulenger deals extensively with the manuscripts used; *Saint Basile, Aux Jeunes Gens*. (Paris, 1935), 33ff.
5. Papers presented at this conference were published in a two-volume work edited by P. J. Fedwick, *Basil of Caesarea, Christian, Humanist, Ascetic* (Toronto, 1981). The editor did, however, deal with Basil's view of Christian education in a separate paper, "Basil of Caesarea on Education," in *Atti del Congresso Internazionale su "Basilio di Cesarea: la sua età e il Basilianesimo in Sicilia"* (Messina: Centro di Studi Umanistici, 1983). In his sketch of the education which Basil himself enjoyed, Fedwick shows how influential the thought of Origen proved to be, mediated through Gregory of Thaumaturgus and Basil's grandmother Macrina. He also

demonstrates how, both in his writing and in his career in the church, Basil sought to integrate the moral and formative aspect of education with the more intellectual, the rhetorical or literary training needed by the student of the Scriptures.

6. P. de Labriolle, *History and Literature of Christianity*, from Tertullian to Boethius, (New York: Knopf, 1925) 25-26.

7. A. Puech, *Histoire de la Littérature Grecque Chrétienne* (Paris, 1930) vol. 3, 277.

8. H.-I. Marrou, *A History of Education in Antiquity* (Mentor, 1964), 429. Marrou realized that Basil was not interested in giving a treatise on the value of reading the pagan classics as such, but underestimated him in referring to the treatise as a homily on the dangers of the pagan writings and how to avoid these. Cf. P. le Merle, *Le Premier Humanisme Byzantin* (Paris, 1971) 44-48 and A. Cameron, "The End of the Ancient Universities," in *Cahiers d'Histoire Mondiale*, vol. 10 (1967) 653ff., esp. 672.

9. In a recent article, "Christianity and Hellenism in Basil the Great's Address, *Ad Adolescentes*," in *Neoplatonism and Early Christian Thought*, ed. H. J. Blumenthal and R. A. Markus (London, 1981) 189-203, E. L. Fortin went so far as to conclude that Basil could advise his students to regard classical authors as devoted to the praise of virtue only in terms of the biblical principle of the "economy of truth," which might justify a certain distortion of the literature as presented by the pagan authors.

10. Schucan, op. cit. in n. 1, 66ff.

11. L. V. Jacks, *St. Basil and Greek Literature*, CUA Patristic Studies, vol. 1 (Washington, 1920) 112-17.

12. Fortin, op. cit. in n. 9, 195ff. For other discussions of Basil's use of pagan authors and his appreciation of them, see (in chronological order) T. L. Shear, *The Influence of Plato on St. Basil* (Baltimore, 1906); S. Giet, *Les Idées et l'Action Sociale de St. Basile.* (Paris, 1941) 217-32; E. Valgiglio, "Basilio Magno *Ad Adolescentes* e Plutarco *De Audiendis Poetis*," in *Rivista di Studi Classici*, vol. 23 (1975), 67-86; E. Amand de Mendieta, "The Official Attitude of Basil of Caesarea as Christian Bishop towards Greek Philosophy and Science", in *The Orthodox Church and the West* (Oxford, 1976).

13. If one reads Basil's treatise with the expectation of finding reasons to continue the reading of the pagan classical authors within the context of contemporary Christian education, one may well be disappointed in the treatise. The work will be of interest only when understood as a contribution toward the development of a Christian position in late Greco-Roman antiquity, seen against the background of a resurgence of traditional pagan religious positions in the schools.

14. Fortin, op. cit. in n. 9, 199, briefly refers to Basil's treatise as a *praeparatio evangelica*, involving a transmutation of traditional values. This evaluation of the pagan writers as a propaedeutic for Christian wisdom was shared by many of the Greek church fathers, especially Clement of Alexandria and Origen (see page 43 in this chapter).

15. For interesting information on the vigorous condition of education, especially as it was still in pagan hands, see Cameron, op. cit. in n. 8, 664-73.

16. Le Merle, op. cit. in n. 8, 45ff.

17. Schucan, op. cit. in n. 1, 49ff.

18. References given are from Boulenger, op. cit. in n. 4. The edition of N. G. Wilson, *Saint Basil on the Value of Greek Literature* (Duckworth, 1975), is based on substantially the same text.

19. Such is the evaluation of Basil's accommodating attitude by various scholars like Cameron (op. cit. in n. 8, 672) or Marrou. "[E]nable them to get the best out of all they had learned. A Christian upbringing was something superimposed on a humanistic education which had taken place without it, something that had not previously been subjected to the requirements of the Christian religion" (Marrou, op. cit. in n. 8, 429).

20. An anti-intellectual attitude among Christians, and consequent opposition to the children receiving any more than a rudimentary education in the pagan schools, is documented in M. L. W. Laistner's *Christianity and Pagan Culture in the Later Roman Empire* (Cornell, 1951), 50ff. He quotes the *Didascalia Apostolorum* 12 against the use of books of the pagans, but does balance this with references to those fathers who realized that children would need an education for the demands of literacy. Cf. Marrou (op. cit. in n. 8, 426-27 and 439-43) who also describes the opposition of Christians to an education based on the pagan literature and the reluctance of the Eastern monastic movement to take on responsibility for the education of children.

21. One risks stating the obvious. Nonetheless, one may question whether a person as knowledgeable on education in antiquity as Cameron would have made a statement on Basil's treatise that it "was no reasoned defence of secular education: it was a superficial justification of the *status quo*" (op. cit. in n.8, 672) had he realized that Basil was not primarily addressing those who like himself had benefited from a good education, but those who were innately suspicious of the products of such an education for the Christian community.

22. Dating of the treatise is discussed in A. Moffatt, "The Occasion of St. Basil's *Address to Young Men*," *Antichthon* 6 (1972): 74-86. Moffatt argues for a setting of Julian's edict of 362 A.D., forbidding Christians teaching in the pagan schools, unethical on their part, since they do not endorse the gods to whom the literature refers. Basil would accordingly be using this address to convince the parents to send their children to the schools regardless of the absence of Christian teachers. Many features of the argument are attractive, including her arguments for a preponderance of Christianity in the Cappadocian province (82), but there is little internal evidence in the treatise to substantiate such a setting. One would have expected Basil to refer to the edict or at least to have shown more vehemence in denying the implications of the edict for education.

23. See nn. 19 and 21 above.

24. Such an assessment of the purpose of Basil's treatise surfaces even in an otherwise excellent article of S. Gero, "Christianity and Hellenism from the First to the Fourth Century," *Didaskalos* 5 (1975), 123-35. According to Gero, the treatise can be summed up in the "well-known adage, *Gather the roses, not the thorns*" (129).

25. Schucan, op. cit. in n. 1, 30ff.

26. It is significant that Basil does not justify Cleinias's supposed conscious imitation of biblical principles (7.47ff.) with an appeal to the commonplace that the Greek poets and sages derived their wisdom from Moses, a theme which was to remain popular well into the medieval period. Cf. E. R. Curtius, *European Litera-*

ture and the Latin Middle Ages (Harper, 1963), 219ff. Basil would certainly have
been familiar with such a theme from his reading of Clement and Origen.
27. The Platonism of the church fathers, whether Greek or Latin, has received
much attention in literature of the past few decades. Of special interest are discussions such as those of W. Jaeger, Early Christianity and Greek Paideia (Oxford,
1961) or E. P. Meyering, Orthodoxy and Platonism in Athanasius, Synthesis or
Antithesis? (Leiden, 1968). Whether use of Plato was ultimately to be more beneficial or harmful to the cause of Christianity is a question we cannot possibly hope
to resolve within the present context. In the desire to encourage the youths to
continue their studies in philosophy, Basil turned especially to Plato as a model. In
the contemporary discussions on the use of Plato by the church fathers, one should
not lose sight of the positive contributions of the philosophical distinctions and
formulations for the search for truth in the religious controversies of the time. Even
though we may wish to distance ourselves from the format of theological discussions
and do not, therefore, accept the results of the controversies at face value, we must
nevertheless recognize the historic role of the discussions of the fourth century for
the development of doctrine and a worldview acceptable for the Christian church.
28. Wilson's commentary on 3.6-11 refers the reader to Seneca's *Letters* 41.7,
acknowledging nonetheless that "I have not been able to trace this analogy to a
particular source"; had he checked Clement of Alexandria's *Paidagogos*, even this
analogy would have been traced to another source. The reluctance of classical
scholars to check the patristic literature may be the culprit here; studies which do
not hesitate to cross boundaries of literary, philosophical, and theological genres
are most rewarding especially for late antiquity, as can be seen from such works
as P. Brown *The Cult of the Saints* (Chicago, 1981).
29. Cameron makes this point in his brief remark concerning Basil that the traditional idea of the "cultured man, eloquent, well read in the poets ... continued to
matter to the vast majority of Christian subjects" (op. cit. in n. 8, 672). One need
not disagree with this statement as such to dispute the implication that this ideal
might become an end in itself for Basil rather than only a means to a different end,
that of convincing others that, as such, a traditional education need not be considered a threat.
30. On a theological education for those who were preparing themselves to serve
the church, see pages 43-44 of this chapter.
31. Awareness of Basil's inclination to interpret "good" or "evil" as virtue or vice,
from the moral perspective, should not blind the reader to the larger perspective
to which he also alludes, namely, obedience to the demands God makes of
humankind. To describe Basil as a moralist is thus not completely justified, although the many references to arete, especially when looked at without due regard
for the larger context, might tempt one to do so (cf. n. 24 above). I have not been
able to discover another modern discussion of Basil's use of the term arete which
in any way recognizes the inner tensions arising in his argument because of the
multiplicity of meanings attributed to the term; he uses it to indicate 1) the fruit
of the soul, that is, the truth, 2) the goal of an education which is concerned with
the care of the soul, as well as 3) the route to be taken to attain that goal (as in
Heracles's choice) or, in other words, the route of obedience to God's law for
humankind. Perhaps it was inevitable that Basil should end up with a certain

circularity of argument, asking the students to identify *arete* in pagan authors while maintaining that the true definition of *arete* is found in the Scriptures which are still too difficult for understanding at their age.

32. See n. 26 above. Is there an indication of a blind spot in Basil's appreciation of non-Christian authors? Perhaps Plato is too important a source to even risk a justification of the use of his writings. A more generous assessment of Basil's use of Plato would recognize his educational background as steeped in the study of the philosopher to such an extent that he used his arguments without being fully aware of appropriating them as an external source.

33. Many church fathers realized that pride in the pagan authors who formed the core of the traditional education was something they consciously had to break with. This is the background of Tertullian's famous remark, "What has Athens to do with Jerusalem?" (cf. Marrou op. cit. in n. 8, 426-27). But even Jerome was not consistent in his repudiation of Cicero: in his letters to Paulinus of Nola, he insists on a traditional educational curriculum for those who wish to become interpreters of the Scriptures (cf. Laistner, op. cit. in n. 20, 65-68).

34. Augustine, as Laistner recognized (see n. 33 above), provided the systematic hermeneutical tool for reading and interpreting the Scriptures, where Jerome gave only sporadic insights. But in comparison with the program outlined by Cassiodorus, Augustine was not as clearly aiming at the establishment of an entire Christian curriculum; cf. M. L. Clarke, *Rhetoric at Rome* (London, 1953), 151-55.

35. Laistner, op. cit. in n. 20, 10-12, 16-21.

36. It should be noted that there is no basis in the *Ad Adolescentes* for advocating for the school texts of the classical authors methods of emendation which involved a wholesale removal of words or passages morally offensive to the editors. There is no indication whatsoever that Basil would have approved of such methods, contrary to what may be a popular misconception of his role. Even in his own time, of course, very few authors were read in their entirety; for the rhetorically oriented education there were many collections of famous passages, *topoi*, by which the authors were frequently identified. Quotations from classical authors in the present treatise often have their origin in such collections, as Wilson has noted. Nonetheless the desire to cut out undesirable passages cannot appeal to Basil as an authority, even though it is not difficult to see how later less careful reading of the treatise might lead to the "cut and splice" attitude, especially when texts were being prepared for very young students not familiar with aspects of Greek morality, like lesbianism or homosexuality.

37. On the role of the *logos protreptikos*, the exhortation to the study of philosophy and the adoption of the philosophic life-style, see Marrou, op. cit. in n. 8, 282-83.

38. E. Lambertz, "Zum Verstandnis von Basileios' Schrift, *Ad Adolescentes,*" *Zeitschrift fur Kirchengeschichte* 90 (1979): 75-95.

39. Ibid., 81, n. 24. On the use of the term "philosophy" among church fathers of the period, see Laistner, op. cit. in n. 20, 53-54. It is of interest that at this time the pastors, especially in the Eastern churches, increasingly were receiving their training in the monasteries.

40. See n. 20 above. On Gregory of Nyssa as philosopher, the discussion of Jaeger, op. cit. in n. 27, 86ff. is of interest; cf. I. P. Sheldon-Williams on Gregory of Nyssa

in the *Cambridge History of Later Greek and Early Medieval Philosophy*, ed. A. H. Armstrong (Cambridge, 1967), pt. VI, 447ff.

41. On the connections of the Cappadocian fathers with the Alexandrian school, see J. Gribomont, "L'Origénisme de Saint Basile," in *L'Homme Devant Dieu, Mélanges H. de Lubac* (Paris, 1964); M. Naldini, "Paideia origeniana nella *Oratio ad adolescentes* di Basilio Magno," *Vetera Christianorum* 13 (1976): 297-318; and Lamberz, op. cit. n. 38, 88ff.

42. Cf. Jaeger, op. cit. in n. 27, 51ff.

43. For Origen's reply see W. Metcalfe, *Gregory Thaumaturgus, Address to Origen* (London: SPCK, 1920), 89ff.

44. For an accessible edition, see M. Harl, *Origène, Philocalie 1-20, Sur les Écritures* (Paris, 1983); it is in the series *Sources Chrétiennes*, H. De Lubac, dir., no. 302.

45. Lamberz, op. cit. in n. 38, 92.

46. The best witness to this tradition and its use of Basil's treatise is Schucan's *Nachleben von Basilius Magnus "ad adolescentes"* (op. cit. in n. 1).

47. On the ideals of the Neo-Hellenists, see R. Pfeiffer, *A History of Classical Scholarship from 1300 to 1850* (Oxford, 1976). His chapter (167ff.) on Winckelmann is of special interest.

48. For the writings of Groen van Prinsterer on the classics, see the study of J. Zwaan, *Groen van Prinsterer and Classical Antiquity* (Amsterdam: A. Hakkert, 1973); his remarks on the "voorbereidingsphilosophie" are on pages 14ff.

Jerusalem versus Rome:
The Religious and Philosophical Context of Augustine's Assessment of the Roman Empire in the *City of God*

Theodore S. de Bruyn

I would like to introduce my reflections on the relationship between Christianity and classical culture in Augustine's *City of God* by reminding us of the audience to which Augustine addressed his *magnum opus et arduum*.[1] It consisted of refugee aristocrats who had fled Rome upon the sack of 410 and were passing time in North Africa. These aristocrats were proud of their Roman heritage and assiduous in its preservation. They were attentive to the cult which had served Rome well in its time of greatness. They were active in the revival of Rome's literary classics. They were familiar with current philosophical explanations of reality. And, most significant for Augustine, they were resistant to the encroachment of Christianity upon their class, some voicing the old claim that the worship of the gods was essential to the security of the empire, others raising philosophical objections to the faith in discussions with their Christian peers in Carthage.

In a society where paganism was by no means dead, such resistance to Christianity was not to be dismissed lightly, particularly among persons of influence and prestige. Augustine accordingly set to work on a reply aimed at these Roman nobles who have set up camp in Carthage. His Christian apologetic turned out to be as complex as their pagan polemic. It is a comprehensive assessment of the religious, political, and philosophical assumptions of the Greco-Roman world.

The first part of the *City of God*, books I to X, is largely a refutation of the more obvious weaknesses in the pagan position. Augustine reviews the history of Rome to show that the worship of the gods neither built moral character nor guaranteed national security. At the same time he reinterprets the history of Rome to undermine the pretensions of the Roman aristocracy about their ancestors. And he explores the relationship between God and humankind to answer philosophical objections to Christianity. But the real power of the *City of God* does not lie in the ostensibly negative approach of the first part of the work. It lies rather in the vision of the two cities, which Augustine unfolds in books XI to XXII. This is the matrix in which Augustine manipulates all the various aspects of his enormous apology. It provides him with a scheme which encompasses all of human history and measures every human aspiration. In its great sweep Augustine picks up the accomplishments of the Romans, determines their value in relation to the whole of reality, and relegates them to their proper place in the history of humankind. With the vision of the two cities, in short, Augustine has a context in which to formulate an integral response to his pagan antagonists.

Augustine's evaluation of the Roman Empire in the *City of God* serves as one example of an assessment of the classical world by a Christian contemporary. In this paper I shall consider this evaluation in the light of Augustine's reflections on Greco-Roman religion and philosophy. First I shall explore some aspects of pagan religion which Augustine consciously repudiates in the *City of God*. Then I shall review his theory of the two cities and his assessment of the empire according to that theory. And finally I shall consider an important aspect of the theory of the two cities for which Augustine is indebted to Neoplatonism.

A. Greco-Roman Religion and Philosophy

As I have said, the immediate problem facing Augustine was the claims Roman expatriates were making for their religious traditions. For this reason Augustine's main interlocutors in the *City of God* are the scholar Varro, author of an exhaustive treatise on the religion of the Romans (VI and VII passim; cf.III.4, IV,1,31ff., VI.2), and the Platonists, whose philosophical tradition, according to Augustine, approximated Christian teaching more closely than any other school (VIII, IX, and X passim; cf. VIII.5). Augustine's audience would no doubt acknowledge these as worthy representatives of their religious views.

From a reading of the first part of the *City of God* it is clear that Augustine considers all pagan religion as one unit. Augustine is aware that Varro distinguishes between three types of pagan religion (VI.5). There are the pagan myths and the deplorable theater that is, for Augustine, synonymous with them. There is the civic cult, the service to the gods on behalf of the household, the town, and the empire. And there is natural theology, the religion of the philosophers, preeminently of the Platonists. But these distinctions prove too fine for Augustine, who exploits the connections between the three types to build his case against pagan religion as a whole. The myths and the theater are easily discredited by their internal contradictions and abominable immorality (VI.9,10,11 and VII passim). Then, the relationship between this sort of debased religion and the observances of the civic cult undermines the latter's credibility (VI.6,7,9; VII.33). Finally, even the religion of the philosophers is tainted by their unwillingness to break entirely with polytheism and the sort of superstition they condemn in the poets (VIII.12; IX.7); thus, Augustine takes Porphyry to task for his involvement in theurgy (X.9,10,26).

But, though Augustine draws out the connections between mythical, civic, and philosophical religion, he has more esteem for philosophical religion than he does for the two other types. Augustine simply ridicules the myths and the cult for what he regards as gross immorality, grave inconsistency, and pathetic impotence. It seems obvious to him that the gods of the Romans could not secure the welfare of the empire, and it is a foregone conclusion that they do not provide the basis for true justice (II.22; cf. II.17,18,22). But the religion of the philosopher, who seeks to live well in harmony with the One of the universe, is less susceptible to satirical review than the religion of the crowd. Accordingly, Augustine treats the religion of the philosopher with greater care than the religion of the crowd.

Various matters come up for discussion in Augustine's consideration of pagan philosophy: the nature and function of the demons (VII and IX passim), the worship due to God (X.3ff.), the true mediator between God and humankind (IX.17; X.20,24,27ff.), and the destiny of the soul (X.30ff.). But behind all the particulars of the debate stand two different conceptions of how the wise person ought to live:

> If, therefore, we are asked what reply the *City of God* gives when asked about each of these points, and first what view it holds about the Ultimate Good and the Ultimate Evil, the reply will be that eternal life is the Supreme Good, and eternal death the Supreme Evil, and that to achieve the one and escape the other we must live rightly. That is why the Scripture says, "The just man lives on the basis of faith." For we do not yet see our good, and hence we have to seek it by believing; and it is not in our power to live rightly, unless while we believe and pray we receive help from him who has given us the faith to believe that we must be helped by him. Whereas those who have supposed that the Ultimate Good and the Ultimate Evil are to be found in this life . . . all these philosophers have wished, with amazing folly, to be happy here on earth and to achieve bliss by their own efforts (XIX.4).

Augustine touches here on many points of difference between Christian and pagan thought.[2] First, in declaring that the *summum bonum* is eternal life, Augustine places the greatest good outside this life, whereas the philosophers represented by Varro aimed at a good within this life (XIX.3). Augustine, furthermore, conceives of eternal life as an eternal union of body and soul in blissful existence. Even the Platonists, who entertained various notions of the eternity of the soul, did not countenance a union of body and soul that was at once eternal and happy. Thus, Augustine takes issue with Plato on the transmigration of the soul and with Porphyry for his idea of the eternal existence of disembodied souls (X.30, XIII.19, XXII.26); in the last book of the *City of God*, he muses that if only Plato and Porphyry had got together, along with Varro, they would have come up with the right idea (XXII.27,28).

Secondly, Augustine maintains that one attains eternal life not by a disciplined effort of reason to discover the good, but by a willingness to believe the Word of God and integrate all human experience in the light of that Word. Augustine is well aware that the Scriptures are the source of so many of the points disputed by the philosophers, but for this very reason he repeatedly affirms the authority of the Scriptures for all that one must believe to attain eternal life (XII.9, XIV.7,8, XV.1, XVIII.40, XIX.18, XX.1) and rebukes the pride of those (in particular, the Platonists) who reject the teachings of the Scriptures because they are incompatible with their "useless learning" (X.28,29).

Finally, Augustine holds that a person cannot know the good or live by it unless that person is enabled by God, who is ready to help those who ask. This is a direct attack on the self-sufficiency of the pagan. Augustine had no mean estimate of the abilities of the rational soul (XXII.24), but he denied it the ability to order the passions so as to attain peace (XIX.14). For this he turns resolutely to the grace of God in Christ. It is particularly distressing to Augustine, therefore, that Porphyry rejected Christ as the way to eternal life (X.28,29). Augustine believed that Porphyry had recognized the need for grace, but had rejected Christ as the mediator of that grace because of the intolerable idea of the incarnation (X.29). Nothing is quite so disastrous for Augustine as the pride of one so close to the truth.

In short, when Augustine compares the pagan philosopher with the Christian pilgrim, he sets Christian teachings of eternal life, faith, and grace over against pagan ideas of happiness and ways to attain it. This means that, despite many qualifications, Augustine comes to the same conclusion about philosophical religion as he does about mythical and civic religion: it is not true religion because true religion is none other than the ordering of this life under divine direction and with divine assistance so as to eventually enjoy peace with God in eternal life (XIX.14); true religion is a life of faith, hope, and prayer.

The fact that Augustine holds that Greco-Roman religion in all its manifestations is not true religion has some bearing on his evaluation of the Roman Empire. Because he maintains that true justice depends on true worship, he concludes that there is no true justice in the empire (XIX.21). Therefore, a definition of the *res publica*, if it is to be applied to Rome, must exclude the term "justice." Accordingly, Augustine proposes a radical qualification of a standard definition of the *res publica*. It is not, as Scipio suggested, "an association united by a common sense of right and a community of interest" (II.21), but rather "an association of a multitude of rational beings united by a common agreement on the objects of their love" (XIX.24). Augustine, in short, desacralizes the empire. For neither its basis nor its welfare does the empire depend upon the worship of the gods; rather, insofar as it is an expression of the *res publica*, it depends merely on the common values of its citizens.

Such a view of the empire opens the way for an assessment of the empire. One is free to question the worth of the values its citizens hold in common. And this is precisely that Augustine does, using his theory of the two cities as the standard by which to measure the empire.

B. Two Cities, Two Loves

At the end of book XIV, Augustine draws one of his many sketches of the two cities (XIV.28).[3] He envisages two communities, two societies, two fellowships which encompass all rational creatures, human and angelic. These two communities are religious communities. They are known by their loves. The one, the earthly city, loves itself above all and directs its will for the enjoyment of earthly goods. The other, the heavenly city, loves God above all and subordinates every desire to the ultimate enjoyment of God. These two communities move together through time from the fall to the last judgment, but because of the difference of their loves they regard their progress in time from quite different points of view. The earthly city has made this life its home. It has settled down to enjoy the goods of this life and believes that by its own efforts it can attain happiness in this life. The heavenly city, on the other hand, regards this life as an exile and longs for the next life as its home. It expects happiness not from the goods of this life but rather from God in the next life and appeals for God's help so that it may finally enjoy God forever. Time is thus the scene of a great drama in which human beings play out their part, joined in an invisible fellowship from the moment when Cain and Abel founded the two cities on earth, guided by God's providence through prosperity and adversity, and eventually gathered together with all their fellow citizens to the peace of eternal life or the torment of eternal condemnation.

This is, obviously, a religious view of human history. It pretends to know the secrets of the heart and to judge according to the secrets of the heart. It is not readily apparent, therefore, to those to whom the secrets of the heart are hidden. How then does Augustine reconcile his view of history with the events of history? In particular, what estimate does Augustine take of the Roman Empire against the standard of the two cities?

The temptation for a Christian living in the fourth century after the Constantinian change was to construe the history of the empire as a history of progress, beginning with the coming of Christ and culminating in the advent of the Christian empire.[4] This perspective was first articulated under Constantine by Eusebius, who depicted the emperor as the earthly image of Christ and the empire as the image of Christ's Kingdom, and, though Christians had seen their share of troubles under Constantine's successors, it was still strong enough at the end of the century that Orosius, writing his *History against the Pagans* at Augustine's suggestion, interpreted the imperial period in Rome's history as a period of divine favor coming to fulfillment when Constantine brought an end to persecution and introduced a millennium of peace. Initially Augustine, too, accepted a modest version of Eusebius's progressive view of the empire, but he abandoned it by the time he wrote the *City of God*. In the *City of God* he in fact takes pains to show that Christian emperors are not guaranteed prosperity in the world and that Christians, far from enjoying a millennium of peace, can be assured of troubles and persecutions to the end of time (V.25,26, XVIII.52). The earthly city and the heavenly city do not admit of easy distinction in the course of human history and cannot be identified with particular historical institutions; rather, the two cities are mixed together in the world just as believers and unbelievers are mixed together in the church (I.35, X.32, XI.1, XVIII.49).

Augustine's assessment of the empire is, therefore, more subtle than a simple equation of the pagan empire with the earthly city and the Christian empire with the heavenly city. His view of Roman politics emerges as a series of qualifications that, even if they are finally damning, nevertheless damn with faint praise. Augustine does not altogether dismiss the accomplishments of the Romans. He acknowledges that some Romans excelled in human virtue (II.9,10, V.12), and he even holds the more outstanding heroes of the Republic, like Atilius Regulus and Scipio Nasica, before his own degenerate contemporaries to wean them from their degraded paganism (II.29; cf.I.15,24,30 and II.5). He also allows that the *pax Romana*, though flawed, is nevertheless a form of peace (XIX.7,12) and, as such, is useful to the citizens of the heavenly city (XIX.17). But according to Augustine the misdirected aims of the Romans finally undermine their accomplishments. He observes that in all their acts of duty and self-denial the best of the Romans were motivated by a love of glory, and as a result he can wither-ingly remark that in the accolades of history they have their reward (V.14,15). What's worse, he maintains that they were consumed with the lust for domination, the characteristic vice of the earthly city (III.14,15, V.19, cf. IV.6,15 and XV.7). And never far from Augustine's mind is the cost at which the Romans acquired their empire (IV.3; cf. III passim): even if their wars were waged for the protection of their state (rather doubtful; cf. V.22), the injustice of their enemies, which compelled them to shed so much blood, should have filled them with great regret (equally unlikely; cf. IV.15 and XIX.7). In the end, when all the credits and debits are tallied, Rome is for Augustine a representative of the earthly city because, like the earthly city, it set its sights on temporal goods and was, therefore, torn by endless strife, litigation and war: Romulus, the founder of Rome, was, like Cain, the founder of the earthly city, a fratricide (XV.4,5).

The achievements of Rome, therefore, are for Augustine only relatively good, better or worse insofar as they are more or less vir-tuous. And in the end the Roman Empire will go the way of the earthly city: its history will end in flames (XV.4; cf. IV.8). But in the meantime Christians are numbered among the citizens of the em-pire. What role, then, do they have in this empire which has only relative value and will finally perish?

It is clear that Augustine would not have the Christian abdicate all responsibility to the Roman Empire. After all, he dedicates the City of God to the imperial commissioner at Carthage, Flavius Mar-cellinus, a Christian (I. pref.). Furthermore, he states that Constan-tine enjoyed such benefits as a long reign, victory in war, security against insurrection precisely in order to show that high worldly office is not closed to those who worship the true God, rather than the demons (V.25). Indeed, Augustine has no doubt that the reign of the good, who worship the true God, is better than the reign of the wicked; it is a blessing not only for themselves, but also for the whole of human society (IV.3).

But Augustine never imagines that Christians would have an easy time in office. He argues that it was to prevent such notions that God allowed early misfortune to befall the Christian emperors Jovian and Gratian (V.25). He also knows from experience the an-guish Christians suffer in trying to fulfill their office in a sinful world. One of the most agonizing passages in the City of God recounts the torment of the Christian judge who, beset by human ignorance and following Roman judicial practice, may be compelled to torture the innocent to death in order to discover the guilty. The best the Christian can do in such circumstances is cry to God: "Deliver me from my necessities" (XIX.6).

Indeed, Augustine's conception of civic duty in a sinful world is precisely this: a necessity. Inasmuch as Christians make use of the goods afforded them by the Roman Empire, and inasmuch as they find themselves in high office, they are obliged to execute that office as best they can, so long as they remain faithful to God and to the church (XIX.17). But inasmuch as in their office they are beset by so much trouble, they are reminded that their ultimate happiness is not found in the honors of this life but in the peace of the life to come. For Augustine even the office of emperor, "the loftiest summit of power," is "nothing but a passing mist"; the reward the Emperor Theodosius enjoyed for his efforts as a faithful son of the church was something immeasurable greater: "eternal happiness" (V.26).

To review, then, the vision of the two cities and Rome's place within that vision: Augustine divides the human race into two great communities which are determined by their loves. The citizens of the heavenly city love God above all. The citizens of the earthly city prefer created, temporal goods. The goods afforded by the Roman Empire belong to the latter; they are created, temporal goods. Whoever values them as the greatest goods is a citizen of the earthly city. But whoever uses them toward the eventual enjoyment of God is a citizen of the heavenly city. Augustine does not, therefore, dismiss the Roman Empire altogether; it has its goods, and even Christians may administer and benefit from its goods. But for Augustine the Roman Empire belongs, finally, to the order of the earthly city; its greatest goods are but temporal, and its greatest virtues (not to speak of its vices) are but human.

This assessment of the empire, along with the repudiation of its religion, is not, however, the last word on the relationship between things classical and things Christian in the *City of God*. There remains the question of the source of the theory of the two cities: to what extent is Augustine indebted to classical thought for the very standard with which he measures the accomplishments of the Romans?

C. Time and Eternity

In considering Augustine's treatment of Greco-Roman religion, I have already observed that Augustine had particular regard for the views of the Platonists. "There are none nearer to us," he says, "than the Platonists" (VIII.5)—by which he usually means the Neoplatonism of Plotinus and Porphyry. Of these two, Plotinus was the first and foremost influence on Augustine.[5] Augustine is indebted to him for, among other ideas, his understanding of eternity and time, which is especially significant for the theory of the two cities.

Augustine seems to have appropriated some basic aspects of Plotinus's view before he wrote the *Confessions*—the parallels between book XI of the *Confessions* and *Enneads* III.7 are striking and significant—and does not appear to have radically changed his approach when he wrote the *City of God*. For Plotinus the distinction between time and eternity is fundamentally a distinction of being.[6] In the hierarchy of reality time is distinct from, but dependent upon, eternity as an image is distinct from, but dependent upon, its archetype. Eternity inheres in the changeless and self-identical life of the Intellect. Time, as its image, inheres in the changing and successive life of the Soul. For Augustine the distinction between eternity and time is also a distinction in being.[7] God, for Augustine, is eternal because God is immutable. Divine being is unchangingly self-identical. Creation, on the other hand, is temporal because it is mutable. Its existence is an endless succession of moments because it came into existence out of nothing and constantly tends toward nothing. Its existence is secure, therefore, only insofar as it depends upon the unchangeable being of its Creator.

This identification of eternity with unchangeability and time with changeability determines the framework for the pilgrimage of the heavenly city in Augustine's theory of the two cities. It is a pilgrimage through the changeable existence of time to the stable being of eternity. In this pilgrimage the object of one's love is all-important because it determines the quality of one's existence.[8] It is imperative for one whose existence is changeable to love God above all, for only then will one participate in the stability of God's unchangeable being. Only then will one enjoy peace in eternal life.

It is no wonder that Augustine had a special regard for the Platonists. They seemed to have caught the essentials of his religious vision: the truth that the Soul can attain beatitude only if it adheres to God, who is unchangeable, in pure love (X.1). But there are still some important differences between the views of the Platonists, particularly the view of Plotinus and the view of Augustine on eternity and time.

First, Plotinus holds that the souls of human beings in their highest aspect participate in the life of the Intellect and therefore rest in eternity, whereas Augustine, in accordance with Christian doctrine, teaches that the souls of human beings are created and therefore temporal (XI.6, cf. XII.15). Secondly, the process whereby the souls of human beings participate in eternity is, for Plotinus, an ahistorical process whereby the Soul concentrates its attention on its eternal aspect by means of contemplation (*Enn.* III.7.5; cf. III.7.12). For Augustine, on the other hand, the process whereby souls participate in eternity is a historical process: the way to eternity is a pilgrimage in time. Thirdly, according to Plotinus, the Soul in its several aspects—the Soul as hypostasis, the Soul as the producer and governor of the material world, the Soul as the highest level of human rationality—remains aloof from the distractions of time and is not morally responsible for them. But Augustine holds human beings responsible for the restlessness they suffer in time because he insists that the deficiencies of their present temporal existence are the result of their turning away from God in the fall (XIII.14, XIV.1,12). Finally, Plotinus believes that the souls of human beings are self-sufficient inasmuch as within themselves they have access to eternity. But Augustine insists that since human beings are mortal and miserable, they need an immortal mediator who has participated in their mortality and can lift them to his own immortality (IX.15,17).

Augustine incorporates all these differences into his vision of the two cities. He places the course of the two human societies from beginning to end within time. He locates the beginning of their pilgrimage through the vicissitudes of time in the fall. He accounts for the divergence in their development from the fall as the consequence of their different loves. He makes the incarnation, death, and resurrection of Jesus Christ the hope of all those pilgrims who journeyed in the ages of promise and prophecy. And he looks to the fulfillment of the work of Christ in the resurrection of all the saints in the New Jerusalem.

All this shows how much Augustine reformulates a Neoplatonic view of reality to fit the scriptural view of history. It is as if Augustine bends the vertical axis of the former to line up with the horizontal axis of the latter. All the main points of reference on the pilgrimage of the heavenly city are events in the history of salvation as reported in the biblical narrative. But the pilgrimage of the heavenly city is still a movement from the vicissitudes of time to the unchangeability of eternity, and in this movement the direction of one's love is crucial; it is the touchstone with which Augustine discriminates between the two cities, the one the society of those who will eventually perish because the object of their love cannot sustain their existence, the other the society of those who will remain secure because the object of their love is God whose being does not change. With this synthesis of biblical history and Plotinian ontology, Augustine measures every earthly accomplishment, including the achievements of Rome.

This, then, is Augustine's debt to "the Platonists" in the *City of God*. From the Platonists, Plotinus in particular, Augustine took over the distinction between forever-changing temporal existence and enduringly changeless eternal being. This distinction he reinterpreted in accordance with the biblical revelation of the history of the relationship between God and humankind from the creation to the New Jerusalem. But the basic point of contrast in the distinction, changelessness versus change, he nevertheless embedded in the overall scheme of the *City of God*, inasmuch as the history of salvation is for him a pilgrimage through the vicissitudes of this life to the stability of the next.

D. Conclusion: A Synthesis
What, then, is the sum of the relationship between Christianity and Greco-Roman culture in the *City of God*?

It is best here to advance by degrees. On the central religious issue Augustine is exclusive: Greco-Roman religion is not true religion. But in the assessment of the empire, which is interwoven with his repudiation of pagan religion, Augustine is measured: he must revise ancient political ideology in order to eradicate false claims for the religion of the Romans, but he does not dismiss the accomplishments of Rome altogether; rather, he places them in a new perspective, the perspective of the two cities, so as to give a right estimate of their relative value in the history of humankind. This perspective, however, is itself significantly indebted to Neoplatonism inasmuch as the Neoplatonic conception of time and eternity underlies Augustine's notion of this life as a pilgrimage to the next life, a pilgrimage in which the decisive factor is the direction of one's love. So there is a progression in Augustine's view of classical culture from the outright rejection of Greco-Roman religion, to the qualified evaluation of the Roman Empire, to the uncritical acceptance in the theory of the two cities of some basic aspects of the Neoplatonic conception of eternity and time.

It seems to me that in this progression Augustine preserves the crucial distinctions between Christianity and Greco-Roman culture, or at least the distinctions which would have been perceived as crucial in his day. Most obviously, he repudiates polytheism and undermines its renewed appeal for the pagan aristocracy at the turn of the century. Perhaps more importantly, he challenges some assumptions of the Platonism of the day with such Christian teachings as creation, fall, incarnation, resurrection, grace, faith, and so on. Above all, he places Greco-Roman culture, and in particular the Roman Empire, within the parentheses of the history of salvation as construed in the vision of the two cities. For Augustine's audience, the coterie of *déraciné* pagan nobles in Carthage, there would be no mistaking of the offense of Christianity.

But it is true, nevertheless, that there is a synthesis of Christian and Greco-Roman thought in Augustine's vision of the two cities, and that this synthesis is important for Augustine's assessment of the Roman Empire. Because Augustine accepts the Neoplatonic definition of the distinction between time and eternity as a distinction between changeable existence and unchangeable being, and because he interprets salvation as the movement from the one to the other, he can evaluate the empire by the temporal nature of its highest values. This means, on the one hand, that Augustine is more balanced in his estimate of the empire than he might have been had he simply identified the worth of the empire with the religion of the empire; with a scheme of the relative value of temporal goods, he can give credit where credit, if only a little credit, is due. But, on the other hand, this also means that Augustine espouses an otherworldly view of salvation which limits the role of the Christian in the empire to that of a homesick exile. As a result the only consolation Augustine can offer his wretched judge is the cry: "Deliver me from my necessities" (XIX.6). Anyone who reads Augustine's account of the treacheries and disappointments of human relationships—treacheries and disappointments from which even the home is not safe—knows that Augustine has good reason to take a pessimistic view of the exigencies of public life (XIX.5-8). But to what extent is this sober view reinforced, or rather exaggerated, by a theoretical subordination of temporal existence to eternal being? Should Augustine have offered his judge more hope of salvation in this life than he did?

But now I am touching on questions beyond the immediate scope of this paper. So let me end with a summary of Augustine's approach to classical culture, as I perceive it, in the *City of God*. Augustine's approach is an apologetic approach which, using terms which would be intelligible to his audience, rejects outright those aspects of Greco-Roman culture which obviously run counter to Christianity but assigns relative value to those aspects which admit of coexistence with Christianity. The occasion for the apology is the arrival of learned pagan Roman exiles in Carthage after the sack of Rome. The monument of Greco-Roman culture to be evaluated is, at least ostensibly, the Roman Empire. The aspects of the empire which Augustine repudiates are those which command exclusive religious loyalty, such as the cult of the gods, and the aspects which he accommodates are those which do not, such as the imperial peace. And the matrix within which Augustine sets this evaluation is one which is significantly, though not uncritically, influenced by a Neoplatonic view of reality.

Notes

This paper is in large part the product of two seminars in which I participated while I was a graduate student at the Toronto School of Theology. The first was a seminar on Augustine's political thought, led by O. M. T. O'Donovan, who was then Professor of Theology at Wycliffe College; the second, a seminar on Plotinus, led by Albert M. Wolters, then a Senior Member in History of Philosophy at the Institute for Christian Studies. I am indebted to these two scholars for introducing me to the subject under consideration in this paper.

1. See Peter Brown, *Augustine of Hippo* (London: Faber & Faber, 1967), 299-304 and T. D. Barnes, "Aspects of the Background of the *City of God*," *University of Ottawa Review* 52 (1982): 64-80, esp.72-73.
2. See R. H. Barrow, *Introduction to St. Augustine, The City of God* (London: Faber & Faber, 1951), 187-200.
3. For this section, see R. A. Markus, *Saeculum: History and Society in the Theology of St. Augustine* (Cambridge, Mass.: Harvard University Press, 1970), 45-104.
4. Ibid., 50-54. On Eusebius's view of the empire, see N. H. Baynes, "Eusebius and the Christian Empire," *Annuaire de l' institut de philologie et d'histoire orientales* 2

(Mélanges Bidez, 1933-34): 13-18; and F. Edward Cranz, "Kingdom and Polity in Eusebius of Caesarea," *Harvard Theological Review* 45 (1952): 51-56. For a comparison of Orosius and Augustine, see Theodor E. Mommsen, "Orosius and Augustine," in *Medieval and Renaissance Studies*, ed. Eugene F. Rice, Jr. (Ithaca, N.Y.: Cornell University Press, 1959), 325-48. On the change in Augustine's view see, in addition to Markus, op. cit., 29-35, F. Edward Cranz's important article, "The Development of Augustine's Ideas on Society before the Donatist Controversy, "*Harvard Theological Review* 47 (1954): 255-316.

5. See J. M. Rist, "Basil's 'Neoplatonism': Its Background and Nature," in *Basil of Caesarea: Christian, Humanist, Ascetic. A Sixteenth-Hundred Anniversary Symposium*, ed. Paul Jonathan Fedwick, 2 vols. (Toronto: Pontifical Institute of Medieval Studies, 1981), 1: 148-49. For a review of the scholarship on Augustine and Neoplatonism, see R. J. O'Connell, *St. Augustine's Early Theory of Man, A.D. 386-391* (Cambridge, Mass.: Belknap Press of Harvard University Press, 1968), 6-10.

6. For an introduction to Plotinus's thought, see A. Hilary Armstrong, "Plotinus," in *The Cambridge History of Later Greek and Early Medieval Philosophy*, ed A. H. Armstrong (Cambridge, Mass.: Harvard University Press, 1967), 193-268, and R. T. Wallis, *Neo-Platonism* (London: Duckworth, 1972). The following studies are important for their treatment of *Enneads III.7: Über Ewigkeit und Zeit (Enneade III 7)*, introduction, translation, and commentary by Werner Beierwaltes, *Quellen der Philosophie*, no. 3 (Frankfurt am Main: Vittorio Kostermann, 1967); Hans Jonas, "Plotin über Ewigkeit und Zeit: Interpretation von Enn. III 7" in *Politische Ordnung und menschliche Existenz: Festgabe für Eric Voegelin* (Munich: C. H. Beck, 1962) 295-319; John F. Callahan, Four Views of Time in Ancient Philosophy (Cambridge, Mass.: Harvard University Press, 1948; rev. ed. Westport, Conn.: Greenwood Press, 1979), 88-148. Other helpful studies are A. Hilary Armstrong, "Eternity, Life and Movement in Plotinus' Accounts of *Nous*," in *Plotinian and Christian Studies* (London: Variorum Reprints, 1979); Paul Aubin, "L''image' dans l'oeuvre de Plotin," *Recherches de science religieuse* 41 (1953): 351-57; Pierre Hadot, "*Être, Vie, Pensée chez Plotin et avant Plotin*," in *Les Sources de Plotin*, Fondation Hardt pour l'étude de l'antiquité classique, Entretiens, vol. 5 (Geneva: Fondation Hardt, 1960), 105-157.

7. The following are helpful approaches to Augustine's discussion of time in book XI of the *Confessions*: Rudolf Berlinger, "Le temps et l'homme chez saint Augustin," *Année théologique augustinienne* 13 (1953): 260-79; Robert Jordan, "Time and Contingency in St. Augustine," in *Augustine: A Collection of Critical Essays*, ed. R. A. Markus (Garden City, N.Y.: Doubleday), 1972), 255-79; E. P. Meijering, *Augustin uber Schopfung, Ewigkeit und Zeit: Das elfte Buch der Bekenntnisse*, Philosophia Patrum, vol. 4 (Leiden: E. J. Brill, 1979). On the relationship between eternity and unchangeability, time and change, see Jules ChaixRuy, *Saint Augustine: Temps et Histoire* (Paris: Études Augustiniennes, 1956) and "*La Cité de Dieu et la structure du temps chez saint Augustin*," in *Augustinus Magister*, 2 vols. (Paris: Études Augustiniennes, 1954), 2:923-31; Etienne Gilson, "Notes sur l'être et le temps chez saint Augustin," *Recherches Augustiniennes* 2 (1962): 205-23; and Henri-Irénée Marrou, *L'Ambivalence du temps de l'histoire chez saint Augustin* (Montréal: Institut d'Études Médièvales et Paris: J. Vrin, 1950), esp. 42-45.

8. See John Burnaby, *Amor Dei: A Study of the Religion of St. Augustine*, The Hulsean Lectures for 1938 (London: Hodder & Stoughton, 1938).

As the Philosopher Says: Thomas Aquinas and the Classical Heritage

Arvin Vos

A. Thirteenth Century Background

Undoubtedly the most influential factor shaping the thirteenth century was the rediscovery of the classical philosophical tradition, primarily in the form of Aristotle's writings.[1] Until the middle of the twelfth century, the West knew only a few of the writings of the classical Greek philosophers—some of the logical writings of Aristotle, the *Timaeus*, and part of the *Phaedo* of Plato. In the last half of the twelfth century and continuing for more than 100 years, from the work of Dominicus Gundissalinus (d. 1151) to William of Moerbeke (d. 1286), a steady stream of translations appeared. Along with Aristotle's writings, the West also received the writings of the great Muslim writers—Alfarabi, Avicenna, Averroes, and others—as well as the Jewish writer Maimonides.[2] The West had known Aristotle's logic through Boethius, but his *Physics* and other writings on natural philosophy, *Metaphysics*, *Ethics*, and *Politics*, along with extensive commentaries on them, were now available for the first time.

The rediscovery of Aristotle's writings was very significant. To understand why we must realize that prior to the thirteenth century the seven liberal arts formed the basis of learning in the West. An educated person knew the liberal arts and theology, the former being considered a preparation for the latter. The most influential work was Augustine's *De Doctrina Christiana*. In it Augustine recommended the study of the liberal arts in order to be able to understand Scripture better. The theoretical and practical aspects of the ancient sciences were left aside, for Scripture was thought to be an adequate, and also more reliable, source for truth.

With the arrival of the new translations, the Latins received what they had long needed: "a cosmology . . . , a scientific and metaphysical description of the structure of the universe."[3] Just the richness of these writings would have caused a significant intellectual upheaval; in fact, they contained more. They contained teachings contrary to fundamental Western Christian doctrines. The problem of the age was to evaluate the newly rediscovered legacy of antiquity. It was not possible to ignore the new learning. To ignore Aristotle's natural philosophy, metaphysics, and ethics would have been obscurantist, and obscurantism is never more than a temporary answer. To ignore Aristotle in the thirteenth century was as impossible as ignoring the natural and social sciences and their associated technology today. Even if it could be done, it would not be desirable, for too many relevant and important questions would be ignored.

Many others before Aquinas were going about the task of assimilation this new learning. Between 1200 and 1255 the study of the liberal arts waned and the arts faculties in the universities became centers for Aristolelian studies. The progress of Aristotle in the curriculum can be seen from the opposition it roused, especially from the prohibitions by the authorities against teaching these writings. By 1255, about the time Thomas Aquinas began to teach at Paris, these prohibitions had become a dead letter. Indeed, "on 19 March 1255 all the writings of Aristotle were put on the syllabus and the Arts faculty became in fact a *Philosophy Faculty* where Aristotelianism was taught."[4]

Significant changes were occurring in the theology faculty during the same period. At the beginning of the century the Parisian theologians were opposed to the employment of Aristotle in theology, but about 1220 professors with an appreciation for Aristotle began teaching theology. In the writings of William of Auvergne and Alexander of Hales, one finds numerous quotations of Aristotle, but it would remain for Albertus Magnus, the teacher of Thomas Aquinas, to bring a full awareness of the resources of Aristotle's thought.[5]

Why did the writings of Aristotle come to dominate the intellectual life of the West during the first half of the thirteenth century? One answer is that his theories of nature, of the human soul, and his metaphysics were superior to what had been available.[6]

There was something about the thirteenth century that made it especially receptive to the Aristotelian viewpoint. It was not a less spiritual age than the centuries dominated by the Augustinian tendency to emphasize the inferiority of the natural world; rather it was a time when Christians were confident that the full resources of nature could be turned to spiritual ends. The cathedrals arose as a manifestation of the same spirit that imbued the philosophers and the theologians in their use of Aristotle. What they found in Aristotle was an appreciation for the resources of nature, the intrinsic principle within things which both makes a thing be what it is and is the source of its operations.[7]

If the new learning was stimulation, it also had its perils. The first exposure to it had resulted in the heretical doctrines of David of Dinant who was condemned in 1210. Later theologians, having a more comprehensive grasp of Aristotle, recognized how formidable a task they faced. There were a number of areas in which the world of Aristotle was irreconcilable with traditional theology:

> [T]he world of Aristotle was itself irreconcilable with the Christian way of conceiving the universe, man, and God. In Aristotle there was no mention of creation. His world was an eternal one, delivered over to the clutches of determinism, without a provident God knowing anything about the world's contingencies. His man was a being bound up with matter, subject like it to corruption, a man whose moral perfection did not involve religious values. The face of Aristotle's philosophy was turned earthward.[8]

There was no simple solution to the problem posed by the new learning. Many thinkers made contributions to the task of assimilation, but here I will consider only the contribution of Thomas Aquinas.

B. Aquinas's Response to Classical Learning

To grasp the perspective of Thomas Aquinas, one must see that he dedicated himself to the gospel and Aristotle—to both and in this order. First, I will examine Aquinas's commitment to the gospel and then his approach to Aristotle.[9]

1. *Aquinas's commitment to the gospel*

In the case of Augustine and Calvin there is a more or less well-documented turn in their lives; in the life of Aquinas there is nothing similar. We find that as soon as he was capable of making his own choices he seems to have had his mind made up. Aquinas's choice, however, was in conflict with his family's goal for him. At the age of five his family sent him to school at the Abbey of Monte Cassino. They intended that he become a monk in this venerable institution. Benedictine monasticism was by now an 800-year-old tradition, and it would be politically advantageous for the family to have a son in this monastery.

In his teens Aquinas was sent to study in Naples where he was taught Aristotle but also came in contact with the Dominicans. The Dominicans, along with the Franciscans, were undoubtedly one of the most dynamic organizations of the time. Dominic, their founder, had seen the devastation of society and the church caused by the Albigensian heresy and the inept attempts of the church to combat it, and had recognized that "the heretics could be won over only by the practice of evangelical poverty, deep learning, and zeal for souls."[10] And so he organized a religious order which had preaching as its goal and study as the means to this end. Like traditional monks, the friars took vows of poverty and chastity, but unlike them they belonged to an order and not a particular foundation. While the monks had traditionally sought seclusion in the countryside, Dominic recruited persons form the university community and located houses near the university. Thomas chose to become a member of this new, radical order, but his family did not approve. In May of 1244 when the Dominicans decided to send Thomas north—likely to get him out of he reach of his family—he was abducted by family members. After being detained for about a year to no avail, his family gave up. When Aquinas was released he immediately rejoined his Dominican brethren and went to Paris, arriving in 1245.

Thomas's determination in the choice of vocation is beyond doubt, but its exact meaning remains to be shown. During the sixteenth century reform would break the bounds of the church, but during the thirteenth century reform still occurred within. Thomas chose for the most vigorous reforming movement of his day—one where dedication to the gospel also involved a life devoted to study.

In the choice to become a friar preacher we see the spirit that animated Aquinas for the rest of his life. Many indications could be cited, but a statement made in the opening of the *Summa Contra Gentiles* (hereafter cited in references as *SCG*) will suffice:

> And so, in the name of the divine Mercy, I have the confidence to embark upon the work of a wise man, even though this may surpass my powers, and I have set myself the task of making known, as far as my limited power will allow, the truth that the Catholic faith professes, and of setting aside the errors that are opposed to it. To use the words of Hilary: "I am aware that I owe this to God as the chief duty of my life, that my every word and sense may speak of him." (SCG I,2.2)

The dedication to the gospel is one focus of Aquinas's life. How is it related to the interest in Aristotle?

2. *Aquinas's interest in Aristotle*

As already hinted, the Dominicans dedicated themselves to study for the sake of preaching. The interest in Aristotle was part of a general interest in the thirteenth century to return to original sources.[11] It should be added that the focus was on dialectic and the sciences, and that literary studies languished in the thirteenth century. Aquinas saw in Aristotle both philosophic method and content that was superior to the Augustinian-Platonic tradition that had dominated the West. I would describe his attitude to Aristotle as that of a critical student—a student for he was eager to learn from him, but critical because he was ready to correct or complete his views whenever necessary. Several points can be made to support this thesis.

First, Aquinas was not a slavish follower of Aristotle. This point is worth making because a slavish attitude toward Aristotle was beginning to develop already in his own time. After studying Aquinas's use of Aristotle, J. Pieper concludes that *"sicut patet per philosophum"* must be rendered: "as has been made clear by Aristotle."[12] Aquinas does not mean that Aristotle said it and therefore it must be true; rather he cites Aristotle because Aristotle said it in a way that sheds light on the issue. That Aquinas did not slavishly follow Aristotle can be seen in the fact that he criticizes "those who vainly endeavor to prove that Aristotle said nothing against the faith."[13] In accord with the practice of his time, he tends to mini-

mize or even fails to mention when he differs with Aristotle, preferring to correct him silently. Because we tend to emphasize how we
differ from others, we easily misunderstand Aquinas's use of Aristotle.

Second, stated positively, Aquinas's attitude is that the purpose
of philosophy is to know reality as it is. In this regard he contrasts
with an attitude that seems to have developed in the arts faculty
during the 1260s. At that time some young arts professors seem to
have made it their goal to be faithful to Aristotle. The extreme is
found in a statement of Siger of Brabant who declares that "he is
going to try to determine the thought of the philosophers more
than to discover the truth, *since he is treating matters philosophically
(cum philosophice procedamus)."*[14] This attitude may appear very
strange until one recalls that the masters in the universities lectured
by reading and explaining the classical authors. Siger and others
like him had an extraordinary esteem for Aristotle which "led them
more or less to identify 'philosophy' with 'the thought of the
philosopher.'"[15] This contrasts with the attitude expressed by
Aquinas in one of his last works. In his *Commentary on the "De Caelo
Et Mundo,"* Aquinas discusses Aristotle's exposition of the various
views of the ancients on the origin of the cosmos. He notes that the
study of arguments which support the positions of opponents is
worthwhile but has limited value. Observing the variety of ancient
views on cosmogony, he states: "[W]e do not have to trouble ourselves too much with respect to these divergences, since
philosophical inquiry does not have as its purpose to know what
men have thought but what is the truth concerning reality."[16] Although Aquinas manifests a critical attitude toward Aristotle, he
tries more than most of his contemporaries to give an accurate and
sympathetic interpretation of the philosopher. Aquinas was concerned to provide for young Dominican students commentaries
which would be purged of the errors promoted by Averroes and
others. Beyond this, Aquinas usually developed his philosophical
thought in the context of theological debate.

Third, Aquinas develops Aristotle's thought in a variety of
ways. One of the best examples of Aquinas's skill in developing and
deepening the philosophy he received is found in his account of
the human soul. Given the assumption that the higher world was
eternal and the lower world subject to degeneration and corruption, Aristotle had a problem in accounting for human nature. The

tendency to adopt the view that there is only one soul, or agent intellect, for all men—at first sight a highly implausible position—arose out of the demands of Aristotle's metaphysics. Aquinas develops resources latent in Aristotle's psychology with the result that he has his own anthropology which is superior not only to that of Aristotle but also to the anthropologies of Augustine and other fathers of the church.[17] In Aquinas's writings one can see the enormous wealth of Augustine's account of the spiritual life being rethought using Aristotelian categories. Especially in his use of the materials from Aristotle's ethics, one sees that Aquinas is not content simply to add a certain spiritual dimension to the Aristotelian account of the moral life, but he works to rethink the meaning of each of the virtues in the context of the Christian view of the goal of human life.

To sum up, Aquinas developed his own philosophy, relying heavily on Aristotle but others as well. He was also critical and, though he preferred to agree with Aristotle, he did not hesitate to disagree when necessary. Aquinas's greatness as a philosopher can be seen in the fact that Siger and others in the arts faculty seem to have changed their positions in response to the criticisms of Aquinas. But for Aquinas his philosophy was not something with which he was concerned for its own sake as an independent study; rather, it was for him primarily a tool in the service of theology.

C. Philosophy and Faith
While I have personally been very impressed by Aquinas's account of human knowledge, it is more appropriate to our theme to focus on Aquinas's understanding of the relation between philosophy and faith and its science, theology. Two main points are to be made: first, that for Aquinas the philosophical order is an autonomous order; and second, that because of the human condition theologians need this order for their own work.

1. The philosophical as an autonomous order
For Aquinas the philosophical order is an autonomous order in the sense that it has its own proper type of argumentation. In this order one operates by the natural light of reason. Recall, first of all, that in the thirteenth century the natural sciences had not yet separated out of philosophy. The philosophical order was thought to include not only metaphysics and ethics, but also the natural philosophy

of Aristotle—physics, biology, astronomy, and so forth. In these areas one must follow the light of reason, seeking relevant evidence, developing a consistent understanding, and exercising balanced judgments.[18] This is complex and difficult, but it is not to be short-circuited by an appeal to faith.

One sees Aquinas arguing philosophically even in those sections of the *Summa Theologiae* where such clarification is necessary to establish his position. For example, the Averroist view that there is one agent intellect for all humankind cannot, says Aquinas, account for our experience—"that we perceive that we abstract universal forms from their particular conditions" (*ST* Ia., question 79, article 4; cf. fn. 17). No doubt there are reasons related to faith that make Aquinas want to reject the view that there is one agent intellect for all humankind, but he goes beyond such observations in presenting his philosophical analysis of the situation as well. Aquinas recognizes that sometimes it is not a point concerning faith that separates him from his opponents, but rather the philosophical assumptions with which each is working.

Showing that a position is contrary to faith is one kind of argument that Aquinas uses, but at other times he deliberately meets the philosophers on their own ground. In the opening chapter of his book, *On the Unicity of the Intellect, Against the Averroists of Paris*, he distinguishes these two ways of arguing:

> Against this doctrine we have already written much. But since the boldness of those in error has not ceased to assail the truth, it is our intention once more to direct an answer to this false teaching in order that its error may be manifestly confounded.

> At this time it will not be our method to show that the aforesaid position is erroneous as being repugnant to the truth of Christian faith: this is at once sufficiently evident to anyone. For if there is no diversity of intellect among all men, and the intellect appears to be the only incorruptible and immortal part of the soul, then it follows that after death nothing of the souls of men survives except the one common intellect. Thus would be destroyed any possibility of retribution, of rewards and punishments, or any diversity in recompense.

However, we intend to show that their position is not less in conflict with the principles of philosophy than it is with the certain testimony of faith.

Since for certain men concerned in this matter the words of the Latin philosophers have no savor, and since they claim to be followers of the Peripatetics (though of their books on this subject they have seen none, except those of Aristotle, who was the founder of the Peripatetic school), we shall point out that their position is altogether at variance with his words and express opinion.

Aquinas wants to meet his opponents on their own ground, hence he uses Aristotle against those who claim to be his disciples.

In principle and in practice Aquinas allows philosophy an autonomy in relation to theology. Philosophy has its own principles, the naturally known first principles, established by the natural light of reason. Revelation also has its own principles, the articles of faith, which are known through the light of faith.[19] Faith and philosophy each have their own principles and argue on their own basis. Philosophy cannot contradict revelation, for "the truth that the human reason is naturally endowed to know cannot be opposed to the truth of the Christian faith" (*SCG* I,7.1). This is a statement of principle and not a claim about fact. Moreover, the claim pertains to what is revealed and not to a particular theologian's understanding of it. In fact, conflicts will always arise as the theologians and philosophers of the thirteenth century knew only too well. But conflict was not accepted as the final solution.

Even if Aquinas holds that philosophy is autonomous, it does not make people self-sufficient; it is not capable of leading them to their ultimate end. For Aquinas we are intellectual beings whose ultimate end is to know God. All human beings are made with the desire to return to their origin, God, but for the rational creature this return is attained in a special way—through knowing and loving him (*ST* Ia. 1,8). Human beings have a natural desire to know God which can be fulfilled only through supernatural aid.[20] Hence a person must have faith.

2. Theology needs philosophy

Beyond the question of the need for faith, there is the issue of whether a science of faith is needed and is possible. The first question of the *Summa Theologiae* is Aquinas's maturest reflections on this issue. Here one can see how radically he was willing to rethink the form of theological discourse in order to present it in a form that would conform to the Aristotelian canons of science.

Sacra doctrina is needed because "God destines us for an end beyond the grasp of reason." But it is not just truths that are beyond reason that need to be revealed, but even those "religious matters that reason is able to investigate" need to be revealed. "For the rational truth about God would have appeared only to a few, and even so after a long time and mixed with many mistakes" (*ST* la. 1,1).

For Aristotle, all science begins with principles that are better known than their conclusions. Using this criterion theology cannot be a science, for it begins with believing. In the Aristotelian framework, however, there are some sciences which borrow their principles from a higher science without proving these principles for themselves—just as natural and social scientists today borrow from higher mathematics and statistics. In this way, Aquinas asserts, the science of theology must be done in the light of divine knowledge and so "Christian theology takes on faith its principles revealed by God" (art.2).

Like other sciences theology has its own perspective or object. Materially it considers everything in heaven and on earth, but it looks at these things from the point of view of what is divinely revealed (art. 3). It is more theoretical than practical because "it is concerned mainly with the divine things which are, rather than with things men do; it deals with human acts only in so far as they prepare men for that achieved knowledge of God on which their eternal bliss reposes" (art. 4). This science is higher than other theoretical sciences because it has a greater certitude, for the others "come from the natural light of reason which can make mistakes" but this doctrine is "held in the light of divine knowledge which cannot falter." Its worth is also greater because it deals with the final goal of human existence, and that governs the ends of all the practical sciences. It is, therefore, the highest wisdom (art. 6); it has God as its object (art. 7). Like other sciences it does not prove its own principles, and in this case the principles according to which it operates are not naturally known, as in the case of sciences based on human reason, but it is founded on what has been revealed, specifically "the revelation made to the Prophets and Apostles who wrote the canonical books" (art. 8). With regard to Scripture, Aquinas asserts that the literal sense is the only one from which arguments can be drawn (art. 10 ad 1m).

Philosophy is given the role of serving as the handmaid of theology. The human intellect is the weakest of all intellects (compared with the angels and God). Hence human beings must begin with sensible things to understand higher realities; the sensible provides models and metaphors by which we can grasp suprasensible realities. So "holy teaching can borrow from the other sciences, not from any need to beg from them, but for the greater clarification of the things it conveys" (art. 5 ad 2m).

As a higher wisdom, however, sacred theology has an additional function—to condemn that which contradicts divine wisdom: "Whatever is encountered in the other sciences which is incompatible with its truth [sacred teaching] should be completely condemned as false" (art. 6 ad 2m). Obviously this is a delicate matter, for theologians are also fallible and still in the process of learning, as later history would show. With regard to developing the sciences, Aquinas insists that establishing the principles of the other sciences is none of the theologian's business. Because theology's own foundation is revelation, the theologian can argue with those who reject this basis in only certain ways:

> [Theology] argues on the basis of those truths held by revelation when an opponent admits, as when, debating with heretics, it appeals to received authoritative texts of Christian theology, and uses one article against those who reject another. If, however, an opponent believes nothing of what has been divinely revealed, then no way lies open for making the articles of faith reasonably credible; all that can be done is to solve the difficulties against faith he may bring up. (Art. 8)

Even with the aid of natural reason, there is a limit to the knowledge that can be gained by the science of faith; we are better able to say what God is not than what he is. Indeed, the account of the divine nature in *ST* 1a. 3-11 is primarily negative theology. There is no possibility of perfect understanding of God in this life (cf. *ST* 1a. 12,11). But as Bernard Lonergan observed, this does not mean that one should "settle down to teaching catechism."[21] There is such a thing as imperfect understanding, and the *Summa Theologiae* is a systematic attempt to proceed to that goal.

D. Conclusion

Aquinas relied heavily on the classical philosophical heritage. In it he saw an understanding of things which he could adapt and develop to his own purposes. The philosophy which he was able to create in reshaping the classical tradition is fundamental for his theology. If Aquinas's theology is impressive, one reason for that is the quality of the philosophy which it employs.

The key element in that philosophy is the determination to do justice to the nature of each and every thing. In a Christian context this becomes the examination of secondary causes. God did not merely make things but also gave them their operations. Aristotle analyzed nature, but he could not order it in relation to its ultimate end, God. So while Aristotle could be used, he also had to be changed, especially with regard to the account of human beings, their moral life and ultimate end. Aquinas does not just add a spiritual dimension to an Aristotelian world, but he reorders every part in terms of the whole.[22] For Aquinas theology is founded on the sacred writings, but it goes beyond the task of determining what the text of Scripture says; it must also relate the various truths of faith to one another so that they may be seen to be a coherent whole. This is one of the achievements of the *via doctrina* as expounded in the *Summa Thelogiae*. Beginning with God, Aquinas explains how all things flow from him and how human beings in particular return to him. In this sweep all history is caught up. More than this, Aquinas is very conscious of placing theology in relation to the other sciences of his day—the newly acquired natural science, metaphysics, and ethics of Aristotle. And rightly so, I would add, for in every age there arises anew the task of reinterpreting one's religious experience in and to a new cultural situation.

The final question we were asked to consider is whether the classical heritage can be integrated in the author's Christian position. In the case of Aquinas the answer is easy, since he succeeded, it must be possible.

Notes

1. Tracing the rediscovery of the ancients has been a complex task, and many historians have made significant contributions. For a survey see F. van Steenberghen, *The Philosophical Movement in the Thirteenth Century* (New York: Thomas Nelson & Sons, 1955), 3-17; also John F. Quinn, *The Historical Constitution of St. Bonaventure's Philosophy* (Toronto: Pontifical Institute of Medieval Studies, 1973), 17-91.

2. Although no direct translations of Plato's writings were influential at this time, he had an enormous indirect influence because writers accepted Proclus's *Elements of Theology* as a work of Aristotle. Plato's *Meno* and *Phaedo* were translated in the thirteenth century but never became well known. Only in the fourteenth and fifteenth centuries did Plato have a significant direct influence.

3. E. Gilson, *History of Christian Philosophy in the Middle Ages* (New York: Random House, 1955), 238.

4. Ibid., 95. One perplexing fact is that the papal prohibition against teaching Aristotle's natural philosophy was never withdrawn, and it was even repeated as late as 1263. Steenberghen sees in this merely typical bureaucratic blundering which had no practical effect (op. cit. in n.1, 46).

5. It now appears that even Bonaventure was not hostile to Aristotle as scholars have supposed. In the latest major work in this area, Quinn asserts that Bonaventure is not hostile toward Aristotelian philosophy; rather Bonaventure always treats Aristotle "with benignity" and adds his "authority to that of Scripture and of the Fathers, particularly Augustine" (op. cit. in n.1, 851).

6. "Aristotle was like a phenomenon of nature: a personification of intellectual energy of elemental power, within whose field of radiation fundamental problems and situations seemed to be clarified of their own accord" (Josef Pieper, *A Guide to St. Thomas*, New York: Mentor-Omega, 1962), 45-46.

7. "In brief, what now appeared was a world that was *real,* a world *capable of being understood.* A mother-science of physics was begotten, and from it were to spring forth all the other particular sciences dealing with nature, starting with a science of man, the science of that being whose nature was free, yet bound up with the world system that surrounded him" (M.-D. Chenu, *Toward Understanding St. Thomas,* (Chicago: Henry Regnery Co., 1964), 34.

8. Ibid., 35.

9. I am developing a point made by Pieper, op. cit. in n.6, 27.

10. James Weisheipl, *Friar Thomas D'Aquino* (Garden City, New York: Doubleday, 1974), 21.

11. At St. James where Aquinas stayed in Paris, there was even an attempt to produce a corrected Vulgate version of the Bible. There was an interest in going beyond the opinions of the church fathers as cited by Peter Lombard and others; they sought serviceable editions of the original works. Thomas is reported to have said that he would gladly have given all the wonders of Paris for a copy of Chrysostom's commentary on Matthew. See Chenu, op. cit. in n.7, 48).

12. "Not because it is Aristotle who said it, but because he said it in a way that throws light on the problem—that is why it is so. . . . It is so because it is true. A writer who quotes in this manner is not really quoting an authority; he is not tying himself to the author's apron strings. On the other hand he does not hesitate to cite an author if it seems to him that this author is right and has contrived to express the truth in exemplary fashion. He takes the liberty of concurring with someone who . . . has told the truth" (Pieper, op. cit. in n.6, 50).

13. Ibid. This quote is originally from Aquinas's commentary on Aristotle's *Physics,* bk. VIII, lect. 2.

14. B. Bazan, *Siger De Brabant, Quaestiones in Tertium* ... , 101:6-9; quoted by F. van Steenberghen, *Thomas Aquinas and Radical Aristotelianism* (Washington, D.C.: Catholic University of America Press, 1980), 86.
15. Steenberghen, op. cit., 86.
16. Ibid., 87.
17. For an account of this matter see Steenberghen, op. cit., "Monopsychism," 29-74. In Aquinas, see *Summa Theologiae* la. (questions) 75ff. (hereafter cited in references as *ST*).
18. While true as far as it goes, this formulation does not give an indication of the concrete conditions in which reason operates. Aquinas is well aware that learning is not easy and subject to many forms of bias. Even the philosophers disagree with one another and on important issues. Since the fall, there is no pure reason. On the effect of sin, see *ST* la2ae. 85 and each of the sections in *ST* 2a2ae where the vices opposed to each virtue are discussed.
19. For a comparison of these two types of principles see *ST* 2a2ae. 1,7.
20. Cf. *ST* 2a2ae. 2,3 and note in Blackfriars translation, vol. 31, 72-73. Here again it is important to recognize that because of the fall the present state of humankind is "unnatural." See *ST* la. 94-96 for an account of the original state.
21. Bernard Lonergan, *Verbum: Word and Idea in Aquinas* (Notre Dame: University of Notre Dame Press, 1967), 213.
22. The criticism often made is that Aquinas simply added grace to nature, the supernatural gifts to the natural gifts, so that nature remained basically unchanged. I think this criticism is based on a misunderstanding that has a variety of sources. For my analysis of this issue see chapter 6, "Nature and Grace," in *Aquinas, Calvin and Contemporary Protestant Thought* (Grand Rapids: Eerdmans, 1985), 123-160.

Aquinas and the Classical Heritage: A Response

Jan A. Aertsen

Arvin Vos has written an excellent paper on Thomas Aquinas and the classical heritage. His paper shows admiration for and affinity with Aquinas's achievement. I share this admiration; Aquinas is a great thinker. Now it is a mark of great thinkers that the content of their thought is so full and rich that one can put emphasis on different aspects. And this is what I intend to do in my response by making some comments and raising some questions. My reflections, stressing a number of underlying ideas, are primarily meant as a supplement to what has been said.

In order to present my remarks in a systematic and coherent way, I take as a starting point a statement of Aristotle which I will develop in four steps, more or less related to the main parts of Vos's paper: (1) the background of the thirteenth century; (2) Thomas's attitude towards Aristotle; (3) the relationship between faith and reason; and (4) the conclusion concerning the question whether the classical heritage can be integrated in the Christian position.

A. The Background of the Thirteenth Century
My starting point is the famous opening sentence of Aristotle's *Metaphysics* (980 a 21): "All men by nature desire to know."

It is a text which would find a strong response in the thirteenth century, for it is the desire for knowledge which gave rise to the university, one of the most important medieval innovations. Aristotle's statement plays a prominent part in Thomas's works. On several occasions he resorts to this saying. In all human beings there is a natural desire for knowledge, that is, for the science of the causes of a thing. Its expression is philosophy. And Aristotle is "the Philosopher," exemplar of the human desire to know.

There is, however, in the Middle Ages another influential tradition, especially within monastic circles, viewing the desire for knowledge as a vice, as *curiosity*.[1] The authority of this tradition is Augustine, who extensively deals with this subject in the tenth book of the *Confessions*. The "temptation" of "curiosity" is that people seek knowledge for the sake of knowledge; it becomes an end in itself. As is argued in *De doctrina christiana*, in Christian scholarship science has an instrumental sense; it must be subservient to human salvation. Its justification lies in the utility for this religious end. Augustine says in his *Confessions* (X, chap. 35): "Man desires nothing else than to know for the sake of knowing." This phrase reminds us of the opening sentence of the *Metaphysics*. But for Augustine it is the curiosity of the worldly man, of man having succumbed to the world. Aristotle's "by nature" has been eliminated.

These very words make the desire for Thomas legitimate; it is a *natural* desire, and as such it is good. So "nature" is the key word. It is defined by Aristotle (*Physics* II, 1) as the intrinsic principle of movement. Things have an activity and causality of their own; they possess an ontological consistency.

It is remarkable that the introduction of Aristotle's works during the thirteenth century had such a rapid success. Arvin Vos states:

> Why did the writings of Aristotle come to dominate the intellectual way of life of the West during the first half of the thirteenth century? One answer is that his theories of nature, of the human soul, and his metaphysics were superior to what had been available.[2]

But here a question arises: what is the criterion through which the superiority is measured? For, to quote Father Chenu, one of the outstanding scholars in Thomistic studies:

> [T]he world of Aristotle was itself irreconcilable with the Christian way of conceiving the universe, man, and God.... Aristotelian science was playing against Christian wisdom.[3]

If this is the case, what is then the motive for the reception of Aristotle?

It is the idea expressed in the concept of nature, namely, that things possess an ontological consistency, which appealed to the thirteenth century. We can notice here a new religious commitment. This world is not merely a "sign," a symbol of a higher world. The Creator has provided the universe with an intelligible structure, with natures knowable in themselves. Science has not a merely instrumental sense. And human reason is able to get true knowledge of things by its natural light. The rejection of the theory of divine illumination, so essential for Augustine, is another example of this shift in worldview.

B. Thomas's Attitude Towards Aristotle

Next we turn to Thomas's commentary on the *Metaphysics*. How does he approach the opening sentence? Strictly speaking, Aristotle does not prove his statement. He gives only an indication, a sign. An indication of the natural desire for knowledge is our appreciation of the senses, even apart from their usefulness. They are loved for their own sake. In contrast to Aristotle, Aquinas gives three arguments for the natural desire to know. I shall not dwell on the first two reasons, being purely Aristotelian. I should like to draw your attention to the last argument, the most interesting one from a philosophical point of view. It runs something like this:

> The third reason is that it is desirable for each thing to be united to its source (principle), since it is in this that the perfection of each thing consists. This is also the reason why circular motion is the most perfect motion, because its terminus is united to its starting point.

> Now it is only by means of his intellect that man is united to his source. For knowledge is an assimilation of the knower to the known.

> Therefore man naturally desires to know.[4]

The interesting thing to note here is that in this argument in support of Aristotle's dictum Thomas introduces an idea from another philosophical tradition. For the motif of circulation (*circulatio*), the identity of beginning and end, is of *Neoplatonic* origin (as Aquinas himself states elsewhere).[5]

Various passages in Thomas's works indicate that he adopted
and adapted this doctrine. See, for instance, *Summa Contra Gentiles*
II, 46:

> An effect is most perfect when it returns to its source; thus,
> the circle is the most perfect of all figures, and circular motion
> the most perfect of all motions, because in their case a return
> is made to the starting point. It is therefore necessary that crea-
> tures return to their principle in order that the universe of
> creatures may attain its ultimate perfection.

The *circulatio* of created reality is a central feature of Thomas's
thought. It also becomes explicit in the structure of his main work,
the *Summa Theologiae*.

> The first part deals with God, and the "procession of all crea-
> tures from Him";

> The second with the movement of the rational creature
> toward him;

> And the third with Christ, who as man is the way of our tend-
> ing to God.[6]

The entire structure is clearly dominated by the motif of circulation (*circulatio*).[7]

Stressing this Neoplatonic theme has a further objective. I am
inclined, perhaps more than Arvin Vos was, to put emphasis on the
Platonic element in the classical heritage adopted by Thomas.

One of the great innovations in the area of Thomistic studies
after the Second World War is the rediscovery of this Platonic
legacy, especially the notion of "participation."[8] This is the more
striking because Aristotle sharply criticized this concept. And
Thomas knew that very well. In a sense Aquinas subscribes to
Aristotle's criticism: there are no self-subsisting separate Forms of
natural things, such as "Animal itself" and "Man itself." Still, he accepts the application of this doctrine to the so-called transcenden-
tals, "being," "good," and "true," that is, to concepts which
transcend the "categories," the particular modes of being. There is
something which is essentially Being, Being itself. All other things
are being by participation, they have received being. "Participation" is the way in which Thomas philosophically interprets the
Christian idea of creation. To summarize in a rather schematic man-

ner: on the level of *nature* there is a strong impact of Aristotle's views, but on the transcendental level, that of *creature*, of Platonic views.[9]

Thomas's application of the *circulatio*-doctrine to the desire for knowledge implies that only God, Being itself and the Origin of all things, can be the final end. The natural desire turns out to be a natural desire to know God. Human happiness is to be assimilated to God through knowing.

C. Faith and Reason

The crucial question now arises: can human beings attain this final end, God? It would appear that this question must be answered negatively. This impossibility originates from the structure of human knowledge. Human beings depend upon the sensible experience for their (intellectual) knowledge.

Consequently the science attainable for human reason by its natural powers concerns the essences of *material* things (because they are knowable by the senses). Human beings cannot obtain essential knowledge of immaterial beings, like God. The question as to *what* they are remained unanswered. The highest knowledge of God which philosophers can reach on the basis of the visible effects is *that* he is. But the natural desire to know cannot be satisfied with such a knowledge, just because the essential question (the question as to *what* he is) remained unanswered. A human being's final end lies solely in the knowledge of God's essence, that is in theological terms, in *the vision of God*.[10]

As a result of this conclusion, philosophy is caught up in a serious crisis. Philosophy offers no prospect of a fulfillment of human life. At great length Thomas sketches in his *Summa Contra Gentiles* what he himself calls the "distress" and "despair" of philosophers, including Aristotle.[11] Here we see the limits of the classical heritage for Thomas.

The impossibility of the vision of God is, however, contrary to the *Christian faith*. Aquinas points out that the possibility is promised to us in sacred Scripture: "We shall see him as he is" (I John 3:2). When writing on "Blessed are the pure in heart, for they will see God" (Matt. 5:8), Thomas, in his commentary on Matthew, synthesizes the eschatology of Christian faith with the finality of the natural desire to know. The Christian faith liberates us from the "distress" of philosophy.

D. Integration of the Classical and Christian Positions
The final end which Scripture promises surpasses a person's natural powers. It is quite literally *super*natural. Human beings can attain their supernatural end only when some principles are added to their nature whereby they are elevated above their own nature. This divine gift is gratuitous and is, therefore, called "grace." And Aquinas states:

> The gifts of grace are added to those of nature in such a way that they do not destroy the latter, but rather perfect them. Therefore also the light of faith which is gratuitously infused into our minds does not destroy the natural light of cognition.[12]

Grace perfects nature. Here we find the clue to the final question whether the classical heritage can be integrated in the Christian position. According to Thomas the Christian life is the fulfillment of the natural order, the completion of the natural desire for knowledge manifested in the classical philosophical heritage.

True human existence is only possible "by God's grace." Roman Catholicism and the Reformation have different views on the relation of nature and grace. In Thomas's view grace is a perfection elevating human beings above their own nature. But as the above mentioned structure of his *Summa Theologiae* indicates, the circular movement of reality—all things are from and to God—stands in a concrete salvation history: the Word became flesh in order to show humankind the way back to its Origin. "The way for all men to come to happiness is the mystery of Christ's Incarnation and Passion." [13]

Notes
1. Cf. H. Blumenberg, *Der Prozess der theoretischen Neugierde* (Frankfurt am Main, 1973) 103 ff.
2. See above, 70-71.
3. M.-D. Chenu, *Toward Understanding St. Thomas*, trans. A. M. Landry and D. Hughes (Chicago, 1964) 35.
4. Cf. *Sententia super* Metaphysicam I, lect. 1,4.
5. See his *Expositio super Dionysium De divinibus nominibus.* cap. 1, lect. 3, 94.
6. *Summa Theologiae* 1. (question) 2, prol.
7. Cf. my paper "The Circulation-motive and Man in the Thought of Thomas Aquinas" in *Acts of the Sixth International Congress of Medieval Philosophy* (Louvain-la-Neuve, 1986) 432-39.

8. Cf. L.-B. Geiger, *La participation dans la philosophie de St. Thomas d'Aquin* (Paris, 1942); C. Fabro, *Participation et Causalité selon St. Thomas d'Aquin* (Louvain/Paris, 1961).

9. For a fuller account see my study *Nature and Creature: Thomas Aquinas's Way of Thought* (Leiden: Brill, 1987).

10. *Summa Theologiae,* 1-2. (question)3, art.8.

11. Cf. *Summa Contra Gentiles* III.48.

12. *Expositio super librum Boethii de Trinitate,* (question)2, art.3.

13. *Summa Theologiae* 1-2. (question)2, art.7.

Erasmus's Christian Humanist Appreciation and Use of the Classics

Beert Verstraete

A. Introduction

The past few decades have brought a much sharpened recognition of Erasmus's pivotal position as a Christian humanist in the history of Western civilization and of his seminal and fruitful influence on our culture. It is no longer possible to assess his role in the turbulent era of the early Protestant Reformation and the Catholic reaction as that of a Protestant *manqué*, who supplied the reformers with the critical and exegetical tools to restore the Christian message to a renewed purity and integrity but lacked the consistency and decisiveness to join their movement. Erasmus, in fact, sincerely believed that the gross abuses of power and the deplorable aberrations in the teaching and liturgical practice of the church could be overcome through internal reform, but that schism and separation would inflict dire calamity on Western Christendom. As a Christian scholar with superb literary gifts, he was able to command a wide audience among the educated public and he endeavored with all his energy to make a significant contribution towards such a reform.

It is equally unjust to view Erasmus as a cryptorationalist, a rationalist before the Age of Reason; this label (if I may call it such) has undoubtedly been fastened upon a very real facet of Erasmus's complex personality and cast of mind, but it does injustice to Erasmus's basically integral Christian worldview. It is, perhaps, a little less unjust to speak of a certain mental dividing line between Erasmus's classical humanism and his Christian convictions. Such an understanding of the intellectual and spiritual tenor of his thought is best expressed by the Dutch historian Johan Huizinga in his still popular biography of Erasmus published more than sixty years ago: "The foundation of his spiritual life was no longer a unity for Erasmus. It was, on the one hand, a strong desire for an upright, pure, and homely belief, the earnest wish to be a good Christian. But it was also the irresistible intellectual and aesthetic need of the good taste, the harmony, the clear and exact expression of the Ancients, the dislike of what was cumbrous and involved. "[1]

I hope to demonstrate, however, that Erasmus uses his classical heritage, especially the great legacy of Greek and Roman literature, within a substantial context of Christian thinking and purpose. After calling attention to the nonhistorical and strictly literary bias of Erasmus's classicism, this paper will first examine the Christian stamp that rests upon even those writings which are heavily classical in their inspiration and serve largely to popularize Greek and Roman literature or to promote classical ideals of culture and education. Second, it will focus on Erasmus's defense of the place of the classics in a Christian society. Third, it will point to the emergence of a more discerning and critical classicism in the later years of Erasmus's career. In the conclusion, I will dwell on the continuing relevance of the spiritual and intellectual problematics raised by Erasmus's Christian humanism to the development of a contemporary Christian hermeneutic.

B. A Christian Approach to Classical Texts
Erasmus's indefatigable work as a popularizer of the classics is well summed up by Margaret Mann Phillips: "Throughout his life he remained faithful to the cause of rediscovering and restoring the literature of antiquity, and a large proportion of his huge output consists of editions, translations, and annotations of classical authors. "[2] It was Erasmus more than any other person who gave the study of the classics such a central and commanding position in Catholic and Protestant school curricula alike for almost four centuries to come. In this respect, he must certainly be regarded as one of the most influential educators of all time. The Greek and Roman literary heritage which, even during the later Middle Ages, had generally been studied and appropriated in a heavily truncated and secondhand fashion—a fact repeatedly deplored by Erasmus—seemed at the beginning of the sixteenth century finally to be coming into its own, thanks above all to his enormous labors.

However, the classicism bequeathed by Erasmus to succeeding generations was of a greatly circumscribed variety. It was a classicism with a strong Roman and Latin coloring, rather than a classicism oriented to the Greeks such as came to enjoy a wide vogue in the nineteenth century. To be sure, Erasmus developed in his thirties an enviable competence in ancient Greek and became intimately familiar with substantial passages of Greek literature from Homer to the Byzantine period. Nevertheless, the approach taken by Erasmus also to the Greek classics demonstrates a rather practical and Latin cast of mind: for him their excellence lies, first of all, in the abundant and indispensable knowledge they provide for almost all aspects of human life and, secondly, in their unsurpassed soundness as models of effective literary communication and pleasing aesthetic form. In fact, Erasmus's perspective on the classics as a whole is literary and strictly nonhistorical and, in this important respect, is very much like that of the large majority of humanists. The historical approach to the study of classical civilization was represented during the sixteenth century only by the so-called antiquarian scholars and, of course, did not come into its own until the nineteenth century. Erasmus, by contrast, is concerned exclusively with the great literary heritage of the Greek and Roman past; this for him is the great treasure house of human knowledge and insight, effective communication, and aesthetic excellence; for him the classics are the *bonae litterae* (a favorite phrase of his), coextensive with all good knowledge and culture and certainly their indispensable foundation.

1. *The* Adagia

One of the most popular of Erasmus's works during his lifetime was the *Adagia* which, like so many of his writings, went through a number of editions, the last one appearing in 1536, the year of his death. It is a huge collection of proverbs and proverbial expressions drawn from Greek and Roman literature (more than four thousand of them in the latest edition), most of them provided with a commentary containing explanatory annotations, literary parallels, and even the occasional excursus not particularly germane to the proverb under discussion. This is probably the most important of those writings of Erasmus which aimed at popularizing the classics among the educated public. It is not surprising that the material on which this work is based is almost exclusively classical, for the express purpose of the *Adagia* is to provide a kind of digest of the practical and moral wisdom of the ancient Greeks and Romans. There is a very occasional citation from Scripture or a church father, but this by itself, of course, does not constitute a Christian perspective. However, in the introduction to the *Adagia*, a distinct note of Erasmus's Christian humanism is heard. Erasmus here contends that a classical proverb or a wise saying by a Greek or Roman author may look forward to the gospel.[3] To underline this contention, he cites the Greek proverb attributed to Pythagoras, "Between friends all is common," and sees in it anticipation of the Christian message that God is love and that Christ is the revelation to humankind of that love, a love which, as he puts it, makes us "united in friendship with Christ, glued to Him by the same binding force that holds him fast to the Father."[4] His concluding comments are: "Finally, love teaches us how, as the sum of created things is in God and God is in all things, the universal all is in fact one. You can see what an ocean of philosophy, or rather of theology, is opened up to us by this tiny proverb."[5]

One might be inclined to judge that this completely allegorical and anagogical interpretation of Pythagoras's proverb does violence to the spirit of classical Greek civilization and establishes only an illusory link between it and the Christian message; that Erasmus, by choosing a Greek proverb as a starting point for that message, in fact, trivializes the gospel. However, we must note that Erasmus offers this proverb only as an opening or doorway to the gospel; there is no question of placing Greek wisdom at the same level as the latter. Erasmus's exegetical principles here may be questionable, but we should not use them to berate his Christian humanism and classicism as a whole. Moreover, as we shall see in the third section of this paper, Erasmus is not always so uncritical.

2. *The* De Pueris Statim ac Liberaliter Instituendis

A second work in which Erasmus's classical literary heritage is very conspicuous, although less lavishly than in the *Adagia*, is the pedagogical and educational treatise, *De Pueris Statim ac Liberaliter Instituendis* (On the necessity for an early liberal education of children; hereafter cited as *De Pueris*), published in 1529. Erasmus had originally composed this work much earlier, probably in 1509 towards the end of his three-year stay in Italy, as a kind of illustrative appendix to his rhetorical treatise, *De Copia Verborum ac Rerum*

(On abundance of expression and subject-matter; hereafter cited as *De Copia*). *De Pueris* was to demonstrate the central literary principle of *De Copia*; namely, how an argument might be expanded from a synoptic outline to a full, rhetorically developed treatment of the subject. Because of various circumstances, Erasmus did not have the chance to complete and publish the work in 1509. However, in the later 1520s, Erasmus became impressed with its considerable pedagogical significance and the possible social and educational impact it might have. At that time he was becoming increasingly preoccupied with the moral and spiritual foundations of Christian family life; this concern also animates *De Pueris*, which constantly reiterates the message that children are the most precious charge entrusted by God to parents who must do everything possible to ensure that their children receive the best possible education.

In essence, *De Pueris* is a Christian humanist reformulation of the classical ideal of a liberal education. Undeniably the classical heritage sounds a very dominant note in this treatise; in fact, it borrows extensively from two important pedagogical and educational works of antiquity, namely, the earlier part of Quintilian's *Institutio Oratoria* and Plutarch's short work, *On the raising of children*, with the argument supported in addition by a wealth of citations from and references to other Greek and Roman authors. The spirit of classical humanism is perhaps best exemplified in the bold statement, *Ratio facit hominem*, "It is reason which defines our humanity. "[6] However, we must not be too quick in interpreting this as a manifesto of classical rationalism or an anticipation of later Western rationalism. What Erasmus basically means by *ratio* in this context is a person's unique capacity for learning; and the weight placed on *ratio* should be seen as somewhat of a rhetorical hyperbole by which he seeks to register his strong belief that the individual becomes the kind of person he or she is by virtue of the characteristically human capacity for learning. Thus, Erasmus's terse saying will not bear the interpretation of a thoroughgoing rationalism.

De Pueris, in fact, displays some distinct touches of Erasmus's deepest Christian convictions. In my estimation, the ultimately Christian basis of this treatise is best revealed in the lengthy section devoted to the issue of corporal punishment.[7] This is certainly one of the most vivid parts of the work, enlivened not only with

the usual classical citations and references, but also with some personal anecdotes which are meant to underline the barbarity of the
kind of physical discipline administered in the schools. Quintilian
had expressed his disapproval of corporal punishment in a few
paragraphs,[8] condemning it as a type of discipline not befitting free
persons. While Erasmus cites Quintilian as his major classical
authority for his own views, he derives the real spiritual impetus
for his impassioned condemnation of the practice from the gospel,
for it is his heartfelt conviction, based on his own personal experience, that the *philosophia Christi* is radically opposed to the
brutalization of children. The well-known injunction to parents in
Proverbs 13:24 not to spare the rod on their children carries no
weight with Erasmus, at least not when it is interpreted literally;
Christians, he emphasizes, must interpret this proverb more
liberally.[9] By way of specific counsel to parents and elders, he
prefers to cite the apostle Paul: "You parents, again, must not goad
your children to resentment, but give them the instruction and cor-
rection which belong to a Christian upbringing"(Eph. 6:4; New
English Bible).[10]

On a broader plane, although admittedly less conspicuously so,
De Pueris also strikes a Christian note in its insistence that the goal
of a liberal education is to prepare the young for a life of service to
the community and to God.[11] For Erasmus, the classical humanist
goal of harmonious self-development—and above all, the development of the life of the mind—is comprehended in the wider goal of
service to God and one's fellowman. He points to Christ as the
supreme embodiment of this ideal; Christ was a teacher who truly
ministered to the needs of his disciples, bearing with their human
weaknesses and gradually leading them onwards to full spiritual
knowledge and maturity.[12] For Erasmus, then, the *philosophia
Christi* is the irreplaceable cornerstone of all learning, all education,
and indeed all human life.

C. The Classics in a Christian Society
Erasmus's lengthiest and most vigorous defense of the classics
comes in the *Antibarbari*, which is, in fact, exclusively devoted to the
question of the role of classical culture in the life of the individual
and in Christian society. The first published edition appeared in
1520, but already in 1495 Erasmus, still in his twenties then, had
produced a version in manuscript form; he had begun to work on

it even before he was twenty. The *Antibarbari* is cast in the form of a dialogue between Erasmus and his friends, with Erasmus acting as the narrator and observer, while his friend Jacob Batt is assigned the role of an enthusiastic and eloquent defender of the classics. The use of the dialogue form recalls classical models and the *Antibarbari*, with its evocative description of background and setting, is particularly reminiscent of Plato's *Phaedrus* and *Symposium*.

It is clear throughout that Batt's defense of the classics is a defense of all good learning and culture. A whole intellectual and cultural heritage is at stake for Batt and for Erasmus; the attacks upon the classics and a classical education are construed as an assault on all learning and intellectual enterprise, indeed all higher forms of human civilization. Batt skillfully disposes of the contention that the gospel is really anti-intellectual. He emphasizes that the Apostle Paul's statement in 1 Corinthians 8:1, "Knowledge puffs up,"a favorite text of the anticlassicists and anti-intellectuals, must be read closely in its context: knowledge in itself is not condemned or slighted here, but only knowledge which is not pursued and displayed in the spirit of Christian love; it is ridiculous, even perverse, to cite this text as an excuse for willful ignorance, mental sloth, and sheer hatred of learning.[13]

Batt speaks in one section of the crucial role played by classical civilization in God's providential plan for humankind.[14] It was no accident that Christ was born in a golden age when human civilization had reached a pinnacle of culture. God through Christ has drawn all things in reality, even those elements hostile or estranged from him, into his service. Even the worst aspects of the pagan religions with which Christianity had to struggle served to throw into relief the glory of Christ. Batt calls attention to the achievements of the Greeks in the arts and sciences and exclaims: "In law, in philosophy, how the ancients labored! Why did all this happen? So that we on our arrival could hold them in contempt? Was it not rather that the best religion should be adorned and supported by the finest studies? "[15] Christianity, then, may be gloriously served by the best fruits of the cultural labors of the ancients. Batt continues by dwelling even more strongly on the positive attainments of classical civilization, attributing them to God's redemptive work through Christ in human history: "Everything in the pagan world that was valiantly done, brilliantly said, ingeniously thought, diligently transmitted, had been prepared by Christ for his society.

He it was who supplied the intellect, who added the zest for inquiry, and it was through Him alone that they found what they sought. Their age produced this harvest of creative work, not so much for them as for us."[16] This section already points forward to an argument used later by Batt, namely, that we may use the classics on the analogy of the Hebrews' spoiling of the Egyptians; there he draws heavily on the reasoning put forward by Augustine in *De Doctrina Christiana*, where he interprets this aspect of the Exodus as a prefiguration of the uses Christians may make of classical culture and learning.[17]

Convictions such as those expressed in the *Antibarbari* regarding the enormous contribution the classics have made and must continue to make to the Christian life always remained at the center of Erasmus's intellectual and spiritual creed and are voiced in numerous other works. A particularly telling and often quoted instance occurs in the colloquy, *Convivium Religiosum* (The godly feast), first published in 1522, where at one point the moral and spiritual greatness achieved by classical civilization is held up as a fine model for Christians, and one of the participants in the dialogue, Eusebius, says: "[P]erhaps the spirit of Christ is more widespread than we understand, and the company of saints includes many not in our calendar."[18] Then, further on, another speaker, Nephalius, is moved by the example of Socrates's unflinching moral and spiritual courage in the face of his death to exclaim: "An admirable spirit, surely, in one who had not known Christ and the Sacred Scriptures. And so, when I read such things of such men, I can hardly help exclaiming, 'Saint Socrates, pray for us!'"[19]

D. The Integration of Christianity and the Classics
Erasmus's integration of his classical heritage into a Christian sense of life and purpose was not an overnight accomplishment and did not mature, perhaps, until he was well into his thirties or even later. Biographers have regarded his encounter with John Colet and other Christian humanists during his first visit to England in 1499 as a spiritual turning point in his life, which set him on the road towards a more serious and integral understanding of his intellectual and literary career as one that needed the context and direction of Christian service.[20] His three-year sojourn in Italy (from 1506 to 1509) may have made him even more keenly aware of the

dangers posed by a sweeping, uncritical classicism and may have strengthened his determination to put his classical learning and literary talents to work for the cause of Christ's gospel and a reformed church and society.

The greater sensitivity in Erasmus's writings to the fundamental claims of the gospel is well reflected in the interesting fact to which Margaret Mann Phillips calls attention in the introduction to her translation of the *Antibarbari*. The 1495 manuscript version contains the following rather provocative statement: "Religion without literary culture has something stupid about it and is violently distasteful to those who have literary culture."[21] Erasmus deleted this sentence from the 1520 published edition and substituted a more moderate statement to the effect that some Christians in the past have felt there was an incompatibility between great learning and pure religion.

One can also observe a more discerning classicism in Erasmus's changed opinion, during his later years, of Seneca's spiritual stature. Already in the preface to his *Lucubrationes* (1515), he attaches severe qualifications to his earlier enthusiasm for Seneca: he faults the Roman author in part for his style but, more seriously, also for the pose of self-sufficiency which pervades his writings. This reassessment hardens in the preface to a new edition of Seneca in 1529 and in a separate preface to the alleged correspondence between Seneca and the apostle Paul, long regarded as authentic but rejected by Erasmus as fictitious. Both in style and content these letters are unworthy of either of these great writers he says. It is absurd to imagine Seneca sending Paul a book to improve his Latin style or the fearless apostle agreeing to a secret exchange of letters for fear of Nero. One may ask if a Christian would have committed suicide as Seneca did and not have mentioned the name of Christ even in his dying moment. Seneca can still be admired for some of his moral insights, but in many respects he is at a far remove from the Christian truth. Erasmus once more condemns the Stoic claim of autarchy made by Seneca: "He says that the wise man owes his happiness to himself alone, and has no need of the gods; indeed, the gods themselves owe something to the wise man. But our faith tells us that sparrows and lilies are in the hand of God, and that man has nothing good in himself, but owes everything in the way of happiness to the free gift of Providence."[22]

In the dialogue *Ciceronianus* of 1528, Erasmus satirizes the neopagan tendencies of some humanists. Bulephorus, the spokesman for Erasmus's views, ridicules them for carrying their classicism to absurd extremes and for refusing to recognize, in their very use of the Latin language, the distinctiveness of the Christian message which cannot be accommodated by a slavish adherence to classical, pre-Christian (e.g., Ciceronian) idiom. A delightful caricature of the literary and puristic aspirations of the neopagan Ciceronians is drawn in a statement of Christian doctrine couched in strictly classical Latin terminology and terms of reference.[23] On a more serious level, however, the *Ciceronianus* makes in its conclusion one of the most powerful statements of the ultimately Christian convictions and sense of purpose underlying Erasmus's mature classicism: *Huc discuntur disciplinae, huc philosophia, huc eloquentia, ut Christum intelligamus, ut Christi gloriam celebremus. Hic est totius eruditionis et eloquentiae scopus.* ("This is the purpose of studying the basic disciplines, of studying philosophy, of studying eloquence, to know Christ, to celebrate the glory of Christ. This is the goal of all learning and all eloquence.")[24]

In noting the emergence of this more mature, Christ-centered classicism in the course of Erasmus's career, I wish to emphasize that his fervent enthusiasm for the classics was never exclusively a reaction against the antihumanistic and anti-intellectual piety which characterized the learning environment of the schools at Deventer and 's Hertogenbosch, where he had received his early education and which also pervaded, to a considerable degree, the mental climate of the monastery at Steyn where he had lived for several years. This piety, which had been fostered in the Low Countries during the fourteenth and fifteenth centuries by the influential movement of the Modern Devotion (finding its most famous expression in Thomas à Kempis's *The Imitation of Christ*), was not altogether uncongenial to Erasmus's maturing spirituality and Christian sense of life, despite its ascetic and anti-intellectual tendencies. In reaction to the increasing formalism of the late medieval church, the Modern Devotion had emphasized the need for a Christ-centered spirituality and walk of life, was less concerned with the externals of ecclesiastical pomp and power, and was more concerned with the individual and an inward-focused spirituality. The more integral Christian worldview and consequently also the more mature classicism, both of which characterize the later Erasmus, may be seen as a reaffirmation of the positive accents of this spirituality.

One of the central issues dominating Erasmus's thinking and his scholarly and popular writings during the 1510s and 1520s, when he was at the height of his influence, was his deeply rooted dissatisfaction with the often arid intellectualism of contemporary Catholic theology and dogmatics. His satirical protests against the more conspicuous abuses of the church are well known: the misuse of authority as well as the encouragement of superstition and an almost mechanical piety. All these are brilliantly pilloried in some of his most famous works. However, his sharp reaction against the dominant trends in the preaching and the theology of the church is equally significant. Erasmus abhorred any explication and formulation of the Christian message which relied on propositional and syllogistic reasoning and thus degenerated easily into a purely speculative dogmatics; such a theology and the style of preaching produced by it were, in his view, contrary to the living gospel of Christ.

In these protests, Erasmus draws with special indebtedness upon his classical background and culture. To understand the Christian truth, he constantly reiterates, one must go back to Scripture, especially the New Testament, where the gospel is most fully inscripturated.[25] Theologians, whose task it is to explicate the Christian message, must have a thorough competence in the biblical languages; for the New Testament, this means an intimate familiarity with the Greek language, not only with its grammar but also with all its literary and rhetorical resources. Only then can they come to know and appreciate the gospel in all its inexhaustible richness and meaningfulness. For this reason, an expert knowledge of the classical languages and literatures is indispensable. At the same time, Christian theologians will also benefit from the splendid heritage of classical literature and rhetoric in order to communicate the Christian message more effectively to those whom they wish to reach. For Erasmus, then, the issue is not only the proper understanding and explication of Scripture but also the effective communication of its message. For this reason, he came to place great emphasis on the necessity of good preaching. In one of his last major works, the *Ecclesiastes* (published in 1535), he expounds at great length on this need and argues that the preacher's effectiveness in the vernacular will be enhanced by a good background in the classics.[26]

Erasmus thus advocates an exegesis and proclamation of the Christian message which is scripturally grounded and philological and rhetorical in method; a logically rigorous and subtle dogmatics, in his estimation, will only obscure and even pervert the gospel. For Erasmus the great church fathers, especially Jerome, exemplify this far superior tradition of theology and preaching within the church; they possessed and used the proper tools of exegesis and communication, instruments which they derived from the great classical literary and rhetorical tradition of which they are the true, Christian heirs. It is not surprising, then, that it became one of Erasmus's great life tasks to prepare editions of the major church fathers for printing, making them more accessible.

Erasmus's advocacy of the philological and rhetorical method in the exegesis of Scripture led him to reject the excesses of allegorical interpretation; in this respect, he is critical of some of the scriptural commentary of Origen and Augustine.[27] One might wonder, however, if his criticism of a thoroughgoing allegorical interpretation of the Bible does not have negative implications for his own rather drastic attempts to demonstrate a spiritual affinity between the Christian message and a classical text, such as we have seen in his introduction to the *Adagia*. Certainly by our hermeneutical and scholarly standards, Erasmus's approach to the classics is lacking in historical sensitivity. All the same, the question needs to be raised whether for any scholar, including the Christian scholar, a purely philological-historical framework of thinking and problematics can really be an adequate *raison d'être* for his or her engagement with the Greek and Roman classics. This is the principal issue that I will explore in my hermeneutical reflections in the concluding section.

E. A Christian Hermeneutic for the Classics

It is, first of all, worth noting that for all its exegetical inadequacies (by our standards), even Erasmus's heavily allegorical and anagogical reading of a classical text may contain a substantial kernel of insight. A remarkable example of such a success, achieved in spite of or perhaps even because of the hermeneutical limitations of Erasmus's commentary style, is his reading of Vergil's *Second Eclogue* in the treatise *De Ratione Studii* (On the method of study), published in 1511. This brief work presents an outline of an ideal programme of studies for the liberal education that every youngster, according to Erasmus, should receive and raises at one point the important pedagogical question whether certain texts which contain morally unsuitable material for young, immature students may still be usefully taught to them.[28] Erasmus's answer is that, with skillful and carefully pitched commentary from the teacher, such material can still be of great educational value to the young person, and he offers Vergil's poem as illustration of how this can be achieved. The poem's erotic (i.e. homoerotic) theme, he suggests, need not be brought into focus in the teacher's commentary; in fact, it can easily be ignored. Instead, the *Second Eclogue* can be studied and appreciated by the young student as a telling demonstration of how two persons with sharply opposed tastes and values, represented in this poem by the rustic Corydon and the sophisticated Alexis, can never form a genuine and lasting friendship.

I certainly do not recommend Erasmus's strategy of circumventing what to twentieth century readers would be a most significant aspect of the theme of this poem. I simply wish to emphasize that the bowdlerization suggested by him has, in all probability, led him to accentuate what is, in fact, a most important facet of meaning in the *Second Eclogue*, for a great deal of the pathos and humor of this poem stems from the insurmountable incompatibility of Corydon and Alexis, and this is an aspect which a modern reader, who is likely to be especially struck and intrigued by the homoerotic ethos of Vergil's poem, might easily neglect or even totally overlook.

I hope that this example illustrates that even a heavily allegorical and anagogical reading of a text, ostensibly quite unsatisfactory to our tastes, can still offer genuine insights by disclosing, as it were, new horizons of meaning and meaningfulness. In fact, the allegorical and anagogical reading of texts is still very much with us and, indeed, has enjoyed a great resurgence in this century. I agree with Richard Palmer that this approach to literature has enjoyed a continuous and still continuing tradition in the West from Greco-Roman times onwards.[29] In our century, in particular, the interpretation of literary texts—whether one thinks of any of the modern schools of criticism (Freudian, archetypal, Marxist, structuralist, or poststructuralist)—has again become remarkably allegorical and anagogical in the broad sense of the word, addressing issues and concerns which lie outside the purview of standard philological-historical scholarship. Even the so-called New Criticism, which dominated literary criticism in the English-speaking world from the 1940s to the 1960s, did not remain closed to these metatextual issues, despite its very strong aesthetic-formalist bias. In the study of Greek and Roman literature, too, there has been a considerable move away from standard philological-historical scholarship over the past few decades—and rightly so, I believe, for the traditional scholarship, indispensible though it will remain for the work of the classical scholar, does not by itself enable us to engage in an integral encounter with the classics.[30] To achieve such an encounter, to which we must surely aspire if the Greek and Roman classics are to have enduring value for ourselves and our culture, we must inevitably take as our basic hermeneutical starting point not the objectives of traditional scholarship but a sense of motivation that is ultimately prescholarly and prescientific in nature and stems from the totality of who and what we are.

Thus, unless we choose to be, at least outwardly and professionally, altogether constrained by the objectives of traditional philological-historical scholarship, we cannot avoid in our work as classicists moving into a mode of interpretation that might very well be called allegorical in the broad and positive sense of the word. We may, of course, never disregard the historical aspect of the text; the text must be allowed, indeed must be interpreted to speak authentically to us in all its historical concreteness. Ideally, we will strike a creative balance in our work of exegesis and commentary between the inescapable historical nature of the text and the equally inescapable reality of our basic hermeneutical starting point which, as I have argued, is ultimately not scientific or scholarly in nature. Then we will be enriched by the horizon of experience opened up for us by the text while the text, in turn, will acquire a new dimension of meaningfulness from our act of interpretation.

The Christian scholar must be especially conscious of the ever-present context of personal motivation in which his or her work of scholarship takes place. This personal motivation must be, at least in part, I very strongly believe, a genuine love of the Greek and Roman classics and the great legacy they have represented for Western or even for world civilization. We need not apologize for our enthusiasm as though it is as such incompatible with the Christian faith. We should remember, perhaps, that while the apostle

Paul clearly condemns the godlessness of his age (Romans 1), he also shows himself to be open to those in his day who were genuinely seeking after God (Acts 17:22ff). His words in Philippians 4:8, "And now, my friends, all that is true, all that is noble, all that is just and pure, all that is lovable and gracious, whatever is excellent and admirable—fill all your thoughts with these things,"should guide us in developing a discerning appreciation of the cultural achievements of the Greeks and Romans. Then we can also still follow Erasmus in reaffirming the lasting value of the classical legacy, and be grateful for his immense labors to make this great heritage more accessible to his contemporaries and succeeding generations.

Notes

1. J. Huizinga, *Erasmus and the Age of the Reformation* (New York: Harper & Row, Harper Torchbooks, 1957) 112. The English translation was originally published as *Erasmus of Rotterdam* (New York: Charles Scribner's Sons, 1924).

2. Margaret Mann Phillips, "Erasmus and the Classics,"in *Erasmus*, ed. T. A. Dorey (Albuquerque: University of New Mexico Press, 1970) 1. On Erasmus's work as a translator of the Greek classics, see the recent study by Erika Rummel, *Erasmus as a Translator of the Classics* (Toronto: University of Toronto Press, 1985).

3. Speaking here of Hesiod and Plato, *Collected Works of Erasmus*, vol. 31, 14, lines 22-27. Wherever possible references to, and quotations from the texts of Erasmus are based on the *Collected Works of Erasmus* (Toronto: University of Toronto Press, 1969-) hereafter cited as *CWE*. For the Latin text, references are to the new edition, *Opera Omnia* (Amsterdam: North-Holland Publishing Co., 1971-) hereafter cited as *ASD*.

4. *CWE* 31, 15, lines 31ff.; quotation from lines 42-43.

5. *CWE* 31, 15, lines 53-55.

6. *ASD* I 2, 31, line 23.

7. *CWE* 26, 326-33.

8. Quintilian *Institutio Oratoria* I.3.13-17.

9. *CWE* 26, 332

10. On statements of the apostle Paul with regard to this issue, see *CWE* 26, 328.

11. On the raising of children for service to the state (or community) and God, see *CWE* 26, 306.

12. *CWE* 26, 328-29.

13. *CWE* 23, 71, line 11 to 73, line 37. For a penetrating analysis of the *Antibarbari* as a whole, see "Under the Pear Tree,"in Marjorie O'Rourke Boyle, *Christening Pagan Mysteries: Erasmus in Pursuit of Wisdom* (Toronto: University of Toronto Press, 1981) chap. 1.

14. *CWE* 23, 59, line 9 to 61, line 25.

15. *CWE* 23, 60, lines 17-20.

16. *CWE* 23, 60, lines 21-26.

17. *CWE* 23, 97, lines 6ff.; Batt draws on Jerome for a similar metaphor or analogy, namely that of the captive woman representing secular learning and culture (*CWE* 23, 91, lines 16ff.)

18. *The Colloquies of Erasmus* (hereafter cited as *Colloquies*), trans. C. R. Thompson (Chicago: University of Chicago Press, 1965) 65. One should make special note, in this connection, of Erasmus's attempt to establish a spiritual rapport between Epicurean ethics and the Christian message in his colloquy *Epicureus* (The Epicurean), published in 1533; see Thompson, *Colloquies*, 535-51, with his introduction. There is an excellent study by Marjorie O'Rourke Boyle in *Christening Pagan Mysteries* (67ff.; cited in note 13) of the argument of the *Epicureus*, which Erasmus wrote against the background of his controversy with Luther.

19. Thompson, *Colloquies*, 68.

20. See R. Bainton, *Erasmus of Christendom* (New York: Charles Scribner's Sons, 1969) 56ff. and J. Huizinga, *Erasmus and the Age of the Reformation* (cited in n.1) 29ff. Both authors, of course, rightly emphasize that one cannot speak of a sudden reorientation in Erasmus's career.

21. *CWE* 23, 10; I have somewhat altered her translation of the quotation given.

22. For a detailed discussion see Phillips, "Erasmus and the Classics,"(cited in n.2) 12-17; the quotation is given in her translation.

23. *CWE* 28, 389. On Erasmus's Latinity and his flexible, non-antiquarian use of the language, see D. F. S. Thomson, "The Latinity of Erasmus,"in *Erasmus* (cited n.2) 115-37.

24. *ASD* I 2, 709, lines 25-27; *CWE* 28, 447.

25. Erasmus's best known statement on the Scriptures is the *Paraclesis*, prefaced to his first edition of the Greek New Testament in 1516; for a convenient translation, see *Christian Humanism and the Reformation*, ed. J. C. Olin (New York: Harper & Row, Harper Torchbooks, 1965) 92-106. The most thorough exposition of his biblical hermeneutics comes in the *Ratio Verae Theologiae*, prefaced to his second edition of the New Testament in 1518; for a lengthy and penetrating discussion, see Margaret O'Rourke Boyle, "Ratio,"in *Erasmus on Language and Method in Theology* (Toronto: University of Toronto Press, 1977), chap. 5; see also R. G. Chantraine, "The *Ratio Verae Theologiae* (1518),"in *Essays on the Works of Erasmus*, ed. R. DeMolen (New Haven and London: Yale University Press, 1978) 179-85; on Erasmus's indebtedness as a Christian scholar and humanist to Jerome as well as on his edition of the New Testament, see B. Hall, "Erasmus: Biblical Scholar and Reformer,"in *Erasmus* (cited in n.2) 81-113; for a detailed study of Erasmus's struggle with the scholastic theologians at a critical point in his career, see A. Renaudet, *Érasme: Sa Pensée Religieuse et Son Action D'Après Sa Correspondance (1518-1521)*, (Paris, 1926, Geneva: Slatkine Reprints, 1970), although, in my view, the author is less than fully appreciative of the real Christological strengths of Erasmus's piety.

26. On the *Ecclesiastes*, not only as a manual for preachers but also as a major and final statement of Erasmus's theology, see R. G. Kleinhans, "*Ecclesiastes sive de Ratione Concionandi*,"in *Essays on the Works of Erasmus* (cited in n.25) 253-68.

27. For Erasmus on the allegorical interpretation of Scripture, see C. Béné, *Érasme et Saint Augustin* (Geneva: Librairie Droz, 1969) 264-72.; see also Boyle, *Erasmus on Language and Method in Theology* (cited in n.25), 117ff., where Boyle rightly stresses the Erasmian insistence on biblical polysemy founded on the "literal bedrock"(121)

which is Christ. Erasmus's evangelical rather than speculative method of allegorical exegesis is well exemplified in his work, *De Sarcienda Ecclesiae Concordia* (On mending the peace of the church), published in 1533. It takes the form of a lengthy commentary on Psalm 84 which pursues the theme of the unity of the church, sorely threatened now, and its restoration through internal reform. For a convenient translation, see *The Essential Erasmus*, ed. J. P. Dolan (New York: Mentor Omega Books, 1964) 331-88.

28. *CWE* 24, 683-87.

29. Palmer sees a close spiritual and intellectual affinity between the allegorical interpretation of the Homeric epics by some Greek philosophers and the "demythologizing"theology of Rudolf Bultmann; see his, "Allegorical, Philological, and Philosophical Hermeneutics: Three Modes in a Complex Heritage,"in *Contemporary Literary Hermeneutics and Interpretation* ed. S. Kresic (Ottawa: University of Ottawa, 1981) 15-37, esp. 25-26. I highly recommend this paper as a whole, as well as Palmer's earlier book, *Hermeneutics* (Evanston: Northwestern University Press, 1969), to which I am very much indebted for the development and formulation of some of my principal views on literary interpretation. Palmer, following Hans-Georg Gadamer, does an excellent job in exposing the hermeneutical limitations of positivistic philological-historical analysis as well as of a strictly aesthetic-formalist approach (e.g., the New Criticism) to literature. Let me state at this point that I also profited a great deal from the intensive discussions at the 1984 Conference, "Christianity and the Classics,"held at the Institute for Christian Studies in Toronto.

30. I have discussed the influence of contemporary literary-critical theories and methodologies on the study of classical literature and Roman literature in particular in an article, "New Approaches in the Literary-Critical Study of Roman Poetry,"in *Echos du Monde Classique / Classical Views* XXX N.5.6 (1987) 341-54.

Calvin: The Theology of a Christian Humanist

Arvin Vos

A. Introduction

> We must list among the Christian humanists not only Erasmus, Vives, Budé, More and Hooker, but also Calvin, the elegant Latin writer and commentator of Seneca . . . .[1]

To forestall misunderstanding, the title of this paper requires two clarifications. First, I will not be concerned with Calvin's writings as such; my sole concern in this paper is to indicate how Calvin's theology reveals the influence of Renaissance humanism. Renaissance humanism was the means by which Calvin acquired his knowledge of and appreciation for the learning of classical Greece and Rome. In literary form, mode of argumentation, and themes, Calvin's writings reveal the influence of the humanist tradition. To approach Calvin from this point of view is, admittedly, to take a limited perspective on his work, but an appreciation of this aspect of Calvin's thought will lead to a better understanding and appreciation of the whole.

The second clarification concerns the term "humanist." Today "humanism" has a variety of meanings, including "the quality of being human" or "any system or way of thought or action concerned with the interest and ideals of people" or "the study of the humanities." Prior to our century, humanism had only the last meaning—the study of the humanities. Certainly this was the meaning of the term in the fifteenth and sixteenth centuries. Then *humanista* and its vernacular equivalents were used "for the professor, or teacher, or student of the humanities."[2] This usage was rooted in a far older tradition:

> The term *humanista,* coined at the height of the Renaissance period, was in turn derived from an older term, that is, from the "humanities or *studia humanitatis.* This term was apparently used in the general sense of a liberal or literary education by such ancient Roman authors as Cicero and Gellius, and this use was resumed by the Italian scholars of the late fourteenth century. By the first half of the fifteenth century, the *studia humanitatis* came to stand for a clearly defined cycle of scholarly disciplines, namely grammar, rhetoric, history, poetry and moral philosophy . . . .[3]

New in the fifteenth century was the emphasis on reading and interpreting the writings of the classical Latin and Greek authors in their original language.

In the Italian universities *humanista* came to be applied to professors of the humanities just as *legista, jurista, canonista,* and *artista* was applied to other disciplines. "Humanist," then, indicates not a philosophical but an educational program centered about literary studies. Of the traditional topics in philosophy only a limited portion of moral philosophy was included—none of which had any great depth.[4]

As an educational program humanism did not include law, medicine, or theology, but this does not mean that it was without influence in these areas. We know, for example, that in his study of law at Orleans Calvin was exposed to two opposing methods— an old school which followed the tradition of using glosses on the *Corpus Juris Civilis* which was then used as a basis for understanding and revising contemporary law, and a new school which ignored the medieval additions and returned to the *Corpus* itself. In this latter case the language, style, and historical context of the work, in addition to its content, became the focus of study. The new school also acquainted the student with the language, history, and social customs of ancient Rome.[5] Even though the new method was not as practical in orientation as the old, it made its way into the schools nevertheless.[6] To conclude, my aim is to indicate how Renaissance humanism, which consisted primarily in a literary program of study which looked back to ancient learning for its inspiration, influenced the thought of Calvin.[7]

B. Humanist Elements in Calvin's Writings

Among the humanists, the one who was probably the most influential on Calvin was Erasmus. Even though Calvin does not seem to have interacted with him personally, among both his friends and teachers there were followers of the great humanist. For a number of years Calvin lived in a setting where Christian humanism was espoused by both friends (de Hangest, Olivetan, Cop, Daniel, Duchemin, Wolmar) and by teachers (Cordier, Alciate, Danes, Vatable). They were all Erasmian or Fabrisian. Through contact with them, Calvin became "a biblical humanist", that is, a proponent of renewal of the church from within through a return to the original sources—Scripture and the fathers.[8]

1. Calvin's correspondence

As a young man Calvin was fascinated by humanism. This is seen most clearly in his correspondence. His letters are in the best humanist style, even to the point of being dated according to the old Roman usage.[9] They also manifest a concern for religious issues, which is not surprising since most of his humanist friends were adherents of a party that wished, like Erasmus, to reform the church from within.

2. Commentary on Seneca's De Clementia

As a writer Calvin's first book was a commentary on Seneca's *De Clementia*. It is an example of the type of work which the humanists were fond of doing—commenting on an ancient text which contained a doctrine of interest. Calvin explains Seneca's teaching by comparing it with those of other classical writers, including the philosophers Plato and Aristotle, but he also evaluates it from the point of view of Christian teaching—the writings of the apostle Paul and Augustine. Calvin's close study of the text is ample evidence of his mastery of humanist tools of learning.

3. Biblical commentaries

The tools which Calvin employed in writing the commentary on Seneca were soon turned to the task of interpreting Scripture. The results were remarkable, to say the least. In his biblical commentaries Calvin penetrates to the world of the author and the meaning that the text had in its original setting far better than his medieval predecessors did. Thomas Aquinas's commentaries on the Pauline epistles are perfunctory by comparison. He tends to treat Paul's letters as if they were philosophic texts, rather than letters to individual persons in particular settings. Even Augustine does not match Calvin in his ability to get at the author's meaning. Calvin's commentaries are his greatest achievement. In part Calvin was able to produce such significant commentaries because of his understanding of the Christian life, but without the skills he acquired as a humanist scholar he would not have gained the skill necessary to understand and explain the biblical text.

4. *The* Institutes
While Calvin's letters and commentaries show clearly the impact of humanism on his thought, its influence is also to be found in the *Institutes*. Here the influence is more subtle but significant nevertheless. It is seen both in the form of the work and its content.

With regard to form, numerous scholars have commented on Calvin's elegant Latin. Its literary style contrasts strongly with the academic theology of the day, the treatises of the schoolmen. The Latin of the *Institutes* is evidence of Calvin's familiarity with classical Latin. The form of the *Institutes* is not due simply to Calvin's interest in humanism, for the work has a history that is significant. It started as a simple handbook of faith, treating the law (decalogue), the creed, prayer, the sacraments (a critique of the false sacraments), and government. Calvin chose to revise this work, inserting in later additions vast amounts of theological discussion. The fact that he chose to retain this form rather than write another work in the mode usual for theological discussion at the time—a disputation for example—is evidence of his allegiance to the literary form so prized by the humanists.[10]

With regard to the content of the *Institutes*, perhaps the most significant way in which Calvin's humanism affects the work is in his attitude toward and use of philosophy. The *studia humanitatis* included a study of morals but excluded other areas of philosophy and related disciplines—logic, physics, astronomy, biology, psychology, metaphysics, and mathematics. As a theologian Calvin does not write a separate work on the moral life, but in the *Institutes* he shows himself to be familiar with the topics discussed by the humanists in this area. When examining the "understanding of earthly things" which are significant for this present life, he mentions government, household management, mechanical skills, and the liberal arts (II.ii.13). When illustrating the "universal apprehension of reason and understanding by nature implanted in men" Calvin's first example is "the ancient jurists who established civic order and discipline with such great equity" (II.ii.13). He also adds a note of approval for "the philosophers... in their fine observation and artful description of nature" (ibid.). This stands with a similar positive comment for the rhetoricians ("those who conceived the art of disputation and taught us to speak reasonably"), for medicine, and the mathematical sciences.

Calvin regards these discoveries of the philosophers as manifestations of the Spirit. Still, they are only a knowledge of earthly things, and they do not advance one in the understanding of "heavenly things". Calvin does not express skepticism about the sciences, medicine, the jurists, and so forth. He simply makes the point that these things do not help one to understand God better.[11]

When we note which of the ancient authors are quoted by Calvin, another aspect of his humanism manifests itself. Cicero was a favorite author among the humanists, and Calvin is no exception. While Plato is probably most approved of by Calvin, Cicero is most cited among the Latin authors. Seneca, the Epicureans, and the Stoics are also mentioned a number of times when Calvin is contrasting the wisdom of the Scriptures with that of the philosophers, showing how Scripture is superior to the findings of the philosophers (cf. I.iii.3). Although Plato's teaching is highly respected, Calvin does not demonstrate a familiarity with his actual writings. Almost entirely missing also is Aristotle, whose views were so influential in the schools.

Calvin condemns the sophistries of the schoolmen and he will not be delayed by the "minutiae of Aristotle" (I.xv.7). On occasion he employs a philosophical distinction when it suits his purpose (such as the mention of the four kinds of causes in the discussion of righteousness in III.xiv.17), but for the most part he is concerned that he not be distracted by what appears to him as needless subtlety. In discussing the soul he admits that the discussions of the philosophers may have merit, but they are not needed for theology.

> I leave it to the philosophers to discuss these faculties in their subtle way. For the upbuilding of godliness a simple definition will be enough for us. I, indeed, agree that the things they

teach are true, not only enjoyable, but also profitable to learn
and skillfully assembled by them. And I do not forbid those
who are desirous of learning to study them. (I.xv.6)

There follows a very brief account—approximately three
pages—of the faculties of the soul which Calvin eventually reduces
to understanding and will (I.xv.7). The brief treatment which Calvin gives these matters can be contrasted with what was typical of
the schoolmen. Most familiar perhaps is the discussion of Aquinas.
In the *Summa Theologiae* (1a. 75 to 89) there are eighty-nine articles
devoted to a study of the soul, its union with the body, its powers
in general and individually, and the operations of these powers
both in the present life and after death.

To sum up, Calvin takes a typically humanist attitude toward
philosophy. The texts that he knows and his attitude toward them
are typical of humanists—Cicero and Seneca rather than Aristotle.
The detailed analyses of the schoolmen are deemed a perilous dis-
traction. In one way, the tension between Calvin and the schoolmen
can be attributed to the competition between two intellectual traditions, but added is the antipathy that stems from the fact that the
schoolmen are leaders of the opposition to the reform movement
which Calvin has joined.[12]

Among humanists there was an emphasis on humankind, their
dignity and place in the universe. Calvin shares this interest, but it
is coupled with an emphasis on humanity in relation to God. Like
other humanists, then, Calvin is relatively unconcerned with the
sciences of the day. Unlike the medievalists, then, who were concerned to find a place for theology in the table of the sciences, Calvin
does not reflect on the relation of theology to the other disciplines
or compare its method with their methods. Any concern he
manifests in this regard is limited to showing that sacred wisdom
is superior to any philosophy or science (natural philosophy) in
what it can reveal about God.

These are some general features of Calvin's thought which are
influenced by humanism. They pertain more to the form of his
thought than its content. This is as one would expect, given the fact
that humanism is primarily an emphasis on literary studies and is
not to be identified with any particular philosophical position. If
one looks for the antecedents of Calvin's thought, one is more
likely to find them in Luther, Augustine, and other church fathers

rather than in any influence of the Greco-Roman heritage. Even his rather dualistic and spiritualistic anthropology—the soul is "an immortal yet created essence", "something essential apart from the body" (I.xv.2)—owes more to Augustine and to other Christian thinkers than it does to Plato. Hence, I do not think it possible to trace central themes in Calvin's thought to the influence of humanism. Humanism with its emphasis on literary studies enriches Calvin's thought both in that it enabled him to be a superior interpreter of Scripture and gave him the capacity to present his own thought in a most effective form.

C. Calvin and the Renaissance Ideal of Knowledge

Calvin did not intend to found a new church, but his goal was rather to renew the old.[13] This goal is reflected in his aim not to present a new teaching but to purify the teaching of the church by removing accretions added by the medieval church. Calvin used the tools of humanism to achieve this goal. One factor in the revitalization of theology was its grounding in a new exegesis of Scripture. The new method was more sensitive to the nuances of the text than scholastic exegesis had been. This was, I think, the great gain of the Reformation so far as theological method is concerned. By the fifteenth century much of the discussion in the schools had become arid, for points of contention among the schools dominated while the focus on Scripture languished. To this situation the influence of humanism served as a corrective. Not only Protestants but also Catholic scholars, such as Erasmus, wished to redirect theologians back to their foundations.[14] For Calvin the schools represented this ossified tradition and were the opposition to much needed reform of the church. In this context he rejects their methods entirely as a way of doing theology. He adopts and uses the tools of humanism. Humanist learning provided Calvin with a greater capacity to interpret Scripture, but the acceptance of humanist ideals was not all gain. From our perspective we can see that there were some things which were also lost.

In part, philosophy is a repository of materials which are useful for the theologian when discussing God, human nature, the spiritual life, and so forth. Philosophy also has another use, based on the fact that it is reflective about its own method. It can enable theologians to become more reflective about their own theological method. In rejecting the traditional use of philosophy by theology,

Calvin fails to recognize that it is useful to reflect on how we come to know earthly things so that we can become more aware about how we know God. In short, there is almost no reflection on theological method in Calvin's writings such as is found among the schoolmen. Moreover, its relation to other disciplines and the relation of its method to that of natural philosophy and related disciplines are not examined. When such relationships are not reflected on, there is a tendency for theology to become isolated.

Something else was lost in addition. The relation between theology and natural knowledge—philosophy—was sketched only negatively, that is, in terms of what reason cannot do. For the period following, however, this would prove to be seriously inadequate. The rise of the natural sciences would pose all sorts of questions in this regard.

Related to philosophy is also the ideal of systematic or comprehensive knowledge—not system in the sense of the idealist philosophies, but rather some order in the process of knowing and in what is known. The closest Calvin gets to this ideal is found in the *Institutes*, but it does not constitute a systematic theology. Some interpreters have turned this fact into a theological principle. There is, I think, a better way to understand this matter.

Intellectual traditions founded on the understanding of a text have their own stages of development. Simple reading of the text comes first—more or less elementary commentaries. At the second stage difficult issues are isolated and discussed in their own right. The disputed questions of the medieval schools illustrate this stage. In the final stage the relations of each issue to the others and the whole is worked out, and it is ascertained both whether the method used is consistent and the results attained form a coherent whole. Aquinas's *Summa Theologiae* is an example of this stage of development.

At the time of the Reformation the deepened understanding of the biblical text resulted in a new beginning of this kind of development. Calvin was at the forefront with regard to commenting on Scripture. The *Institutes* represents a movement toward the second and third stages of development.

To carry the point further, it appears to me that in one respect at least the development from Calvin to the Reformed scholastics was not a regrettable decline, but rather an inevitable transition. The same thing had happened earlier in the history of the church, and it would no doubt happen again. In addition to commenting on the biblical text, there is the need to discuss theological issues in an orderly way. Calvin's education in the humanistic tradition did not prepare him for this work; indeed it probably kept him from proceeding in that direction. Later theologians took up where he had left off, for theology itself had to be restated on the basis of the new biblical exegesis.

To conclude, Calvin was influenced by the Renaissance. Humanism opened up a new method of interpretation through its focus on literary studies. Just as it influenced the study of law, so through Calvin and others humanist learning reshaped theology. Not philosophical but literary categories and methods were utilized in doing theology. And this development had both strengths and weaknesses.

Notes
1. Paul Oskar Kristeller, *Renaissance Thought* (New York: Harper & Row, 1961) 87.
2. Kristeller, op. cit., 9.
3. Ibid., 9-10.
4. "Most of these [moral] treatises . . . are the works of consummate writers and scholars, but must appear somewhat amateurish to a reader acquainted with the works of the greater Greek, scholastic, or modern philosophers. They often seem to lack not only originality, but also coherence, method, and substance, and if we try to sum up their arguments and conclusions, leaving aside citations, examples, and commonplaces, literary ornaments and digressions, we are frequently left with nearly empty hands" (ibid., 17-18). But since profundity has never been a prerequisite for popularity, this does not mean that humanist writings were without influence. Indeed, just the opposite was true.
5. On this matter see T.H.L. Parker, *John Calvin* (Philadelphia: Westminster Press, 1975) 13-15.
6. Negatively stated, the meaning of "humanistic" as an educational program must be distinguished from present usage in which "almost any kind of concern with human values is called 'humanistic' and consequently a great variety of thinkers, religious or antireligious, scientific or antiscientific, lay claim to what has become a rather elusive label of praise" (ibid., 8).
7. In the nineteenth century some historians associated the Italian Renaissance with a pagan tendency and interpreted the Protestant and Catholic Reformations as religious revivals which challenged the un-Christian culture of the humanists. It is true that during the Renaissance there developed a renewed interest in the pagan gods and heroes, but this does not mean that there was opposition to Christian teachings and practice. No one proposed a revival of the ancient pagan worship. Although new studies may have competed for public attention, they were not antireligious in the way Enlightenment and post-Enlightenment thought would later be. According to Kristeller, if one chooses to call "Christian humanists

all those scholars who accepted the teachings of Christianity and were members of one of the churches, without necessarily discussing religious or theological writings in their literary or scholarly writings, [then] practically all Renaissance humanists, before and after the Reformation, were Christian humanists...." (Kristeller, op. cit. in n.1,86). What Kristeller is not taking into account is that there is quite a difference between merely accepting or tolerating Christian teachings and devoting one's energies to promoting them.

8. On the role of each of these individuals and their positions, see Alexandre Ganoczy, *Le jeune Calvin: genèse et évolution de sa vocation réformatrice* (Wiesbaden: Franz Steiner Verlag, G.M.B.H., 1966), chap. 1.

9. Ganoczy, op. cit., 193.

10. In this connection it should also be mentioned that Calvin never had a formal theological education. The indications are that he studied in the arts faculty at Collège Montaigu but did not enroll in theology. Cf. Ganoczy, op. cit., 186.

11. Calvin's position in this regard seems quite traditional with parallels in both Augustine (*On Christian Doctrine* II, xxvi, 54 and xxxi, 49) and Thomas Aquinas (*Summa Theologiae* 1a. 1, 8 ad 2m and 2a2ae. 2,8) Recently William Bouwsma has argued that Calvin struggled with a crisis of knowing that dominated the Renaissance period and that his doctrine of faith was shaped by this problem. I think Bouwsma has misunderstood the traditional view of knowledge and hence sees a crisis in knowing that did not really exist. For Bouwsma's account, see "Calvin and the Renaissance Crisis of Knowing," *Calvin Theological Journal* 17/2 (November 1982), 190-211.

12. Kristeller is no doubt right when he claims that the humanist polemic against the schoolmen is often an expression of "departmental rivalry" (op. cit. in n.1, 42), but in Calvin's case it is likely that the opposition he and his friends experienced from the authorities in Paris, including the professors at the Sorbonne, likely had an even greater influence on Calvin than did humanist prejudices. See Ganoczy, *Le jeune Calvin* (op. cit. in n.8, chap. 1) for a detailed account of the religious struggle going on between those favoring and those opposing reform.

13. On this point sections 6 and 7 of the "Prefatory Address to King Francis give the best brief statement by Calvin of his mission. It was part of the first edition of the *Institutes* and it remained unchanged.

14. One must not assume that the scholastics were uniformly opposed to the new learning. It is surprising to learn, for example, that in 1572 in the library of the Academy founded by Calvin there were twelve titles by Cajetan. Although Cajetan's commentary on Thomas Aquinas's *Summa Theologiae* is found there, the largest part of these volumes are scriptural commentaries which he wrote late in his life. See Alexandre Ganoczy, *La bibliothèque de l'académie de Calvin* (Geneva, 1969), 96-97.

Aristotle and Early Reformed Orthodoxy: Moments of Accomodation and Antithesis

Donald Sinnema

The late sixteenth century emergence of Reformed orthodoxy[1] was marked in part by a growing scholastic orientation. Studies in recent years have identified several basic tendencies of this scholastic orientation. They include its attempt to present the Christian faith as a logically coherent and rationally defensible system of belief, a dependence upon the methodology and philosophy of Aristotle, an increased role given to reason and logic in presenting and defending religious truth, an interest in metaphysical and speculative questions, and a nonhistorical view of Scripture as a self-consistent account that can be reduced to a creedal statement.[2]

The present study focuses especially on the second tendency. While Reformed orthodoxy showed a renewed interest in the classical tradition as a whole, it is clear that the works of Aristotle received particular attention. In contrast to Calvin, whose writings reveal traces of Platonic and Stoic influence, later Calvinists clearly preferred Aristotle.

The whole field of Renaissance Aristotelianism has become the object of intense study in the past thirty years.[3] It is now recognized that Aristotelianism thrived in the period 1500 to 1650, although this era also saw sharp criticism of it from the side of the new science. Moreover, new emphasis has been placed on the diversity within Aristotelianism in this period. Under the influence of humanism, Aristotelianism in Italy was interested in returning to an Aristotle purer than that of medieval scholasticism, and it tended to be more secular, independent of theological considerations. The neo-scholastic movement in the Iberian peninsula combined a humanistic approach to Aristotle with medieval scholastic theology. In Protestant Germany Philip Melanchthon, influenced by the rhetorical tradition, produced his own brand of Aristotelianism which rejected metaphysics except insofar as it was absorbed within dialectics and rhetoric. Reformed orthodoxy displayed an openness to all of these trends. Thus, beyond the influence of Melanchthon, especially in German Reformed circles, Calvinists could appeal, for example, to Zabarella, the great Aristotelian philosopher of Padua,[4] and to the Spanish Jesuit Suarez.[5]

In exploring Reformed orthodoxy's many-faceted relationship to Aristotle, it is best to examine selected examples which clearly illustrate the issue. The question of how orthodox Calvinist theologians in the latter half of the sixteenth century related to Aristotle provides a convenient focus. One might fruitfully examine Calvinist philosophers or other teachers in the arts faculties of Reformed universities, whom one would expect to be open to Aristotle since his works remained the mainstay of their disciplines. However, these important aspects of the issue lie beyond the scope of this study. I limit myself to selected Calvinist theologians, especially as they were active in nontheological areas. Since one would expect the theologians to be particularly sensitive to the influence of pagan authors on Calvinist religion, they provide a good sample.

First, it will be helpful to sketch the academic setting of Reformed orthodoxy as found in late sixteenth century Reformed universities, Leiden University serving as an example. With such a background in mind, this paper will focus on Zacharias Ursinus's rejection of Ramism as well as Theodore Beza's attitude toward Aristotelian logic and then examine two Calvinist approaches to teaching physics[6]—those of Girolamo Zanchi and Lambert Daneau.

A. The Academic Setting

Central to the academic environment in which the late sixteenth-century Calvinist theologian operated was the Reformed university. Generally speaking, the curriculum of Protestant universities at this time, Lutheran as well as Reformed, followed the four-faculty pattern of the medieval university. At the first level was the arts faculty, where one studied the liberal arts (such courses as logic, rhetoric, physics, mathematics, Latin, and Greek). The arts program served as propaedeutic training to prepare students for the three higher faculties: theology, law, and medicine. The arts courses, as taught in Reformed universities, were based largely on classical authors, especially Aristotle.

It is true that the reformers Luther and Calvin shied away from Aristotle. With fierce assaults Luther often rejected him. Yet his harsh judgments were modified in other statements. In his tract *To the Christian Nobility* (1520) he advised that Aristotle's *Physics, Metaphysics, De anima,* and *Ethics* be discarded because of the evil effects these books had on the Christian faith. Nevertheless, Luther did admit that Aristotle's *Logic, Rhetoric,* and *Poetics* might be retained as useful tools in training young people to speak and to preach properly.[7] For Luther, Aristotelian philosophy had some validity in the natural realm, but in theology it had no place whatever.[8]

Luther's colleague and successor Philip Melanchthon showed more interest in Aristotle and the classics. Faced with the pressing need for classroom materials in the new Protestant schools, Melanchthon wrote textbooks for many of the disciplines. These tended to be compendia of Aristotle's works, corrected and supplemented at points by the truths of biblical revelation.[9] A similar pattern of increased appreciation for Aristotle and other classical authors may be found among the Calvinists, as the curricula of Reformed universities make evident.

Leiden University provides a good example of a Reformed university in this period. It was founded in 1575 by William of Orange, partly for nationalist reasons—to avoid sending students to foreign centers, especially to the Catholic university at Louvain—and partly to help meet the urgent need for ministers in the northern provinces of the Netherlands.

The Reformed character of the university was evident especially in its theological faculty, occupied by professors related in spirit to Calvinist Geneva and Heidelberg. In the nontheological faculties, however, a Reformed perspective was not as obvious. There the Renaissance spirit of Erasmus held sway and the concern to have professors of high reputation overshadowed the concern for a Reformed outlook. The Greek professor Vulcanius, for instance, did not even profess the Reformed religion, and it was easy for the great classicist Justus Lipsius to return to Catholicism upon leaving Leiden.

The combination of Christian and classical spirits was apparent already at the inauguration of the university in 1575. In the ceremonial procession that paraded through the city of Leiden, allegorical figures represented the four university faculties. At the head of the procession, after a squad of soldiers bearing the town colors, was a float carrying Lady Sacra Scriptura, accompanied on foot by the four evangelists Matthew, Mark, Luke, and John. This depicted the theological faculty. Then the law faculty was represented by Justice, riding blindfolded on a unicorn and carrying a sword and pair of scales. Accompanying it were the four famous Roman jurists Julianus, Papinianus, Ulpianus, and Trobonianus. Then came Medicine, carrying a book and medicinal herbs, accompanied by the classical physicians Hippocrates, Galen, Dioscorides, and Theophrastus. Finally, representing the arts faculty was Pallas Athena, accompanied by the philosophers Aristotle and Plato, the orator Cicero,and the poet Vergil. The rest of the procession consisted of Leiden dignitaries and soldiers.[10]

The curriculum at Leiden reflected the same pattern combining Christianity and the classics. After an initial Ramist emphasis in the curriculum, a request from students in 1582 urged the use of the actual text of Aristotle, not compendia, as the basis for instruction in logic and physics. The university Senate agreed. Soon Aristotle's *Organon* and the commentaries of Zabarella became the fundamental texts in logic.[11] The earliest surviving list of lectures, dating from 1587, provides a revealing glimpse of the curriculum. In theology and the sacred languages four professors lectured on the minor prophets, Daniel, Isaiah, Matthew, and Hebrews. Four law professors lectured on the *Institutiones* of Justinian, the first part of the *Pandectae*, and the *Feudorum Iura*. Two professors in medicine gave lectures on Hippocrates's *Prognostica* and Fernelius's *Physiologia* and supervised the practical study of this art. Finally, five arts professors lectured on Aristotle's *Logic, Physics*, and *Politics*, the (pseudo-Aristotelian) *De Mundo*, Cicero's *Epistolae ad Atticum*, Florus's *Epitome Rerum Romanorum*, Homer, cosmography, and astronomy.[12]

In the late sixteenth and early seventeenth century, Leiden University was dominated by the presence of two great classicists, Justus Lipsius and Joseph Justus Scaliger. Both had been brought in to enhance the reputation of the university. These men edited many Latin and Greek texts of the classical authors and wrote commentaries on many of these works. Their work in classical philology was continued by the "little Scaliger" Daniel Heinsius who, incidentally, stood on the Calvinist side against the Arminians at the Synod of Dort (1618-19), serving as secretary to the civil delegates.[13]

Such was the academic setting in which Calvinist theology was taught at Leiden. The average student training for the ministry would first take arts courses as a preparation for theology and then spend two years in the theology faculty. This pattern was fairly typical of Reformed universities elsewhere—such as those at Heidelberg, Geneva, Marburg, Herborn, and Franeker.[14]

The Calvinist theologian thus taught in an environment permeated with the ancient classics, with Aristotle dominating the arts faculty. Seldom did the theologians experience the teaching of theology and the classics together as incompatible. In fact, it was not uncommon for Reformed theologians themselves to teach courses also in the arts faculty. For example, at Strasbourg Peter Martyr Vermigli lectured on the *Nicomachean Ethics*, while Girolamo Zanchi lectured on Aristotle's *Physics*. At Heidelberg Zacharias Ursinus lectured on Aristotle's *Logic*. Before beginning careers in theology, Caspar Olevianus taught Melanchthon's *Dialectices* in Trier and Pierre Du Moulin lectured on Aristotle's *Logic* and *Physics* at Leiden. In Basel Amandus Polanus taught logic. Bartholomew Keckermann taught various philosophical disciplines in Danzig, as did Johann Heinrich Alsted in Herborn. Antonius Walaeus lectured on the *Nicomachean Ethics* in Middelburg. Other examples could be cited.

B. Zacharias Ursinus's Rejection of Ramist Dialectic

A major challenge to the Aristotelian predominance in logic appeared with the rise of Ramism in the mid-sixteenth century. Peter Ramus (1515-72), teaching in Paris, strongly attacked Aristotle and the scholastic curriculum based on him as cumbersome and confused. Yet the Ramist reform was more a simplification and revision of the Aristotelian system than an abandonment of it. Working in the humanist rhetorical tradition of Rudolph Agricola, Ramus simplified logic, eliminating what he considered redundant and reducing all argumentation to one art of discourse which he called dialectic or logic. Thus he developed a rhetorical logic with the aim of facilitating the learning process and serving a practical application of any subject matter.[15]

In about 1561 Ramus converted to Protestantism, in a mild Zwinglian form, and subsequently he began to exercise great influence on the Reformed tradition, especially on Calvinist secondary schools. He expanded his influence on the Reformed community during a tour of Swiss and Rhenish cities in 1569-70, when he visited such centers as Strasbourg, Basel, Heidelberg, Frankfurt, Zurich, Geneva, and Lausanne, befriending leaders in the Reformed community. His sympathizers soon numbered many prominent Reformed theologians, including Immanuel Tremellius, Caspar Olevianus, Heinrich Bullinger, Johann Sturm, Johannes Piscator, and Johann Heinrich Alsted.[16]

Other Calvinist theologians, however, firmly rejected Ramism on the basis of an Aristotelian orientation in philosophy. Prominent among these theologians were Theodore Beza of Geneva and Zacharias Ursinus of Heidelberg.

Ursinus (1534-83), the primary author of the Heidelberg Catechism (1563) and a professor of theology at Heidelberg's Collegium Sapientiae, expressed his hostility to Ramism especially during Ramus's visit to Heidelberg from October 1569 to the early months of 1570. Ramus was invited by the Palatine Elector Frederick III to fill an available teaching position in ethics, but Heidelberg University did not accept this appointment. For a short time Ramus was permitted to lecture on an oration of Cicero, and then he requested that he be allowed to teach his own dialectic. At this point, in a statement presented to Frederick early in 1570,[17] Ursinus strongly opposed Ramus's request. Ursinus considered it not only inadvisable but also in many ways destructive to introduce the new dialectic and rhetoric of Ramus into the schools. He offered five reasons for this conviction.[18]

First, he argued, in the schools youth should be taught what is true and useful, not corruptions of the arts and disciplines. The Ramist innovation in philosophy is not genuine dialectic and rhetoric but a sophistic distortion of them. It omits some fundamental parts of these arts and so twists what is left that the youth are not able to draw methodical and solid teaching from it. It fails to distinguish properly between dialectic and rhetoric. Moreover, erroneous opinions are scattered even upon the very foundations of these arts. What is derived from true and ancient teaching is scarcely explained in a way that youth may learn to distinguish true from false, certain from uncertain, good consequences from bad ones, or to judge and speak rightly. Rather, everything is directed to idle babbling and is deformed by novel and obscure terms and phrases that students cannot understand or put to good use.

Second, the Ramist innovation will be harmful also to all other studies, especially to philosophy and theology, and thus in turn to the church, the state, and society. Those who are steeped in this new method while young will be intractable since their mental abilities have been distorted and they will not be able to judge things rightly or to teach others. If they are gifted they will plead their cause by sophistical babbling rather than by reason and the strength of the truth. Thus they introduce error and dissension into ecclesiastical and political affairs. It is especially deplorable if, when Ramism is introduced, the large costs spent on maintaining the schools are wasted or badly invested in what produces not fruit but harm to the church and to posterity.

Third, Ramism is to be avoided especially in regard to the precepts and method of speaking and teaching. It troubles the youth and hinders them in their studies in various ways. First, they are not able to grasp the difference between the older and the new terminology. Second, the Ramist reform distorts rather than improves things. In place of the old well-established and clear terminology it substitutes a terminology that is strange, obscure, and difficult to understand. Third, the youth also hear conflicting precepts and opinions from different teachers. Thus, having to unlearn under one teacher what they learn under another, they are set back in their studies and in the end develop few mental abilities.

Fourth, the proverb, "The work commends the craftsman," confirms all of this. "By Aristotle, a distinguished man of genius and instrument particularly formed and raised up by God for this work, and by other wise and famous masters, [dialectic and rhetoric] were with the greatest zeal and understanding brought together and arranged in proper order, not by their whim or will but rightly by the leading of reason implanted by God and of wide-ranging experience."[19] For many centuries the most learned and eminent men among the pagans and Christians alike rose up by the help of ancient philosophy, especially by this work of dialectic and rhetoric; and whatever there is of learned men that survives comes from the old school. But none of the new sophists, who applaud their own ignorance and heap up innovations, nonsense, and confusion, is even worthy of them. It is clear that Aristotle,

Themistius, Alexander of Aphrodisias, Ammonius, Porphyry, Eustrathius, Philoponus, Simplicius, Cicero, Quintilian, Hermogenes, and other learned ancients had greater knowledge of things than these reformers with all their madness and pride-swollen heads.

Finally, there is already more than enough disagreement and quarreling everywhere, an evil which is everyone's responsibility to avert, not to increase by pointless innovation. The truth is so firm that it easily stands in the face of this nonsense. Once Ramism is introduced, nothing but harmful contentions, sects, and aggravated minds can be expected.

Ursinus went on to suggest what kind of compendia of dialectic and rhetoric should be lectured on in schools for children. It was his intention, he argued, that Ramist dialectic and rhetoric should not be introduced in these schools, not that compendia or rudiments of these subjects should not be used. It would be absurd and fruitless to present to boys the works of Aristotle himself which are not written for the mental capacity of youth. Therefore, it is necessary that compendia and rudiments, which simply contain the basic points and foundations of the arts, first be presented to youth, so that those wishing to advance to higher studies may be led to search the very sources (*ad ipsos fontes*)—the books of ancient and other authors where the arts and disciplines are treated more copiously and completely. Aristotle and similar authors should be reserved for the universities and for those who have moderately well mastered the principles of the various disciplines.

It is clear, he contended, that such compendia should not conflict with the sources since they ought to lead youth to these sources. Otherwise, they are not compendia but harmful losses (*dispendia*) which corrupt mental ability. Similarly, it would not be advisable for boys to study Calvin's *Institutes* but rather a simple epitome or catechism which is not opposed to the Scriptures or to books that explain the truth in an ample way. The dialectic and rhetoric of Ramus is no more a compendium of genuine dialectic and rhetoric than the catechism of the Jesuits is an epitome of orthodox doctrine. Those who depart from the dialectic and rhetoric of the ancient authors substitute empty babbling and sophistry for the proper way of debating, teaching, learning, and speaking. In Ursinus's view, Satan began to introduce this evil in recent times in order to bring a greater barbarism and thicker darkness to things human and divine than ever before.

Ursinus pointed out that it was not his intention to depend wholly on the authority of the ancient philosophers. One must carefully consider the reasons and defenses of their philosophy and reject anything false or overly subtle, introduced by ignorance of the divine Word or by the darkness of the human mind. "But what is true and useful (such in fact is the main body of ancient philosophy) we acknowledge and retain as exceptional gifts of God who wills that these gifts be communicated to us and be preserved for us through them."[20] Ramist sophistry destroys these gifts and tramples upon that pleasant garden.

Ursinus then countered the Ramist argument that Ramist logic is preferable because boys can thoroughly learn it in the course of six months. First, he replies, the Aristotelians refute this with the argument that evil is always grasped more quickly than the good. What is false does not deserve commendation because it is easier; nor does what is good deserve rejection because it is more difficult. Second, daily experience demonstrates that those educated by the Ramist method turn out to be nothing but impudent babblers who do not rightly know how to form an argument, much less to distinguish good from bad argumentation, or to prove the one kind and to refute the other.

On the other hand, boys who have learned the true precepts of the arts in a year or a year and a half know how to judge clearly and eloquently. The fact that many of them are slow to achieve success is not the fault of dialectic but happens partly because some simply do not have the mental ability for studies and partly because some schoolmasters cram long dictations into the rudiments in order to display their own erudition. Thus it often happens that boys do not understand the text or the dictations, and they are not able to apply the rules they learn. There are modern compendia available, composed by learned men, which can be finished in a year of teaching. What is needed to avoid delays in instruction, Ursinus concluded, is not the Ramist reform but teachers who accommodate themselves to students without hindering their progress by their own prolixity.

Ursinus's objections proved to be convincing. Ramus did not receive permission to teach his dialectic in Heidelberg and he soon traveled on. Ursinus, however, did not rest satisfied with this vic-

tory. In the next few years of his teaching at the Collegium Sapientiae he wrote a commentary on Aristotle's *Organon* to help his students learn Aristotelian logic and to counter the influence of
Ramism.[21] Johann Jungnitz, a former student of Ursinus and the
editor of the commentary, later wrote:

> Ursinus not only zealously impressed upon his students that
> they should diligently learn, practice, and use the logic taught
> most perfectly by Aristotle, but he also devoted some labor to
> the explaining of Aristotle and composed these paraphrastic
> questions in his spare hours, in order that his students might
> apply themselves more willingly, cheerfully, and resolutely to
> that study, and not be deterred by obscurity, and in order that
> he might close, as much as he could, the doors of that study
> to the new-fangled logic (*novitiae logicae*).[22]

Ursinus composed his commentary on the *Organon* in dialogue
form. The title suggests it was intended to serve as a learned commentary also for advanced students. The work itself covers
Porphyry's *Isagoge* (a common introduction to Aristotle's
Categories), the *Categories*, *On Interpretation*, and the two books of
the *Prior Analytics*. Because of a busy schedule and illness before
his premature death in 1583, Ursinus was not able to extend the
commentary to the rest of Aristotle's logic. Nor did he have the op-
portunity to polish what he had written.[23] After his death Jungnitz,
as professor of logic at Heidelberg, edited the work and had it
published in 1586. Jungnitz included Ursinus's 1570, objections to
Ramist dialectic and rhetoric and he added a dedicatory epistle in
which he presented a concerted defense of the use of logic in theology.
    Ursinus's commentary deserves a careful study to determine
its precise stance toward Aristotle. However, it is well known that
Ursinus's thinking was shaped by his early training under
Melanchthon,[24] so one would expect his thinking in the area of
logic to reflect Melanchthon's type of Aristotelianism.

C. Theodore Beza and Aristotelian Logic

A position similar to Ursinus's is evident in Theodore Beza's attitude toward the use of Aristotle's logic in theology. Beza (1519-
1605) was John Calvin's successor at Geneva. He continued to head
the Geneva Academy for forty years after Calvin's death and exer-

cised an enormous influence on the Reformed world through his extensive correspondence.

Like Ursinus, Beza rejected Ramism because of his esteem for Aristotle. Having visited Geneva from April to June 1570, during which time he lectured briefly on Cicero, Ramus requested a teaching position at the Geneva Academy. Beza turned down Ramus's request especially because of the latter's anti-Aristotelian sentiments. In a letter dated December 1, 1570 Beza gave Ramus the following reasons:

> The first is that there is at the moment no vacancy in our school, and our resources are so meager that we cannot enlarge the number of professors....The second is that we are resolved and determined not to deviate from the position of Aristotle, even a trifle, both in teaching logic itself and in explaining the other disciplines.[25]

This gives a clear indication of the position Aristotle held in the Geneva Academy under Beza. The number of Aristotelian books in the library of the Academy at this time suggests the same attitude. A 1572 catalogue lists, out of nearly 725 books, more than 50 books by or about Aristotle.[26]

For a closer look at how Beza viewed the use of Aristotelian logic in theology, it is worth examining his preface to an introductory work on systematic theology, titled *Christianae Isagoges* (published in 1583), by his colleague Lambert Daneau.[27] After bewailing the miserable state of medieval theology, its neglect of the Scriptures, and its debates over thorny questions drawn from Lombard's *Sentences*, Beza states that the Lord brought renewal—surprisingly, he does not point to the preaching of the Word—by the restoration of languages and the good arts in the schools, especially "that true and genuine logic explained by the Peripatetics alone." For this he credits Lefèvre d'Étaples in the French regions and Melanchthon in Germany. According to Beza, this renewal of languages and good arts prepared the way for the driving out of the "idolomania" of popular medieval religion.

Those who think that logic should be banished from theology are seriously deluded and are dangerous to the human race, Beza argued. By the art of logic we are taught to define things truly and divide them properly and to discern false from true conclusions by a certain and invariable method. Surely nothing is to be taught confusedly and in a disorderly manner in the church, nor is anything to be concluded rashly and foolishly. What kind of madness is it, Beza asked, to keep away from sacred studies, as if it were something profane, that divinely taught knowledge which alone points out clearly both the orderly way of teaching anything and the way of discerning things consistent from things inconsistent?

Beza was cautious to point out that in saying this he did not mean to mix the sacred with the profane or to bind divine wisdom to the rules of dialectic. Neither theological principles nor the main points of religion which are deduced from the theological principles should be drawn from the books of the philosophers, which gave rise to nothing but the falsely called knowledge rebuked by Paul (1 Tim. 6:20). In other words, Beza denied that the content of theology may be derived from pagan philosophy.

Yet, for the purposes of orderly reasoning and teaching, Beza gave Aristotlelian logic a firm place in theology.

> This I say, this I impress again and again upon all students, if indeed they wish to be considered teachers of the truth and refuters of falsehood in the Church, that especially in this time they should continue diligently to learn, practice, and use logic, not that new-fangled logic of the very clever sophists [an allusion to Ramist logic (D.S.)] . . . which turns men into pseudo-dialecticians in three days, while overturning the foundations of both the art itself and of nature, but that true and genuine logic such as has been taught most perfectly by Aristotle.[28]

When students have learned this art, Beza pointed out, they need go no further than the apostle Paul for the perfect example of the practice of logic. None of the books of the most learned men compares with Paul, whether one considers the general order of his teaching, the arrangement of his arguments in confirming truth or in refuting falsehood, or finally the cogency of his demonstrations. I wish therefore, wrote Beza, that this art or science of logic "be learned either from the most perfect teacher of it himself, Aristotle, or (if anyone does not think that he needs to know the individual details which Aristotle teaches so precisely and accurately) from any learned compendium, but that the practice of the art be observed in our Paul."[29] Beza dared to promise that those who diligently do this will become excellent theologians in a short time, and also truly Christian if they arrange their life and morals according to this rule.

Both Ursinus and Beza considered logic a gift of God which, to be sure, does not contribute to the content of theology but is very necessary for theology on a formal level as an instrument and standard for correct thinking. In their view, logic provides the divinely given rules by which the theologian may distinguish true conclusions from false ones, things consistent from inconsistent, and things certain from uncertain. It provides the norms for good and necessary consequence so that theological doctrines may be correctly deduced from the theological principles drawn from Scripture. It teaches how to define theological points rightly and divide them properly into their parts and offers the method for an orderly teaching of theology. Thus logic serves to confirm theological truth and to refute falsehood. Although it was recognized that many things in theology are beyond the grasp of reason and logic, the concern for the necessary use of logic within theology contributed to the tendency to assume that the Christian faith can be presented as a logically consistent and rationally defensible system.

For both Ursinus and Beza the only true and genuine logic was that of Aristotle. This was a prominent stance within orthodox Reformed circles, shared, for example, by such leading theologians as Pareus in Heidelberg, Lubbertus, Gomarus, Voetius, and Maccovius in the Netherlands, Du Moulin in Sedan, and Chamier in Montauban. Ramist logic made strong inroads among Reformed thinkers, but this revision of the Aristotelian system was motivated more by humanist and pedagogical concerns than by any biblical concern to carry the reformation to this nontheological field.

It may be noted that there were other Reformed voices who, from a concern for fidelity to Scripture, strongly mistrusted the growing trend to use Aristotelian philosophy in theology. A leading example is Heinrich Bullinger of Zurich. In one instance Beza sent him an anonymous writing on the Lord's Supper and commented that the author's way of writing was obscure and confused, like that of Jakob Schegk, a German Lutheran philosopher at Tübingen who had written on theological topics from a distinct Aristotelian perspective. In a reply to Beza, dated December 1, 1568, Bullinger stressed that the author was also sophistic:

I add, also sophistic, because if those philosophical geniuses continue to examine all the dogmas of our religion according to the Aristotelian method, we will again have a scholastic doctrine, yes, a new Aristotelian doctrine, and many Aquinases, Scotuses, Alberts, and Seraphics [Bonaventures]. How many questions, I pray, is that man engaged in within the bounds of his writing? It seems that he is now prepared for a thoroughly sophistic debate on many sides. To say it frankly, I abhor these things with my whole heart and I now often remember the saying of Tertullian, that the philosophers are the patriarchs of heretics. And what, may I ask, will be the aim of these debates? From them the students will understand nothing, and if they understand anything, they will learn to doubt everything. Truly extraordinary is the aim of that Aristotelian theology![30]

D. Girolamo Zanchi on Aristotelian Physics

When Reformed theologians gave logic a formal instrumental role in theology and assumed it did not contribute to the content of theology, it was easy to consider Aristotelian logic as nonthreatening to the Christian faith. In the area of Aristotelian physics or natural philosophy, however, one might expect greater criticism from orthodox Reformed theologians since this physics presents a worldview which, if accepted, has a direct impact on the content of theology. Yet, we see very divergent Reformed attitudes to Aristotle's physics, ranging from an almost uncritical acceptance to rejection. This is evident in works by Girolamo Zanchi and Lambert Daneau, two Calvinist theologians who taught physics from very different approaches.

Zanchi (1516-90) had received a scholastic training in his native Italy and then was introduced to Reformed literature there in the 1540s. In 1551 he left Italy, studied for several months under Calvin at Geneva, and in 1553 took a teaching position in theology at the Strasbourg Gymnasium, where Johann Sturm's reforms had introduced a curriculum strongly based on Aristotle.[31] Later Zanchi taught at the Calvinist centers of Heidelberg and Neustadt in the Palatinate.[32]

At the request of Sturm, the rector at Strasbourg, Zanchi took on the task of lecturing on Aristotle's *Physics* in addition to his regular teaching in theology. The course began in mid-February

1554 with Zanchi lecturing on the *Physics* and his colleague Peter Martyr Vermigli lecturing on the *Nicomachean Ethics* on alternate weeks. As a complement to his lectures, Zanchi prepared a Greek edition of Aristotle's *Physics*, to which he added a seventy-page preface. In the late summer of 1554 this work was published by Wendelin Rihel.[33] The preface is worth examining since it contains the material of Zanchi's first lectures in which he attempted to justify the study of Aristotelian philosophy by theologians.[34]

Zanchi began by explaining that he had been assigned the task of teaching Aristotle's *Physics* at Strasbourg in the absence of a regular person in philosophy and that by the encouragement of God's will, the Scholarchs of the school, the students, the rector Sturm, and other friends he willingly took on the assignment. Entering upon the theme of the preface, Zanchi noted that four kinds of people condemn or censure the study of Aristotle's *Physics*. Some think a study of this philosophy is an utterly unworthy endeavor for the Christian. Some even reject it as useless in human affairs and detrimental to Christianity. Others do not reject such study as unworthy or useless, but approve the way of Plato rather than that of Aristotle. Finally, there are some who approve Aristotle's philosophy but do not want his books read in the schools because direct study of his works is too time-consuming and because he speaks obscurely; they prefer to use a compendium of Aristotle in the schools.[35]

To the first objection that physics is unworthy, Zanchi replied that the study of physics and of nature is almost divine and so it is most worthy for the Christian. He attempted to prove this by affirming that God himself is the author and giver of this philosophy. To demonstrate this Zanchi traced the lineage of physics from its origin in God, the fountain of all good. This science or knowledge of divinely created things and of their causes first flowed down from God to Adam. The first man was thus the first natural philosopher, as is evident in the fact that he assigned names to creatures, a task he could not have done had he lacked a knowledge of their natures and properties. From Adam's descendents this knowledge passed on to Noah, and from there to the Chaldeans, Armenians, Babylonians, Assyrians, and Phoenicians. The Chaldeans—apparently by way of Abraham—handed it on to the Jews. Solomon was the greatest philosopher of nature ever, as is clear in 1 Kings 4, and people came from all nations of the earth to hear his wisdom. If Solomon's books on physics had not been lost, there would be no need to read Aristotle. From the Jews this knowledge passed on, so says Eusebius, to the Greeks and thus it was received by Thales, Anaximander, Xenophanes, Pythagoras, Plato, and Aristotle.[36]

On the basis of this tradition Zanchi disagreed with the idea that physics was first discovered by human observation—by the Greeks. Rather, he argued, it was revealed by God to humankind and was then increased by human study. Indeed, we are much indebted to the Greeks who, by their contemplation of things and investigation of nature, dug up this almost buried philosophy, polished and increased it, and committed it to writing for all posterity. Though physics can be increased by investigation, its first source was God; hence, this study is divine and most worthy for the Christian.

Zanchi added several other arguments for the worthiness of the study of physics, some of which are based on Platonic thought. Thus, for example, he stated that the Platonists speak of three worlds: an angelic and ultramundane world where God and the angels enjoy eternity, a celestial world of the sun, moon, and stars, and the lowest sublunary world where humans dwell. The human being is a microcosmos made up of three parts which correspond to these three worlds—the head to the angelic world of intelligences, the mid-section containing the heart to the celestial world, and the lower body to the lowest world of generation and corruption. As a microcosmos of the three worlds, a human being ought to understand these worlds. Since natural philosophy teaches a knowledge of the lowest world and much about the celestial world, it is certainly worthy of study. Zanchi's final argument on this point was that the purpose or end to which this philosophy leads, shows it to be worthy. Its purpose is that human beings may be led to know, love, and worship God, the author of all natural things.[37]

In reply to the second objection that physics is not useful, Zanchi first pointed out that it is not necessary to explain all the uses of physics for the mechanical and liberal arts. He simply focused on how this study contributes to humankind both as rational beings and as Christians. Inasmuch as human beings are rational, this physical philosophy helps to perfect their minds since this philosophy teaches a certain knowledge of things, the sign of a healthy mind. This knowledge also gives rise to the moral virtues which are necessary for a happy human life. Insofar as human beings are Christian, physics is useful because they may ascend by a knowledge of natural things to a knowledge and love of God, since all creatures are a mirror of their Creator. Such knowledge also helps Christians understand the many metaphors drawn from nature in the Bible. Moreover, it directs the student of nature to godliness which is the end of all human endeavors, a fact recognized by the sounder philosophers—he names Pythagoras, Epictetus, Plato, and Aristotle—even though they did not truly know God.

To the related objection that physics may be detrimental to Christianity, hindering understanding and belief in the gospel, Zanchi replied that natural philosophy drawn from created things in no way conflicts with the Christian religion. It is the perversion of true philosophy that is detrimental. In itself philosophy is good and very beneficial to Christianity. Where the apostle Paul, in Colossians 2:8, refers to philosophy as vain deception, he is not speaking of true philosophy, for in Romans 1:20 he himself commends such true philosophy by declaring that the invisible things of God are seen, being understood from the things that have been made.[38]

To the third objection that Plato's way, rather than Aristotle's, is to be preferred, Zanchi replied that the way Aristotle followed in teaching philosophy is much more useful than that of Plato. Here Zanchi did not mean to find fault with Plato's philosophy; nor had he undertaken the task of comparing Aristotle with Plato. For such comparisons Zanchi recommended Trapezuntius's arguments for Aristotle against Plato and, on the other hand, Bessarion's defense of Plato. Zanchi simply contended that in the schools the teaching of Aristotle was preferable, especially for four reasons. First, the subject-matter of physics is treated most exactly by Aristotle, something not done by Plato or by any other philosopher before or after Aristotle. Plato's *Timaeus* does not measure up to Aristotle's many books on physics which are the result of his investigation into all things, even the most minute things of nature. Second, Aristotle proves his case by clear demonstrations. Though very learned, Plato does not offer clear reasons to prove what he says; yet, no one can be found more eloquent than Plato. Third, Aristotle uses a clear way of speaking which is of great advantage to students. Plato's writing, on the other hand, is full of irony, a style better suited to ridicule than to teaching. Last, no one has followed a better method of teaching than Aristotle. He treats all things in their proper order, first things first, and in proving his case he follows a very useful and necessary order. Students should study Aristotle, if for no other reason than that they may become accustomed to this "best and most excellent Aristotelian method."[39]

To the fourth and final objection that a compendium should be used in teaching rather than Aristotle himself, Zanchi answered that when compendia—which are usually more of a *dispendia* (loss) than compendia—are used, the original source is often neglected. Thus many never become truly learned, just as those who only study theological compendia and do not examine the Scriptures— the very source of theology—never become true theologians. Zanchi did not disapprove all use of compendia, especially if they were clear and explained the true mind of the author, but they must lead to the study of Aristotle himself. If someone objected that direct study of Aristotle takes too much time, Zanchi replied that he who learns well learns quickly enough. To those who objected that Aristotle is obscure, especially in his physics, he replied that Aristotle is sometimes obscure due to the meagerness of the things he treats and sometimes due to the fact that many of his books have perished and those that are extant contain some errors. Similarly, he claimed, it could be argued that Plato and Cicero should not be read, for there is no one who is not obscure somewhere. By using method, diligent study, and good interpreters, by listening to teachers, and by asking God, obscurities could easily be removed.[40]

After thus defending the study of Aristotle's *Physics*, Zanchi discussed at some length the title of the book, its author, and its content and offered an overview of Aristotle's books on natural philosophy. At the end of the section on Aristotle's life he declared that the Stagirite's doctrine is taught by a better method than any other at any time and is proved by many and the most certain reasons, all of which agree with each other. Thus it is that no philosophical writings can be found more suited to educating people quickly and very well than the writings of Aristotle. "Therefore mortals are much indebted to him after God, the best author of all good things, and after the holy Scriptures." Zanchi then discussed whether it is true that Aristotle is to be numbered among the blessed. Though some affirm this, Zanchi himself did not consider him to be a Christian or his teaching to be theology. It is sufficient to say that "he was the outstanding, best, and most perfect philosopher, and his teaching was the most excellent of its kind, insofar as it confines itself to the natures of created things." Therefore it is to be diligently learned.[41]

This is high acclaim for Aristotle. Zanchi seems to have accepted his *Physics* almost without criticism. It was possible for him to take such a stance since he regarded Aristotle's wisdom as ultimately derived from God.

Zanchi's preface is tempered somewhat by a letter of commendation written by the rector Johann Sturm to Zanchi, which is included in the work. In friendly jest Sturm took Zanchi to task for preferring Aristotle to Plato. He countered Zanchi's arguments for the superiority of Aristotle and argued that there is nothing in Aristotle's doctrine which is not already in Plato, at least in some form. Sturm preferred to give Aristotle and Plato equal value and have them taught together in the school.[42]

It should also be noted that some twenty years later while teaching at Heidelberg Zanchi again dealt with physics, this time in the context of the theological doctrine of creation. In a major work titled *De Operibus Dei intra sex dies creatis* (posthumously published in Neustadt, 1591), he analyzed God's work of creation following the six days of Genesis 1. Although Zanchi corrected Aristotle on some points, for example on his view of the eternity of the world, Aristotle remained an authority for Zanchi. Now Aristotle is presented as agreeing with Moses. Though Moses' account is briefer, both follow the same methodical order. "The same method that Aristotle observed in explaining natural philosophy, Moses by the inspiration of God's Spirit had followed long before in describing God's physical works."[43] Philosophy now stands in a harmonious and complementary relationship with revelation in Scripture. This reflects the Thomist synthesis of Aristotle and the Christian faith, and in fact this work is part of a larger dogmatic project patterned on Thomas's *Summa Theologiae*.[44] Zanchi's Aristotelianism derives largely from his Italian background.

E. Lambert Daneau's Christian Physics

With Lambert Daneau we find a totally different approach to physics. Daneau (1530-95) was a French Calvinist who had studied in Geneva under Calvin and Beza and then spent several years as a pastor in France. In 1572 he began to teach theology at the Geneva

Academy, serving as a colleague of Beza. He left in 1581 to take up a teaching position at Leiden for a year and then taught and did pastoral work at several locations in France.[45]

While at Geneva Daneau taught theology and also a course in physics. He published the results of his teaching in 1576 under the title *Physica Christiana*, the first work of this kind.[46] The striking feature of this work is that Daneau sought to base physics not on Aristotle but on Scripture, particularly on the first chapter of Genesis.

In his letter of dedication Daneau noted that on the question of the origin of the world there is a great diversity among the pagan philosophers and even among Christians. That the philosophers were so divided Daneau considered understandable since they lived in darkness, destitute of God's Word, the true light of knowledge. The disagreements among Christians, who have the certain basis of truth in the Word, cannot so readily be excused. The reason for these disagreements is that many Christians were instructed in the precepts of pagan philosophy and were deceived by it. This happened not only in the early church, when many were trained in the schools of the philosophers and could not easily change their opinions after their conversion, but also in Daneau's own age. Therefore, Daneau did not doubt that his work on Christian physics, in which he "corrects the doctrines of the philosophers from the Word of God," would incur the censure of many.[47]

In the introductory chapters to the *Physica Christiana*, Daneau spelled out his view of physics and further revealed his attitude to the works of pagan authors. He began by defining physics as "the true knowledge or investigation (tending toward the praise of God the creator) of the creation of the world, of the distinction of this whole world and its parts, of the causes by which it so came into existence, and likewise of the effects which follow from them."[48] This four-fold definition Daneau derived from the Scriptures—from Proverbs 30:4 and Genesis 1, to which he adds the more explicit passage in Wisdom 7:17-18.

To the question why he called such study "physics," a term of the pagan philosophers, Daneau replied with two reasons. First, Christians should not be afraid to use common words that the pagans use since both enjoy the same sun, air, earth, water, and so on, and Scripture itself—in Ephesians 2:3 and 2 Peter 1:4—as well as the early church fathers do not shun the term. Second, *phusis* in Greek is commonly applied to things that consist not only of essence (i.e., God) but of essence combined with accidents, such as are all things perceived by the eyes. For these reasons Daneau deemed it appropriate to call the study of the visible world "physics."[49]

In Daneau's view there were two kinds of Christian physics: general and particular. General physics deals with the general and most principal parts of the world, their origin, nature, and causes. That is, it studies heaven and the four elements (fire, air, water, and earth). General physics, for the most part, is contained in the first chapter of Genesis.

Particular physics focuses on the specific natures, potencies, properties, and effects of every kind of thing that may be distinguished in the created world. In the second part of his work, Daneau treated such physical things according to the order of the six days of creation. Particular physics is not wholly contained in the Scriptures since Solomon's copiously written books on natural things were unfortunately lost; yet even in Scripture certain parts of this physics may be found dispersed like sparkling gems. Such knowledge is better found in the books on medicine and in the "histories" of plants and animals. Thus we see that Daneau did admit a source of knowledge beyond Scripture itself, at least on the level of particular physics.[50]

General physics, however, is chiefly to be learned from the Bible, not from the pagan philosophers, for they could not attain to anything more than obscure sparks of knowledge. Just as practitioners of crafts can best explain their own work, so a knowledge of God's created work is best learned from God himself in Scripture. Here the establishment of this world, the general forms of things, their natures and many kinds are copiously taught, distinguished, and explained in an orderly way. Moses is the key source of this study. For what else does Moses do in Genesis 1, Daneau argued, than explain briefly (and yet truly and in order) the origin, operations, natures, and effects of things, that is, explain physics? It is true that matters of physics are not explained in detail by Moses. He writes in a bare and simple style, stripped of all ornament, so that all may understand more easily. Yet Moses was very learned in all the noble arts, especially in physics and medicine, having been educated in Egypt where these arts flourished. But above all, he received his knowledge of the creation of the world and of the causes of things by revelation from God.[51] This analysis, it may be noted, differs from that of Zanchi, who began with a revelation to Adam.

Although Daneau acknowledged that physics and theology are distinct disciplines, he argued that this does not mean that both cannot be contained in Scripture. In fact, he said, physics is, in a certain way, a part of theology and serves it since it is a very excellent way of knowing God and of advancing his glory. For God's power, wisdom, and eternity are perceived in visible things.[52]

How did Daneau explain the knowledge of the natural world acquired by the Greeks? He contended that such leading Greek philosophers as Plato and Pythagoras traveled to Egypt in order to learn physics. On the authority of Diogenes Laertius, Daneau was certain that it was from foreign peoples, especially the Syrians, that is, the Jews, that the knowledge of physics spread to the Greeks.[53] Therefore, it would be a blasphemy to say that Plato and Aristotle knew more about this than did Moses whom God himself taught.[54]

Whatever knowledge of physics comes from outside of God's Word, Daneau argued, is not as certain as that which derives from his Word because it is confirmed only by human senses or reason, neither of which are firm and immovable grounds. Yet reason and the senses are not totally deceptive and false since God did not give these abilities to human beings in vain. Therefore, all knowledge supported by reason or the senses should not be condemned as vain and false. "For who will rightly say that the knowledge of so many excellent things and arts is to be despised which God, outside of his written Word, has granted to men, even to pagans—such as the many things Plato, Aristotle, Galen, and other ancient and more recent philosophers have discovered and taught? Whoever despises this despises God's gifts, which certain godly men have sometimes also been adorned with."[55] In this way Daneau credited to the Greeks another source of knowledge besides the tradition of wisdom passed on to them from the Jews.

Daneau devoted a specific chapter to the difference between Christian and pagan physics. There is a very real difference, he said, between Moses and Aristotle concerning physics. First, they differ regarding the purpose of this knowledge. The purpose of Christian physics is that God may be acknowledged and praised as the Creator of all things and be worshiped more ardently. On the other hand, Aristotle and pagan physics are concerned only with things themselves or "nature" and do not ascend to the Creator. They are preoccupied with secondary causes rather than primary causes. Although the earliest Greek natural philosophers made mention of God as Creator, inasmuch as they received their insights from the Egyptians and the Jews, it is Aristotle's tribe which came to dominate the field of physics. In this tradition, going back to the Ionian philosophers, the principal causes of the bringing forth of things came to be ascribed to created things themselves. This Daneau saw as the dominant trend in the schools of his day.

Second, they differ in regard to causes. Christian philosophers advance only true causes, those from the fountain of truth in Scripture. They acknowledge God as the primary efficient cause of all things and his voice and command as a most powerful cause by which a certain potency is infused in all things. That potency, which is prior to all other imaginable causes, is a second and instrumental cause wholly dependent on God's power and command. The pagan philosophers, however, do not recognize God as cause. They consider the potency given to things as the first cause of all things and thus substitute the effected cause for the efficient. They dream up causes, think of matter as eternal, and with form added make these the first principles of natural things.

Third, they differ in their method and order of teaching the art of physics. Although Christians often describe visible things in different ways, sometimes proceeding from highest to lowest (from God to creatures) and sometimes from lowest to highest (from creatures to God), as in Psalms 104 and 136 and Proverbs 8:23ff, they always acknowledge Moses' account in Genesis 1 to be the true order of things and of their creation. The pagan philosophers, on the other hand, cannot agree on method. Some begin with first matter, others with the four elements, others with a chaos, others with heaven, and others with a boiling abyss. Even within some sects of philosophers there is a lack of agreement.[56]

Daneau considered the subject studied by physics to be creatures that are visible and perceived by the senses.[57] Here again he disagreed with philosophers like Aristotle who think that physics deals with things inasmuch as they have movement. For Daneau, movement is too broad a category, for it includes angels who are not visible and thus are not studied by physics.[58] As Daneau proceeded to his actual treatment of physics, into which I shall not delve here, he continued to find fault with the pagan philosophers. For example, he strenuously rejected Plato's theory of ideas in which natural things are not real substances but mere shadows of their true natures in heaven. "Let us bid Plato farewell, for he is not only an Academic, and is doubtful of mind and uncertain in everything, but he is also a pagan."[59] He also rejected Aristotle's idea that privation is a principle of natural things.[60] Likewise, he objected to Aristotle's notion of the eternity of the world and maintained that it had a definite beginning in time—to be specific, on a Sunday in the month of Tishri (August/September), 3980 B.C.[61]

Although on the basis of Scripture Daneau made certain corrections on particular points, he was not able to move beyond the basic structure of pre-Copernican cosmology and he actually reconfirmed it by clothing it with biblical authority. For Daneau the earth remained in a stationary position at the center of the spherical world (cosmos), and heaven was a sphere that did not undergo change. The two principal parts of the world, which he identified as the biblical "heaven" and "earth,"[62] reflect Aristotle's division of the world into heavenly and sublunary realms. Moreover, in the structure of his analysis, Daneau uncritically adopted other Aristotelian modes of thinking, for example, the basic distinction between general and particular physics and the concepts of substance and accident. Aristotle's four causes also figure prominently in Daneau's work; there are specific sections analyzing the efficient causes of the world, its form, its matter, and its end.[63]

Though Daneau was not able to escape the prevailing worldview of his time, we see here a genuine attempt to reform pagan classical physics and to treat physics from a Christian point of view. He was convinced that God's Word provides the foundation and source not only for theology but also for other sciences, and so he attempted to write not only a Christian physics but also a Christian ethics and a Christian politics.[64]

This project was, however, largely a biblicist effort, for Daneau attempted to draw physics, for the most part, directly from Scripture. Only where this biblicist approach did not work—in the details of particular physics—did he look to the works of the natural philosophers. Instead of seeking a knowledge of physics from the natural world itself by empirical investigation, he simply substituted authorities by replacing Aristotle and other classical authors with Scripture as the main source of this knowledge.

F. Conclusion

It is evident that the classics and especially Aristotelianism in various forms pervaded the theological environment of early Reformed orthodoxy. This was particularly true in the arts faculties of universities where theological students were taught the classics, even by theologians, before proceeding to specialize in theology. Logic as the art of reasoning was commonly assumed to be a necessary tool for theologians and, though Ramist logic made strong inroads in Reformed circles, many leading orthodox theologians were committed to Aristotelian logic. Since it was thought that logic, as a gift of God, does not influence theological content, it was easy to assume that Aristotelian logic was neutral with respect to the Christian faith. In relation to Aristotelian physics where an impact on the content of theology could be expected, there was more polarity in orthodox Reformed attitudes.

In general, Reformed orthodoxy in the latter half of the sixteenth century reveals two divergent tendencies in its attitude to Aristotle. On the one hand there was an accommodating attitude to the works of Aristotle. This is clear in the ready acceptance of Aristotelian logic by such leading figures as Ursinus and Beza, and it comes to clearest expression in the attitude of Zanchi who in his mature years attempted to develop a synthesis of Aristotle and Christianity.

On the other hand there was an antithetical attitude which shied away from Aristotle for various reasons. Ramist logic, though outwardly antithetical, was actually a simplified restructuration of the Aristotelian system motivated more by humanist pedagogical concerns than any concern for biblical reformation. The antithetical tendency is also evident in Bullinger's reluctance to use non-biblical philosophical terminology, but in its most extreme form this attitude became an appeal to Scripture not only as the norm but also as the primary source of nontheological knowledge. Daneau attempted to base all science on the Scriptures; yet, he could not escape the prevalent worldview of his day. Zanchi and Daneau represented the greatest polarity of the two tendencies. Most orthodox Calvinists of this period stood somewhere in between.

The tendency to accommodate Aristotle to the Reformed faith was a significant factor in the late sixteenth century emergence of Reformed scholasticism, a movement that would become an important source of rationalist theology a century later. The antithetical tendency as represented by Daneau was a worthy attempt at the reformation of nontheological sciences, but it proved to be abortive largely because of its extreme biblicism. Both tendencies failed to realize that in a Christian perspective on the sciences the Bible or some classical authority does not function as the primary source of knowledge, but rather that the Scriptures provide light and guidelines for a scientific investigation of God's creation itself.

Notes

1. By the term "Reformed orthodoxy" I refer to the late sixteenth- and early seventeenth-century consolidation and defense of Reformed theology that followed the more creative period of early reformers like Huldrych Zwingli and John Calvin.
2. Recent studies which attempt to identify the basic characteristics of Reformed scholasticism include: Brian Armstrong, *Calvinism and the Amyraut Heresy* (Madison: University of Wisconsin Press, 1969), 32; John Bray, *Theodore Beza's Doctrine of Predestination* (Nieuwkoop: B. DeGraaf, 1975), 12-13; and John Patrick Donnelly, "Italian Influences on the Development of Calvinist Scholasticism," *Sixteenth Century Journal* 7 (1976): 81-101.
3. Paul Oskar Kristeller, F. Edward Cranz, Charles Lohr, and Charles Schmitt have been leaders in this field of study. See especially Kristeller's *Renaissance Thought: The Classic, Scholastic, and Humanist Strains* (New York, Evanston, and London: Harper & Row, 1961), ch. 2; C. Schmitt, "Towards a Reassessment of Renaissance Aristotelianism," *History of Science*, 11 (1973): 159-93; and C. Schmitt, *Aristotle and the Renaissance* (Cambridge and London: Harvard University Press, 1983).
4. For example, Fortunatus Crellius, a Calvinist philosopher at Neustadt, introduced Zabarella's version of Aristotelian logic to Germany in his *Introductio in Logicam Aristotelis* (Neustadt, 1581), just three years after the publication of Zabarella's own *Opera Logica* in 1578. The Calvinist theologian Girolamo Zanchi, a colleague of Crellius, wrote a letter of commendation which is printed in Crellius's work. Zanchi praises Crellius for presenting the true teaching of Aristotle with brevity and clarity. He promotes the use of Crellius's summary of Aristotle for the lower classes but insists that more advanced students be taught Aristotle himself, who presents logic more methodically, copiously, and perfectly than anyone.
5. In Leiden University, for example, the influence of Suarez's *Disputationes Metaphysicae* (1957) is evident in student disputations in the years 1607 to 1609. In 1616 the philosophy professor Gilbert Jacchaeus published his *Institutiones Primae Philosophiae* which correspond in plan to Suarez's work. See Paul Dibon, *La Philosophie néerlandaise au siècle d'or* (Amsterdam: Elsevier, 1954), 1:64-71. The Dutch Calvinist theologian Jacobus Revius later published *Suarez Repurgatus sive Syllabus Disputationum Metaphysicarum Francisci Suarez* (Leiden, 1644), a critical adaptation of Suarez which he produced for use as a textbook in the Calvinist schools.
6. Physics, in this paper, refers not to the modern science of physics but to the classical study of the natural world, also called natural philosophy, a field that covers a broad variety of modern sciences ranging from astronomy and meteorology to geology and biology.

7. Martin Luther, "To the Christian Nobility", in his *Works* (Philadelphia: Fortress Press, 1966), 44:200-201.

8. Brian Gerrish, *Grace and Reason: A Study in the Theology of Luther* (Chicago and London: University of Chicago Press, 1979), 32-42.

9. Jaroslav Pelikan, *From Luther to Kierkegaard* (St. Louis: Concordia, 1963), ch. 2.

10. M. W. Jurriaanse, *The Founding of Leyden University* (Leiden: E. J. Brill, 1965), 10.

11. Dibon, op. cit. in n. 5, 12-14, 50. For the teaching of physics see Edward Ruestow, *Physics at Seventeenth- and Eighteenth-Century Leiden: Philosophy and the New Science in the University* (The Hague: Martinus Nijhoff, 1973). The second chapter of this study focuses on the Aristotelian physics of Franco Burgersdijck, whose influence dominated philosophic instruction at Leiden for a quarter of a century after the Synod of Dort (1618-19).

12. P. C. Molhuysen, *Bronnen tot de Geschiedenis der Leidsche Universiteit* (The Hague: Martinus Nijhoff, 1913), 1 (Bijlagen): 157-58.

13. On the activity of these men see J. Waszink, "Classical Philology," in *Leiden University in the Seventeenth Century*, ed. T. H. Lunsingh Scheurleer and G. Posthumus Meyjes (Leiden: E. J. Brill, 1975), 161-75.

14. H. H. Kuyper, *De Opleiding tot den Dienst des Woords bij de Gereformeerden* (The Hague: Martinus Nijhof, 1891).

15. On Ramist dialectic, see Walter Ong, *Ramus, Method, and the Decay of Dialogue* (New York: Octagon Books, 1979); Wilhelm Risse, *Die Logik der Neuzeit* (Stuttgart-Bad Cannstatt: Friedrich Frommann Verlag, 1964), 1:122-200.

16. The Ramist influence on Calvinism is explored by Jürgen Moltmann, "Zur Bedeutung des Petrus Ramus für Philosophie und Theologie im Calvinismus," *Zeitschrift für Kirchengeschichte*, 68 (1957):295-318.

17. Johann F. Hautz, *Geschichte der Universität Heidelberg* (Mannheim: J. Schneider, 1864), 2:55-58. For a recent biography of Ursinus, see Derk Visser, *Zacharias Ursinus* (New York: United Church Press, 1983).

18. Zacharias Ursinus, "Bedencken ob P. Rami Dialectic und Rhetoric in die Schulen einzuführen," in his *Organi Aristotelei, Libri Quinque Priores, a Doct. Zacharia Ursino Vratislaviensi, per quaestiones perspicue & erudite expositi, ita ut provectioribus quoque, docti commentarii usum praestare possint* (Neustadt, 1586), fols. **1-****1. No page numbers are given. Reference is to the signatures. I used the copy of the Zentalbibliothek of Zurich.

19. Ibid., fol. ***3. The translation is my own.

20. Ibid., fol. ***4

21. For the full title of Ursinus's commentary, see note 18. The editor Johann Jungnitz states that Ursinus composed the commentary while teaching at the Collegium Sapientiae under the rule of Frederick III (dedicatory epistle, ibid., fol. *2). Since the commentary is also a response to Ramism, the probable date of its composition is sometime between 1570 and 1576.

22. Ibid., The "new-fangled logic" is clearly a reference to Ramism.

23. Ibid.

24. Erdmann Sturm, *Der junge Zacharias Ursin: Sein Weg vom Philippismus zum Calvinismus (1534-1562)* (Neukirchen-Vluyn: Neukirchener Verlag, 1972); Derk Visser, "Zacharias Ursinus," in *Shapers of Religious Traditions in Germany, Switzer-*

land, and Poland, 1560-1600, ed. Jill Raitt (New Haven and London: Yale University Press, 1981), 121-39.
25. Theodore Beza. *Correspondance* (Geneva: Librairie Droz, 1983), 11:295.
26. Alexandre Ganoczy, *La Bibliothèque de L'Académie de Calvin* (Geneva: Librairie Droz, 1969), 123-27.
27. Lambert Daneau, *Christianae Isagoges ad Christianorum theologorum locos communes* (Geneva, 1583), prefaced by Beza (dated August 20, 1583).
28. Ibid., fols. *iii-*iiii. For an explanation of the pagination see note 18.
29. Ibid., fol. *iiii.
30. Bullinger's letter is printed in Beza's *Correspondance,* (Geneva: Librairie Droz, 1978) 6:197. From similar motives Bullinger objected to the use of the nonbiblical term "substance" in describing the Lord's Supper, especially after the 1571 Synod of La Rochelle rejected the opinion of those who did not accept the term.
31. On the Gymnasium at Strasbourg see Miriam Chrisman, *Lay Culture, Learned Culture: Books and Social Change in Strasbourg, 1480-1599* (New Haven and London: Yale University Press, 1982), ch. 12.
32. On Zanchi's life and intellectual development see Christopher Burchill, "Girolamo Zanchi: Portrait of a Reformed Theologian and His Works," *Sixteenth Century Journal* 15 (1984): 185-207; Joseph Tylenda, "Girolamo Zanchi and John Calvin: A Study in Discipleship as Seen through Their Correspondence," *Calvin Theological Journal,* 10 (1975): 101-41.
33. For some of these details see Burchill, op. cit., n. 32, 189. Following the preface is a note to the reader, dated July 15, 1553 (*sic,* 1554), in which Zanchi tells that he had lectured on the material of the preface in the Gymnasium. When the publisher Wendelin Rihel was ready to print the Greek text of Aristotle's *Physics* for use by the students, he urged Zanchi to have this material printed as the preface to this edition. Zanchi notes that it was being published in the same order and style as he had presented it almost extemporaneously in the school, since he did not have the time to polish it. If his preface was well received, he adds, and if he would continue to lecture on Aristotle's *Physics,* he would perhaps in due time publish commentaries on the *Physics.* Such commentaries never appeared.
34. G. Zanchi, *Aristotelis de Naturali Auscultatione, seu de Principiis, cum praefatione Doctoris Zanchi* (Strasbourg, 1554). References are to the signatures. To my knowledge the only North American copy of this rare work is found in the Newberry Library in Chicago. John Patrick Donnelly calls Zanchi's preface "perhaps the most concerted defense of Aristotle written by a sixteenth century Calvinist" (op. cit., 94).
35. Zanchi, op. cit., n. 34, Preface, fol. a3.
36. Exactly how it passed from the Jews to the Greeks Zanchi does not say. Other Calvinist theologians assert that the Greeks received their knowledge from the Jews by way of the Egyptians, who learned it from Abraham or from Moses and the Israelites. See, for example, Theodore Beza, *Jobus partim commentariis, partim paraphrasi illustratus* (London, 1587), 23. On this point Beza refers to Josephus's *Jewish Antiquities,* which states that Abraham "introduced [the Egyptians] to arithmetic and transmitted to them the laws of astronomy. For before the coming of Abraham the Egyptians were ignorant of these sciences, which thus travelled from the Chaldaeans into Egypt, whence they passed to the Greeks." Trans. H. Thack-

eray, Loeb Classical Library (London: William Heinemann, 1930; and New York: G. P. Putman's Sons, 1930), 1:8.

37. Zanchi, op. cit., n. 34, Preface, fols. a7-b1.

38. Ibid., fols. b1-b7.

39. Ibid., fols. b7-c1.

40. Ibid., fols. c1-c3.

41. Ibid., fol. d6.

42. Ibid., fols. f2-f8.

43. Zanchi, *Opera Theologica* (Geneva, 1618), 3:217. This work is analyzed by Ernst Bizer, *Frühorthodoxie und Rationalismus* (Zurich: EVZ-Verlag, 1963), 50-60.

44. John Patrick Donnelly, "Calvinist Thomism," *Viator*, 7 (1976): 441-55.

45. On Daneau's life see Paul De Felice, *Lambert Daneau* (Geneva: Slatkine Reprints, 1971). The only comprehensive study of Daneau's theology is Olivier Fatio's *Méthode et Théologie: Lambert Daneau et les débuts de la scholastique réformée* (Geneva: Librairie Droz, 1976). Fatio's work makes only passing references to Daneau's *Physica Christiana*, but it contains a short section on Daneau's use of classical authorities in his various writings. His conclusion is that Daneau oscillates between the principle that pagan authors have a remnant of the divine light and the principle that Scripture speaks infinitely better than they do even in their own discipline. The first principle justifies his ample use of classical authors; the second justifies his critique of them and his project to substitute for them a science drawn entirely from Scripture (99-102).

46. Lambert Daneau, *Physica Christiana, sive de rerum creatarum cognitione* (Lyon, 1576). Later printings appeared in 1579, 1580, 1588, 1602, 1606, and in Daneau's collected works, the *Opuscula Omnia Theologica* (Geneva, 1583). The second part of his work, concerning particular physics, was published in Geneva in 1580 and was reprinted in 1582, 1589, 1606, and in the *Opuscula*. An English translation of the first part appeared in London in 1578 under the title, *The Wonderful Workmanship of the World*. For an analysis of the *Physica Christiana* from the perspective of the rise of rationalism, see Ernst Bizer, op. cit., n. 43, 32-50. Bizer argues that Daneau and other early orthodox Reformed theologians pave the way for the later age of rationalism because they already teach certain themes that lay a foundation for the rationalist view. One such theme is that reason and revelation are not contradictory, so rational proof can be used as a way to reinforce the certain teachings of Scripture. Another sets the stage for natural theology by emphasizing that nature ought to be studied because by a knowledge of nature one gains a knowledge of God, his wisdom, power, and eternity.

47. I cite from Daneau's *Opuscula*, 226.

48. Ibid., 227.

49. Ibid., 227-28.

50. Ibid., 228.

51. Ibid., 229-30.

52. Ibid., 230.

53. For this point Daneau appeals to the first book of Diogenes Laertius's *Lives of Eminent Philosophers*. This third-century history of philosophy was an important source for Daneau's knowledge of Greek philosophy. A Greek-Latin edition of this

work, edited by Henry Estienne, appeared in Geneva in 1570, a few years before Daneau's work.

54. Daneau, *Opuscula*, 229-31.

55. Ibid., 232.

56. Ibid., 231-32.

57. This delineation of the subject matter of physics Daneau again derives from Scripture—from Romans 1:20 and Hebrews 11:3, to which he adds Wisdom 7:17-19 and 13:2.

58. Daneau, *Opuscula*, 233-35.

59. Ibid., ch. 10.

60. Ibid., ch. 24.

61. Ibid., ch. 39.

62. Ibid., ch. 28.

63. Ibid.; see especially chapters 17, 21, 27, and 31.

64. Daneau's attempt to base the disciplines of ethics and politics on the Scriptures is found in his *Ethices Christianae* (Geneva, 1577) and his *Politices Christianae* (Geneva, 1596).

Classical Studies and the German Pietists

Peter C. Erb

On an initial glance no two areas appear less suitably linked than classical studies and the German Pietism of the seventeenth and eighteenth centuries. When classical studies were pursued by German Protestants of this period, the activity was, for the most part, carried out by Pietism's orthodox opponents and more often by contemporary "a-religious" Enlightenment and pre-Enlightenment scholars for whom the religious controversies of the time were the mark of lesser minds and who, if forced to choose a religious position, certainly did not move in the direction of the Pietist "enthusiasts." For such opponents of the movement, Pietism (as is the case with its "evangelical" North American descendants) was placed on the side of Jerusalem and not Athens.

Even though there is some truth in this initial view, it is far too great a generalization. Like most of the other depictions of Pietism which developed in the struggles between the systematicians of the nineteenth century and the Pietist renewal of the same period, the partial truths it enunciates are almost completely destroyed by the falsehoods which are pressed at the same time. Thus the common tendency to distinguish Pietism from orthodoxy in a radical manner has been shown to be incorrect; the Pietists owed much of their theology to scholastic structures and orthodoxy too laid emphasis on practical religion.[1] The practical concerns of Pietism, however, are a major element in its use of the classics.

A. The Pietist Movement in General

As a movement Pietism can be precisely dated. It began in Frankfurt am Main in 1675 when the Lutheran senior of the ministerium, Philipp Jacob Spener, published an introduction to a new edition of the works of Johann Arndt. The introduction, entitled "Pia desideria," was an immediate best seller and within a year it had gone through numerous editions; within a decade its principles had affected all the major Protestant denominations in Germany, the Lowlands, and Scandinavia.[2]

Spener's work was based on a five-point theology. It called for (1) a renewal of Christian life on the part of (2) experientially reborn Christians (*Wiedergeburt*), (3) truly repentant for past sins (*Busse*), (4) who committed their lives to living out their theology in practical love for God (by acts of devotion) (5) and neighbor (by acts of social service). It was expected that such persons would meet weekly in small conventicles (*ecclesiolae in ecclesia*) for Bible study and mutual edification and that they would not support a theology "of the head" or maintain a dogmatic polemicism. Pietism encouraged a renewal of pastoral care and, as a result, of pastoral education which took emphasis off polemically oriented scholastic and confessional theology and placed it on biblical training and practical ministerial skills.

The most significant leader of Spener's brand of Pietism was his disciple August Hermann Francke who founded a university at Halle on Pietist principles. A second wing of the Pietist movement took a radical turn, breaking away from established churches and forming new denominations of their own. In the early 1720s a third type of Pietism arose when the remnants of the Hussite Bohemian Brethren fled Moravia and came to the estates of the Lutheran Pietist Count Nicholas Ludwig von Zinzendorf. A fourth wing of the movement developed in the Reformed church of Germany and the Netherlands and a fifth in the state of Württemberg. It is to the Württemberg movement that the greater part of this paper will be devoted. Finally, in the mid-eighteenth century sectors of Pietism reshaped themselves so as better to face the "modern world"; these we describe together as a sixth group under the title "neo-Pietism."

B. The Spener-Francke Group and the "moral" reading of texts

The earliest form of the movement paid little attention to the classics, so little in fact that one seldom finds any reference in their writings to classical writers. Indeed, when these Pietists do look to earlier texts at all, their attention is almost inevitably drawn to the mystics and spiritual masters of the late Middle Ages. When classical references occur, it is clear that the authors have not been working carefully with complete texts but have recalled a quotation from earlier schoolwork and have used it for a practical moral or religious purpose. Often such quotations are of commonplaces. Thus Francke almost never refers to a classical author in his devotional writing; when called upon to demonstrate his learning before an opponent he misquotes (possibly from memory) a sentence on the nature of praise from Cicero's *Tusculan Disputations*,[3] and makes fleeting references to Seneca.[4] But he is well acquainted with the Flemish mystic Ruusbroec.[5] In all these cases it is evident that the Christian application of sentences from Latin authors was uppermost in the teacher's mind. Thus in his pedagogical writings Francke provides his readers with the following example: "Nepos says, '*Alicuius inopiam suis opibus levare.*' In regard to this one is to ask what it means for the rich to share with the poor from their means. He who fears God stands alongside his poor neighbors with his means."[6]

Other than the "moral" citations of classical authors, most of the other classical references used by the Spener-Francke and the radical Pietist groups are to Aristotle, and these are far from complimentary. They show little knowledge of the Stagirite's thought and even less indication of a willingness to learn from it. For the Pietists here under discussion, Aristotle is tarred with the same brush used on his Protestant scholastic defenders. His work is considered nothing more than sterile formulations of facts, of no practical value other than to help the person quoting them gain academic visibility. Perhaps the best example of this approach can be found in the work of radical Pietists such as Gottfried Arnold,[7] although there are also extensive examples in Spener's work.[8]

Before leaving our discussion of the Spener-Francke school, one other matter should be noted: its pedagogical renewal. There can be no doubt of the significance of the educational methodologies developed at Halle for the next several centuries of German education. Halle practice touched all disciplines, the teaching of the classics with the others.[9]

Chief among the leaders of this pedagogical renewal was August Hermann Francke. For Francke four things were necessary for a good education: training in (1) true piety (*Gottseligkeit*) and (2) useful sciences for (3) proper speech (*Beredsamkeit*) and (4) external manners.[10] For "Christian intelligence" Francke required a basis of knowledge from all the areas of knowledge. It was the teacher's primary task to invite students to a practice of doctrine. The school is to serve as a garden for methodical learning and students are to be encouraged to learn on their own. The teacher is to copy letters on the board, for example, and encourage the students to find them in a book.

Not surprisingly, considering the concern with preaching which the Pietists had, Halle gave special attention to rhetoric, in which students were to be prepared in Latin, Greek, French and German. Of these languages emphasis was placed on the classical languages. Latin was practiced by the student who was required to describe a building or a picture or tell of a historical occurrence. Vocabulary was first learned and then sentences parsed, translated, and a précis of the passage made. On Wednesday and Saturday there were discussions between teachers and senior students in Latin. Latin poetry was saved for the senior classes. There they first learned poetic meters. Latin conversation was required only in the senior grades. For these students news was given in Latin on Mondays between three and five o'clock. Greek studies were similarly carried out with particular attention to the New Testament.

The outline of the training above does not appear peculiar to us, but its emphasis on students' own preparation and on moral applications along with the expected "kindness" of the instructors was a new beginning in education at the time. That the influence of the Halle method was important in the history of German education is clear, but there is still a great deal of work to be done before the full impact of the method can be clearly known.[11]

C. The Young Zinzendorf
Perhaps the most important Pietist to study at Halle was Count Nicholas Ludwig von Zinzendorf and, although he does not deserve a central place in this study, it would be inappropriate to pass him by without at least a brief mention of his *German Socrates*, a youthful piece published first in 1726-27 and reissued in 1732, opposing the censorship rules as applied to religion.[12] In spite of the title, the work does not indicate a close knowledge of the classics.

Zinzendorf chose the character of Socrates solely for the enuncia-
tion of a number of themes reflected by the Greek philosopher's
life. As he wrote at the beginning of his work: "Socrates has arisen
once again in Dresden. . . . I must secretly laugh that my fate is that
of this ancient wise man—the only difference is that I have not yet
been given a cup of hemlock."[13] The whole purpose of Socrates'
life, according to Zinzendorf, was to make the people of his day
"reflect." The German Socrates can do no more, even though his
call to reflection is enunciated by an attack on the orthodox
theologians and the intolerance of the religious authorities of his
day.

D. The Scholarly Pietists of Württemberg

It was among the Württemberg Pietists that the most important
scholarly work was done, and among the chief Pietists of the area
in the eighteenth century were Johann Albrecht Bengel and
Friedrich Christoph Oetinger. The importance of the Württemberg
school cannot be underestimated.[14]

There is no Pietist more closely acquainted with the classics
than Johann Albrecht Bengel (1697-1752), rightly described as the
founder of the modern science of biblical criticism.[15] Bengel's first
publication was his 1719 edition of Cicero's letters, *M. Tullii
Ciceronis epistolae ad diversos vulgo familiares. Recognitae et iis instruc-
tae rebus quae ad interpretationem imitationemque pertinent* . . . (Stutgardiae, 1719), a work obviously intended, as fitting the Pietist
tradition, for use in the schools. Already in this work Bengel is concerned with the importance of alternate readings, and he adds to
the work some twenty-five pages of textual apparatus. Moreover,
the volume is concluded with a dissertation on the relationship between faith and knowledge, learning and piety.

In addition to this work it is useful to review Bengel's early edition of Thaumaturgus. The title makes the "moral" or practical intention of the work clear: *Gregorii Thaumaturgi Panegyricus ad
Originem. Graece et Latine. Recognitus, notis auctus, et omnibus qui
sapientiam, ut illi, christianam, vel cum lingua graeca vel etiam citra eam
docent, discunt et colunt, eo accomodatus instituto, cuius ratio in proemio
explanatur* (Stutgardiae, 1722).

Three years later, in 1725, his edition of Chrysostom's "On the
Priesthood" appeared (again the edition was in Greek and Latin)[16]
along with his first work on the New Testament, the *Prodromus*

Novi Testamenti graeci recte cauteque adorandi (n.pl., 1725) (included with the Chrysostom edition).

The rest of Bengel's career is so well-known and extensive that there is no need to outline it here. Year after year until his death there appeared works on individual books of the New Testament (particularly the Apocalypse), on textual problems relating to the New Testament (one thinks primarily here of the *Gnomon*), and above all the critical edition of the New Testament (first edition in 1734 and six more editions before the end of the century).[17]

The importance of Bengel's edition of the New Testament for critical studies of classical texts at large is as obvious as it is important for later New Testament studies. But in all his work, both religious and classical, Bengel is primarily interested in the application of his well-known adage: *Applica te totum ad textum; applica textum tota ad te*, following the typical Pietist pattern of insisting on a "moral" reading of all materials. In this he and his Pietist co-believers share an interesting analogy with the British a century later when, at the height of imperialism, classicists gave a chauvinistic turn to the Greek revival in England, teaching Homer and the military virtues depicted in the Homeric texts for their "moral" value, in this case morality being defined according to the needs of the empire, extending a little spot of English soil and the Union Jack to the farthest regions of the world.[18]

How Bengel and the Spener-Francke Pietists before him shaped the classical texts to suit their purposes is obvious, but it is too naive to charge them with simply plundering the ancients. A close look at Bengel's *Gnomon of the New Testament* offers a better idea of the "scientific" use Pietists like him made of the classical texts and of the extent of their knowledge of those texts. Thus, for example, throughout the *Gnomon* one can see Bengel's extensive knowledge of the Greek vocabulary of authors earlier and later than the New Testament, and his application of this knowledge to an understanding of the New Testament text.[19]

Among the most original of all the Pietists was Friedrich Christoph Oetinger (1702-82). Next to Bengel the most important Pietist in Württemberg, he maintained a continual interest in patristic sources and was, in addition, strongly influenced by the thought of Jacob Boehme, by the Jewish Cabbala, and a number of speculative writers of the seventeenth and eighteenth centuries such as Newton, Malbranche, Swedenborg, and others. Special attention must be given to Oetinger because of the significance he has as a bridge between the first generation of Pietists, the neo-Pietists (the category into which Oetinger himself perhaps best fits), and the nineteenth century. Oetinger's influence has been traced to Lavater, Goethe, Herder, Hamann, Schiller, Jacobi, Novalis, Hoelderlin, Hegel, Schelling, and Baader.[20] How close a knowledge of classical authors Oetinger had is difficult to say, but his wide use of these authors is worthy of note. That use must be discussed, however, within the framework of his theological system, a system most fully outlined in his *Theologia ex idea vitae deducta*.[21] The volume has often been commented on in the context of nineteenth-century *Lebensphilosophie*. Following his Pietist background,[22] Oetinger begins his work by insisting that theology is not to be gained in the study or academic hall. The science of theology stands far above all other sciences. It flows from one's own life (*Erleben*) and from one's own conversation with God. God is the source of life, working in all and perceptible in all. Because everything arises from God and returns to him, theology is, for Oetinger, "open" to the world and all the sciences which shape the human approach to that world and contain the knowledge gained thereby. At the source of the cosmos is the being of God and in that cosmos God's being is hidden as a mystery.

As a result Oetinger is open to ever new revelations of the power and glory of God in Scripture, human tradition and nature. As G. Schaefer says in his introduction to the *Theologia*, "Oetinger did not belong to a time in which truth was to be sought in a distant unknown future, at an omega point; for him truth was most fully and completely revealed in the beginning, in the earliest times. When Oetinger reaches back to the ancient sources, when he studies the past, he knows he is in the presence of God."[23] God has thus shared a conception of himself with all human beings. God has done this particularly in the Scriptures. It is always to be remembered, however, that the Scriptures are written in human earthly words and there is, therefore, no break between God and the world. Classical studies then play a necessary role in the interpretation of the biblical text, and in this way Oetinger has bound together "secular" philological work and biblical exegesis, just as he has Christian and classical wisdom.

In a similar way nature too points to the glory of God. Nature and Scripture are the two sources of God's revelation, perfecting one another and forming an analogy between God's unrevealed being and his "becoming." Knowledge of God through nature is, however, problematic in a fallen world and it thus has less significance than has such knowledge through revelation. But Scripture must not be absolutized against nature; nature itself is being redeemed and at the end of time both the knowledge which comes through Scripture and that which comes through nature will betoken the same knowledge. For the present, however, there is an organ of the soul in every person which makes knowledge of God through nature possible; this is the *sensus communis*. The *sensus communis* is an intuitive grasp of the whole and requires before its exercise no analytic or rationalistic acts. Reason only follows it.

Oetinger works out the full details of his idea of the *sensus communis* in his *Inquisitio in sensum communem et rationem*.[24] In both the *Theologia* and the *Inquisitio*, Oetinger makes use of classical authors, and in both these works there are many references which remind one of the typical use made of earlier writers already noted in his fellow Pietists. His love of "moral" works, particularly of Cicero, is similar to Francke's,[25] as is his antagonism to Aristotle.[26] A major difference occurs with his special interest in the work of Hippocrates,[27] his extensive reading,[28] and, despite his opposition to Plato,[29] his knowledge of the works of that author[30] as well as many others,[31] and the accuracy of his quotations.

But Oetinger's system forces the reader to rethink the simplistic judgment to which one is lead by the facts outlined to this point. It is a mistake to suppose that the Pietists' dualistic division of true from false Christians, of church from world, of those taught by God and those taught merely from books can be extended to reject classical pagan authors in favor of Christian writers. Rather, classical authors are accepted on their own basis and, although one may have serious reservations with the judgments which Oetinger makes concerning certain of them (Plato is almost always attacked as supporting a position too close to Oetinger's opponents), one does not find him dividing Christianity from pagan classical culture in such a way that a negative judgment always falls on the classical author. When Oetinger is discussing the merits of a particular judgment based on the *sensus communis*, it makes no difference to him whether the person being discussed is Christian or pagan. A judgment based on the *sensus communis* is not necessarily misdirected because one did not have the additional revelation of Christ to go by.

Thus in his *Biblisches und Emblematisches Wörterbuch*, Oetinger takes up a discussion on teaching and the teacher (*didascalia*). The true teacher, needless to say, is Christ, but Oetinger opens the article with a treatment of classical learning:

> Plato says that the person who does not understand Geometry is not able to understand anything. But Socrates thinks otherwise. Socrates speaks according to the *sensu communi*. According to this common sense all men have the ability to learn.[32]

Socrates is thus not set aside because he does not have Christ. Oetinger goes on to point out that all learning which comes through Christ is different and more certain. On the basis of the *sensus communis* all are one, whether pagan or Christian, and all are so to be judged.

There remains one other matter, however—that of the relationship between Christianity and classical culture, as suggested by the work of Oetinger. For some of the nineteenth-century Pietists there is a division between Christianity and the pagan classical world out of which it grew. The division does not seem to be upheld by Oetinger. For him there was a golden age at the beginning of time when men and women were closer to God and when the revelation of nature and of grace were as close as they will be at the end of time. All things came forth from the original source at the beginning and the closer one is to that time, the closer one is to God. The classical period shares with other cultures in this proximity to the beginning, and thereby its *sensus communis* is to be closely considered.[33] It did not have the doctrine of Christ but it was in close proximity to the beginning and many of its members profited from the fact, passing on wisdom to the modern world. The very language developed at the time was the language in which the Word of God was written, binding together the realms of nature and of grace in as intimate and concise a manner as God and man were bound together in the person of Christ. To this golden age of antiquity Oetinger calls humankind back and thus, in many ways, he foresees the use of Greek civilization as a critique for contemporary life as it was developed among the German Romantic poets and theologians. What must always be remembered is that his position is not out of keeping with the Pietists who had gone before him: the nineteenth-century willingness to base a critique of culture within history rather than outside of it has surprisingly more in common with Pietism than earlier interpretations of the movement which saw it merely as a moral and rigoristic attack of Jerusalem against Athens, of Christ against culture.

Notes

1. Note, for example, Martin Schmidt, *Wiedergeburt und neuer Mensch* (Witten, 1979), 5-6.
2. For a fuller bibliography on the movement, see my introduction in *Pietists* (New York: Paulist Press, 1983).
3. In his *Verantwortung* to Johann Friedrich Maier in 1707; see E. Peschke, ed., *August Hermann Francke: Streitschriften* (Berlin, 1981), 288f.
4. Ibid., 310.
5. Ibid., 285, 315, 371-75.
6. See Wolf Oschlies, *Die Arbeits- und Beruf-pädagogik August Hermann Franckes* (Witten, 1969), 104.
7. For details see my *The Influence of Late Medieval Mysticism in the Life and Work of Gottfried Arnold* (Ph.D. diss., University of Toronto, 1976).
8. See references in Jan Olaf Ruttgardt, *Heiliges Leben in der Welt* (Bielefeld, 1978).
9. One must take great care before undertaking an extensive discussion on this topic. Note some of the difficulties in Klaus Schaller, "Pietismus und moderne Pädagogik" in *Pietismus und Moderne Welt*," ed. Kurt Aland (Witten, 1974), 161ff., but an excellent beginning has already been made by Oschlies (see n.6).
10. As quoted in Oschlies, op. cit., n.6, 102
11. Works such as that of Hildegard Zimmerman on *Caspar Neumann und die Entstehung der Frühaufklärung* (Witten, 1969) help us to sketch out the breadth of that influence. Neumann worked most of his life in Breslau and had a great influence in the teaching of Hebrew. His methodology gained much from Halle and he in turn influenced Lutheran Pietists and others.
12. Nicholas van Zinzindorf, *Der teutsche Socrates, Das ist: Aufrichtige Anzeige verschiedener nicht so wohl unbekannter als vielmehr in Abfall gerathener Haupt-Wahrheiten* (Leipzig, 1732).
13. Ibid., 34.
14. Hartmut Lehmann has done an excellent job of outlining the history of the movement there in his *Pietismus und weltliche Ordnung in Württemberg vom 17. bis zum 20. Jahrhundert* (Berlin, 1969). Along with his study Joachim Trautwein's *Religiosität und Sozialstruktur: Untersucht anhand der Entwicklung des württembergischen Pietismus* (Stuttgart, 1972) deserves close attention.
15. On Bengel see especially Gottfried Mälzer, *Johann Albrecht Bengel* (Stuttgart, 1970).
16. Johann Albrecht Bengel, *Johannis Chrysostomi de Sacerdotio libri sex graece et latine* (Stutgardiae, 1727).
17. For a full bibliography see Mälzer, op. cit., 459-69.

18. It would make an interesting study to trace the influence of the Greek revival in eighteenth- and nineteenth-century England and Germany, for example, and analyze the texts chosen in the schools and the use made of the texts. It is not surprising that the Pietists should have turned to Epictetus, Seneca and, of course, Cicero in the eighteenth century and that in the nineteenth century they should have followed the same pattern extending their use of Greek literature to include the Athenian dramatists and Plato (albeit selectively in a manner suitable to their own Burger interests). British school children, on the other hand, were studying Homer, Thucydides, and Caesar. Vergil was read by both, but the emphasis was radically different in each country.

19. For a discussion of the *Gnomon* see Mälzer, op. cit., 377ff.

20. See Henry Francis Fullenwider, *Friedrich Christoph Oetinger. Wirkungen auf Literatur und Philosophie seiner Zeit* (Goppingen, 1975); for an interesting review of Oetinger's influence on twentieth-century writers see Sigrid Grossmann, *Friedrich Christoph Oetingers Gottesvorstellung* (Gottingen, 1979), 14-39.

21. Friedrich Christoph Oetinger, *Theologia ex idea vitae deducta.* Hrsg. Konrad Ohly (Berlin: De Gruyter, 1979), 2 vols. Hereafter cited as *Theologia.*

22. For the outline of Oetinger's theology which follows, see particularly the introduction in the Ohly ed., op. cit., n.21, vol. 1.

23. Gerhard Schaefer, "Vorwort." Ibid., 1:7.

24. Friedrich Christoph Oetinger, *Inquisitio in Sensum Communem et Rationem,* (Tübingen, 1753); reprint with introduction by Hans Georg Gadamer (Stuttgart, 1964); hereafter cited as *Inquisitio.*

25. See Oetinger, *Theologia,* 67, 89, 126, 196, 265.

26. Ibid., 65, 131.

27. Ibid., 66, 69, 97, 131, 195, 234, 248, 259, 264.

28. Note in particular his citations in the introduction.

29. Ibid., 66, 67.

30. Ibid., 24, 122, 34, 136, for references to the *Apology, Parmenides, Phaedrus,* and other dialogues.

31. Oetinger, for example, has a good knowledge of Terence, Pliny, Plutarch, Tacitus, and others. For full references see the index to *Theologia* (op. cit., n.21).

32. Friedrich Christoph Oetinger, *Biblisches und Emblematisches Worterbuch* (Stuttgart, 1776), 402.

33. Oetinger, *Inquisitio,* 2:11. The practical concerns of Pietism, however, are a major element in its use of the classics.

Hegel on Greek and Revealed Religion

William V. Rowe

A. Introduction

The topic of this essay is Hegel's assessment of Greek and revealed religion. Since our general concern has been with Christianity and the classics, this essay will narrow and focus our attention in three respects. In the first place, we will focus on Hegel's view of Christianity and the classics; second, we will discuss only the Greek elements in classical antiquity; and third, we will concentrate on Greek religion.

1. Hegel on Christianity and the classics

Some view Hegel as a Christian philosopher;[1] some consider him one of the most consistent Hellenists in modern thought.[2] Both interpretations are one-sided. Indeed, Hegel considered Christianity the summit, or "truth," of all forms of religious consciousness; in his terms, Christianity is "absolute religion." Though received and expressed in representations (*Vorstellungen*), Christianity in Hegel's view is one with absolute knowing, the most highly developed and concrete standpoint possible for philosophy, the standpoint of "infinity" (unlimited self-relation) which Hegel wished to make his own.

Nevertheless, Hegel is not a Christian philosopher in any straightforward sense of the word. For it is Hegel's desire—or, rather, it is in his view philosophy's requirement—that no religion, revealed or otherwise, dominate thought. Instead thought must think through and raise the content of religion to the level of philosophy. With the fulfillment of this requirement, with the elevation of religion to thought, philosophy attains what Kant knew only as the future of philosophy and Fichte knew as philosophy's authentic name: "science" (*Wissenschaft*). Hence, Christianity may be the truth of all other religions, but religion as such, Christianity included, finds its truth outside itself—where all representation finds its truth—in the Concept. Because of this, the reader of Hegel's treatment of religion is left with a feeling of ambiguity. Does Hegel really wish to transcend religion and leave it behind as he enters the element of thought? Or does he seek to preserve the content of religion through a kind of rational apologetics, ending with a philosophy that amounts to metaphysical religion?[3]

Meanwhile, in his relation to Greek antiquity, Hegel allowed a certain classicism to inspire his work. At times this element in Hegel appears decisive. Certainly Hegel placed the issues of Greek philosophy close to the heart of his own concerns and thoroughly grounded his thought in that of the ancients. He was perhaps the only philosopher of his generation with a sufficient interest in, and knowledge of, Greek philosophy to carry such a project to its conclusion. He admits, for example, that he did not neglect a single fragment of Heraclitus in composing his *Wissenschaft der Logik*.[4]

It is also noteworthy that Hegel composed this work during his Nürnberg years (1808-16) while he was employed as the headmaster of a classical high school. The fact that Hegel regularly communicated to his Gymnasium students the outlines of his speculative logic testifies to the harmony he felt existed between his philosophical standpoint and the motives of classicism.

Nevertheless, as with his relation to biblical Christianity, Hegel's "classicism" appears ambiguous and he is no classicist in the ordinary sense. While modern philosophy grows out of Hellenic soil and while the Greeks had, in Hegel's estimation, grasped and expressed the essence of thought—the Concept—nevertheless ancient thought finds its "truth" outside itself, namely, in the modern philosophy of subjectivity. In the end, therefore, Hegel represents neither Christianity nor classicism as such. Nor is his standpoint merely a combination of these two, but something new, a third point of view. Yet, this third point of view is not simply new; it is not merely other than that of Christianity and not really different from that of antiquity. It could not simply differ from these because, as Hegel is at pains to show, the absolute shape of infinite thought includes both Hellenic antiquity and biblical religion as moments in its content and elements of its standpoint. This explains the ambiguity in Hegel's relation both to Christianity and the classics.

Two other instances of narrowing and focusing are at work in this essay. We are ranging Hegel's treatment of classical antiquity under the rubric of Greek religion. This raises two questions: why the Greeks, and why their religion?

2. The Greeks

In answer to the first question we note that the eighteenth-century revival of humanism north and west of the Rhine displays in Hegel its characteristic preference for the Greeks over the Romans as the principal exemplars of antique culture. It is not that Hegel overlooked the art, religion, and statecraft of the Romans; it is not that he failed to appreciate their role as historical mediators of Greek culture to western Europe nor that he belittled their philosophy. But the foundation of higher study, says Hegel, is always "Greek literature in the first place, Roman in the second."[5] As he comments in the lectures on the *Philosophy of History*:

> Among the Greeks we feel ourselves immediately at home, for we are in the region of spirit; and though the origin of the nation, as also its philological peculiarities, may be traced further back—even to India—the proper emergence, the true palingenesis of spirit must be looked for in Greece itself.[6]

3. Greek Religion

According to Hegel, Greek religion represented the source of Hellenic spirit—or rather the most concrete shape taken by that spirit, one that embraced its art, founded its political life, and led the way in Hellenic cultural expansion and reception by other peoples. A nation's religion is in Hegel's view nothing more than its self-understanding. It is in its religion that a culture places itself on display—primarily for its own benefit, that is, for itself. A culture is "for itself" in its religion.

But it is for itself in an object: namely, in the representations of its god or deities. Hence, religion also places a culture on display for others and is its principal way of doing so. Hegel's treatment of Greek religion is, therefore, our best access to Hegel's view of Greek life and clearly the best preparation for comparing this with his understanding of Christianity.

Hence, we can leave aside the vexing question of Hegel's relation to the philosophy of the Greeks, for although this is a more
decisive question for the development of Hegel's own standpoint,
it would lead us away from our topic. Furthermore, it was Greek
life and not Greek philosophy, the appearance of the "beautiful
totality" rather than the emergence of the Concept, that animated
Hegel's earliest reflection upon the civilization of antiquity. This
emphasis on the totality and concreteness of Greek life is retained
in the passages from the *Phenomenology of Spirit* we have chosen as
our guide to "Hegel on Greek and Revealed Religion."

B. Hegel's *Phenomenology of Spirit*

1. The task of phenomenology
We have chosen the *Phenomenology* because it represents the earliest
of Hegel's mature treatments of Greek religion and Christianity.
In the pre-Jena writings, many of which revolve around the question of the relation between Greek and Christian consciousness,
Hegel's work appears to be animated by the conflict he felt existed
between these two religions. But in the *Phenomenology* the conflict,
while explicitly thematized, is in the same measure laid to rest since
Hegel—or, as he would say, the Concept—has not taken sides in
this issue but is elevated above the conflict. From this new
standpoint, the science of phenomenology is able to describe the
transition from Greek religious consciousness to New Testament
faith as something beneficial and necessary, both for religion and
for philosophy.

This latter point is all the more important for our theme since
it indicates that the new standpoint of the Concept has been reached
by means of a synthesis of Greek and Christian religions. In effect,
these two manifestations of human culture have been appropriated
by the Concept as elements in its own structure. As a result the
heart of Hegel's philosophical outlook is rooted in that complex of
problems we refer to as "Christianity and the classics."

a) Phenomenology as a pedagogical/scientific labor of spirit
But this synthesis is also significant because, in the science of
phenomenology, these two phenomena are necessary elements in the
"curriculum" of spirit, necessary stages in its self-pedagogy. On the
one hand, the standpoint of absolute knowing is important for

Hegel, at least in part, because it unites the disparate spirits of Greece and the New Testament. On the other hand, Greek and Christian religious consciousnesses are important for Hegel because they constitute the pedagogy of spirit, the education or curriculum by means of which spirit is raised and forged into its absolute shape.

Although the themes of Greek and Christian religiosity are treated in numerous early texts, in a fuller way in the lectures on *Philosophy of Religion*, and in a simpler way in the *Encyclopedia*, it is in the *Phenomenology of Spirit* that the pedagogical function of their synthesis is made explicit and presented as scientifically, rationally necessary.

We may seem to overstate the case when we call Greek and revealed religions together the essential pedagogy of spirit. There are many other shapes of consciousness analyzed in the *Phenomenology*, many other moments in spirit's self-manifestation. Just because Christianity and Greek religion constitute respectively the penultimate and antepenultimate stations in spirit's itinerary, this does not make them the essential stages in this process. But the science of phenomenology assigns to the shapes of religious consciousness just such an extraordinary status.

b) The place of religion in the pedagogy of spirit

Both for philosophical and historical reasons, religion is not only the essence but the entirety of this pedagogy. As Hegel says of the other moments in spirit's movement-toward-self (those moments being Consciousness, Self-consciousness, Reason, and Spirit), "Spirit as such contains the previous shapes in universal determinations, in the moments just named. Religion presupposes that these shapes have run their full course and is their simple totality or absolute self."[7]

By this Hegel means that these moments of spirit are actually moments of *religion*, and that religion is spirit itself—the "absolute self"—pure and simple. Religion "presupposes" that these moments or shapes have been run through and determined. This tells us why religion must be treated last in the *science* of appearing spirit. Religion, being nothing in itself and certainly nothing separate from or transcendent in relation to these moments, is simply their totality. But this could only be demonstrated once the seeming self-sufficiency, or autonomy, of each of these shapes was set aside by its undergoing the "experience of consciousness" and by a scientific rehearsal (*Er-innerung*) of their necessary retreat into their true origin.

But if this is the case—that the course followed by the science of phenomenology is that of the systematic retreat of every would-be shape of consciousness into its origin, into the actual totality from which it has been abstracted—then we would expect that the end result of this science is really the original shape of spirit, is really spirit itself, present as spirit and justified as such in the scientific sense. By saying that religion presupposes that its moments have run their course, Hegel means that the scientific self-elucidation/exposition of spirit—the phenomeno-logic of spirit—must have followed this course. But this requirement derives its authority from the fact that religion is really the origin of these shapes into which they are being re-flected, the original *concretum* from which they have been abstracted and in which they now acquire true being only as moments.

c) The place of history in the *Phenomenology*
Because the several shapes of consciousness have their true being as moments of religion, it is only in religion that they have any actuality in time. The course followed by the science of phenomenology is, therefore, not the historical order of spirit's appearing. The moments of spirit which this science runs through separately in each of its sections—Consciousness, Self-consciousness, Reason, Spirit—have a simultaneous existence in time as moments of a religion. Spirit is always both conscious and self-conscious; it is always both rational and spiritual. This is why Hegel distinguishes the science of phenomenology from history proper.[8] Only with the stage of religion does the structural analysis of appearing spirit touch upon the actual history of spirit.

> The course traversed by these moments is, moreover, in relation to religion, not to be represented as occurring in time. Only the totality of spirit is in time, the "shapes," which are "shapes" of the totality of spirit, display themselves in a temporal succession; for only the whole has true actuality and therefore the form of pure freedom in face of an "other," a form which expresses itself as time.[9]

Thus all history for Hegel presupposes religion; all of history is in effect the *history of religion*.

2. *The method of the Phenomenology*
Phenomenology's special status is owing to its function, as Hegel spells it out, of introducing natural consciousness—human knowing's unspiritual habit of stubbornly remaining in one of its finite shapes—to the Concept of science. That is why the *Phenomenology of Spirit* is determined as the "First Part of the System of Science."[10]

a) Introducing science
As introduction, phenomenology is directed at the extra-scientific, or non-scientific, structure of consciousness, that is, to the division of knowing into the duality of consciousness and its object. But as "first part of the system," phenomenology belongs within the ambit of science itself in spite of its subject matter, the experience of consciousness.[11] Hence, there is a certain conflict between phenomenology's function as an introduction to science and its status as the first part of this science as a system. It seems phenomenology is a pedagogy of consciousness, providing it with a "ladder"[12] to ascend into the Concept as the element of science, and yet phenomenology falls within the system of science itself.

This problem is an issue for us because Hegel means by "system" a self-coherent, self-contained, exclusively self-related, hence "absolute," knowing which for that reason cannot be introduced. As a system, science is pure interior: pure, because for it everything "exterior" (world, others) has been canceled as other, interiorized, and made into a moment of the systemic totality of absolute knowing; pure, meaning without an outside and, hence, without a point of access. When Hegel says the system of science cannot be introduced, he means that either it must be introduced from inside science, in which case introduction is superfluous, or that, if an introduction is written, it must fall outside the closed circle of scientific knowing and therefore fail to "lead one into" (introduce) it.

Despite this, the inaccessibility of science is really no problem for the non-scientific standpoint of consciousness because "consciousness" is merely the appearing of spirit, spirit's *phenomenon*, while "science" is simply actual spirit itself.[13] The experience of consciousness *is* science implicitly. Phenomenology's function of introducing science, its vocation of raising phenomenal knowing into its true element, therefore, is not only explained in terms of its possibility by this fact, but phenomenology's success in carrying out this education is guaranteed by it in advance.

b) The experience of consciousness
The pedagogical motive of phenomenology is clear in its determination to examine all of the shapes possible for consciousness, so that every conceivable standpoint from which Hegel's *Phenomenology of Spirit* could be read would, in the course of this reading, find its claim to knowledge refuted and find itself transformed into a moment in a greater totality.

But consciousness' experience of being refuted appears to consciousness in a different light; it appears to be something more than simple doubt concerning a truth claim. This "refutation" could be called an "absolute skepticism"[14] because this experience is the undoing of consciousness in that shape in which it is conscious of itself. Consciousness' experience is the negation of its self-consciousness. So far as this negative process and its negative result are concerned, no pedagogical science, no phenomenology, is required to bring it about. It is simply the structure of consciousness' experience as consciousness, the structure of its consciousness-of-self.

Meanwhile, this experience is not purely negative either since consciousness, by undergoing this experience, has not only learned that it is untrue in itself but has also learned that it possesses a relative truth as a moment in something more concrete. The negation undergone by any untrue shape of consciousness is not complete obliteration and oblivion; it is only the negation of this particular shape. The negativity in the experience of consciousness is not an absolute nothing which, after it has done its destructive work, leaves nothing behind. It is rather a determinate nothing, or in Hegel's terms, a "determinate negation,"[15] a negation just as determinate in content as the content which it negates.

Or, rather, the content of a determinate negation is more determinate than the content it negates because the negation includes the negated; the negation retains the negated as a moment of its own content, thus enhancing its internal structure and differentiation. In a similar way, the negative logical expression "non-A" includes the logical content symbolized by "A," which it has negated, as part of its content. The experience of consciousness itself has this dialectical structure. Hence, the outcome of what at first seems to be a skeptical experience is really something of determinate meaning, something positive in its own right. The experience of consciousness in which consciousness in a certain untrue shape gets refuted and negated is equally the validation of consciousness in a new shape, a shape which, because it is "experienced," is certain of its truth vis-á-vis its previous standpoint.

For this reason, the negative experience of consciousness is really a cleansing, a *catharsis*. Hegel speaks of it as "the Calvary (*Schädelstätte*) of absolute spirit,"[16] a redemptive suffering and dying that becomes a source of life for spirit. Therefore, for the positive outcome of its experience, too, consciousness is not indebted to phenomenology's scientific tutelage. Consciousness cannot avoid undergoing its experience of purification by fire—that is, of determination by negation—and it cannot avoid profiting by and learning from it.

c) Recollecting the whole experience of spirit

Nevertheless, consciousness needs a scientific account (a *Wissenschaft*) of its experience in order to be truly educated. This is because consciousness learns nothing from its experience if it comes to see only one step further along its road to truth, if it passes through the crisis of negation only to identify itself once more with some finite truth. If consciousness is to learn the actuality of its essence, if it is to ascend into the element of science, it is not enough for it simply to pass on to the next, more concrete, although still finite, shape (*Gestalt*). What alone suffices is for it to pass out of its finitude as such and pass into the Concept.

This explains the necessity of a scientific introduction to science. It is the entire human race in the totality of its historical experience, or rather spirit itself appearing as the history of consciousness, that must undergo this discipline and pedagogy. Only spirit as a totality—the spirit that is religion in its concrete temporality and historicity—can undergo the exhaustive experience of consciousness. Any individual through actual experience may undergo one, two, or several of these transitions and transformations of spirit. But for that individual only a portion of the content comprising the absolute can possibly be experienced, only certain moments in the determinateness of absolute knowing can be appropriated by the finite spirit first-hand. The full experience of consciousness belongs to spirit as such and can be appropriated by an individual only if he climbs to that height, occupies that altitude, and breathes that *aether*, which is the true element of spirit. Only here does the individual perceive himself in his perception of the absolute, and only here does the absolute perceive itself in the individual. Only here is spirit what it is, namely, "pure self-recognition in absolute otherness."[17]

"This Aether, *as such*, is the ground and soil of science or knowledge in general."[18]

When spirit is what it is, when it is actual spirit,[19] it is—as this passage also says—*science*.[20] Only when spirit itself exists for the individual in the shape of absolute knowing can spirit be attained by the individual. Only then can the individual—in which alone absolute spirit can attain itself—itself attain absolute spirit. Only in, or as, science is the whole experience of consciousness traversed by spirit and preserved in a kind of memory which Hegel calls "interiorization" (*Er-innerung*). Only in a science of this experience is its pedagogical value made accessible to the individual; only in this form can its content actually be recollected (*er-innert*) by finite spirit.[21]

d) Religion as an experience of finitude
It follows that religion, although it is the concrete existence of actual spirit, still falls short of this actuality in some way. This is because religion is not scientific, is not rooted in the Concept, but dwells in the element of representation (*Vorstellung*), or picture-thinking. In religion, spirit is actual, concrete, and true; but it is such for itself only by way of a *representation*. Religious spirit's being "actual for itself" exists only in an objective representation, that is, in its god or deities. The representational quality of all religious consciousness is both its strength and its weakness. Because religion represents spirit to itself and recognizes itself in this representation, it is the eternal abiding of spirit in the element of infinity. But because it must represent this infinity, and cannot think it, it is still consciousness and, therefore, an experience of finitude.

C. The Phenomenology of Greek and Revealed Religion

1. Consciousness and self-consciousness in religion
For the purposes of this discussion of Hegel's phenomenology of religious spirit we must understand the important distinction he makes between consciousness and self-consciousness. In religion this distinction is an actual difference that is overcome only with the advent of science.

By consciousness Hegel means a form of apparent, phenomenal knowing in which knower and known are externally related. Consciousness is a relation between subject and object in which the object is viewed as other than and external to the subject.

Self-consciousness, on the other hand, is a knowing relation in which subject and object are identical and, therefore, are identified. Self-consciousness is a form of consciousness that is conscious of its identity with the object of consciousness. Self-consciousness is simply consciousness' being conscious of consciousness.

But distinguishing consciousness from self-consciousness as the disjunction and identification respectively of subject and object can lead to misunderstanding. Self-consciousness' identification of what consciousness construed as the disjunction of subject and object does not mean that self-consciousness has overcome consciousness.

There is for Hegel a "subjectivistic" form of self-consciousness in which consciousness achieves an identity of subject and object by distinguishing its consciousness of self from its consciousness of objects. That is, there is a kind of self-consciousness (Hegel calls it "reflective") which consists of a self-relation by way of other-negation, a relating-to-self by means of a withdrawal from the object.

Such a self-consciousness is limited by the fact that consciousness can only find itself in something other than the object of consciousness. Two points about this form of self-consciousness are decisive for Hegel. First, this self-consciousness is not itself a "shape of consciousness." Rather, it occurs only in a larger context, namely, in the context of a negative contrast between consciousness proper (the subject/object split) and self-consciousness (the subject/object identity). This subjectivistic self-consciousness can never be the "infinite" that is sought by spirit as the element of science. In Hegel's opinion, Fichte wrongly sought a foundation (*Grundlage*) for science in this subjective and abstract identity of the I with itself (I = I).

Second, the real reason why this subjective self-consciousness cannot provide a basis for science is that it in turn is based upon simple consciousness. The sense of self found in reflective self-consciousness is achieved over and against a sense of the object. Consciousness as simple consciousness of an object is therefore presupposed in this self-consciousness. Thus, while consciousness is needed by self-consciousness, the latter cannot account for the possibility of consciousness itself.

The task of every form of self-consciousness is to resolve the contradiction in it, not merely between subject and object, but between a consciousness of the subject and a consciousness of the object, between self-consciousness and a residue of consciousness. Hegel calls the resolution of this contradiction "reason." Reason is infinite self-consciousness, a consciousness of self not as negative, not as opposed to the object of consciousness, but in and as this object. Reason is a "pure self-recognition in absolute otherness."

To relate the above to the analysis of religion, we must recall that religion means the "self-consciousness of spirit." This self-consciousness is a one-sided, reflective one; it sustains itself by contrasting itself with a "consciousness of spirit." The "consciousness of spirit" that is here opposed to spirit's self-consciousness understands spirit as something objective. This means spirit is present to consciousness as a "substance" or as the "world" which consists of customs, laws, norms, expectations, and possibilities for consciousness.

In religion, these two—a consciousness of the world (the spiritual object) and the self-consciousness of spirit—are in conflict as "secular" versus "sacred." This conflict can be resolved when spirit reposes in the element of the Concept and expresses itself as the system of science—the infinite identity of subject and object, the "absolute" knowing.

2. Revealed religion

So far as Hegel's account of religion itself is concerned, it is best to start with basics, and the basis of religion—not its abstract principle but its principal shape—is revealed religion. Furthermore, the basis of revealed religion is the incarnate god, absolute spirit present to consciousness as an individual self-consciousness, as a concrete universal. The characteristic mark of biblical religion—that quality by virtue of which this religion is the highest and most inclusive—is revelation. This feature is basic because it represents the advent in religion of knowledge.

The religion of nature as well as the religion of art (Hegel's term for Greek religion) are tied through natural shapes and by the work of art to sensuous consciousness and are limited by it. Over and against this limitation, revelation comes as a liberating force because the "other" in which religious consciousness knows itself is not something immediately, sensuously, present to consciousness but is spirit itself.

a) The "absolute religion"
Revelation, any revelation, is the disclosure of spirit to spirit. The religious consciousness of revealed religion, therefore, is a *self*-consciousness. But, while religion in general is self-conscious spirit, revealed religion is the self-consciousness of this self-consciousness. It is a religion in which spirit is conscious of itself in an entity that, like spirit, is a self-consciousness.

But this self-consciousness is not merely "like" spirit, and spirit is not merely conscious of itself "in" this entity. The entity in which spirit acquires a consciousness of self is not like but identical with spirit because this entity's consciousness of self is this entity's consciousness of spirit. It is no mystery, then, that spirit is conscious of itself through its consciousness of this divine entity, that is, through its faith in revelation.

This is no mystery because the substance of divine spirit is precisely its disclosure of the divine *mysterion* (secret); the divine essence consists in self-revelation. The divine entity whose self-consciousness is spirit's own consciousness of self is not only the divine, it is the divine "Word." Revealed religion, therefore, is "absolute religion" because in revelation the revealed content is fully expressed. Revelation is not a veil that somehow signals the presence of a something hidden; it is the unveiling in which the divine is made known. Revelation is the key element in this religion, according to Hegel, because in and as revelation religion as such is manifest (*offenbare*) to itself as a consciousness of the self-conscious absolute spirit and, hence, as an absolute knowing.

In other words, not only does finite religious spirit behold its own essence in the God-man, it also beholds in him its own consciousness. The consciousness of the God-man, when he is conscious of himself and of his identity with absolute spirit, is identical with the religious consciousness by which he is beheld in finite consciousness.

We will return to this point presently. Here, let us simply note the following. The fact that the God-man's consciousness is just as religious as the consciousness of his finite votaries or disciples is the first meaning of the expression "revealed religion." Even before this religion is *geoffenbarte*, or "positive" religion—meaning revealed in specific historical events or with a determinate doctrinal content—it is *offenbare*, or "manifest" religion. In manifest religion the nature and actuality of religion itself is revealed to religious consciousness.[22]

The God-man reveals by exemplifying the reverence, obedience, piety, submission in suffering, and even faith of finite consciousness—in short, by representing the whole religious consciousness that is this shape of religion. Revelation itself has taken on this shape, hence the Self made known in it is one with the self to whom it is revealed, and the revelation itself is the actuality of this oneness, not only the seal upon, but the accomplishing of this union. Revelation is just this raising of finite consciousness to a participation in and identification with the absolute. Revealed religion joins these two—finite and infinite spirit—from both sides. This joining occurs, therefore, not simply as revelation but as the *religion* of revelation, the union of God's revealing and man's believing. This joining and union make Christianity "absolute religion."[23]

b) The incarnate God

The divine nature is revealed only when it takes on the actual being of a self-conscious Self. This means, as we saw, that finite consciousness, in being conscious of this Self as its religious object, is equally conscious of itself. Or, finite consciousness is conscious that it is one with the divine essence. But this oneness also works to the benefit of the other side of the equation. The divine self-consciousness too knows—and knows only—what it has revealed to consciousness: that is, it knows only itself.

We may also express this as follows. Only in its unity with finite consciousness does the divine essence, whose being consists in a being-known and in a being-known-by-self, actually become what it is: namely, spirit that is absolute. Spirit that is absolute has reconciled its other to itself. Absolute spirit is spirit that has no "other" and so is infinite.

Therefore Hegel's phrase, "the self-revelation of spirit," does not merely mean that the divine nature has disclosed itself to finite consciousness. "The self-revelation of spirit" also means that the incarnation reveals the divine nature to the divine being himself. The incarnate God is the divine essence made into an object for the divine being. Hence, the divine spirit reaches the highest height—the realization of its essence—when it has descended into the depths of the finite world. Only here does spirit coincide absolutely with its absolute self-revelation.

> By thus *coming down* it has in fact attained for the first time to its own highest essence. For it is only when the concept of essence has reached its simple purity that it is the absolute *abstraction* which is *pure thought* and hence the pure individuality of Self, just as, on account of its simplicity, it is also the *immediate* or *being*. Thus the lowest is at the same time the highest; the revealed which has come forth wholly on to the *surface* is precisely therein the most *profound*. That the supreme Being is seen, heard, and so forth, as an immediately present self-consciousness, this therefore is indeed the consummation of its concept; and through this consummation that Being is immediately present qua supreme Being.[24]

c) Revelation as oneness of humanity and god

The unity of consciousness and self-consciousness in revealed religion is best expressed by saying that absolute spirit's being-for-consciousness and its being-for-itself are the same being. "Being-for" in both cases is a knowing. The knowing that is called revelation is just the unity and identity of these two knowings as one knowledge, a knowledge that is absolute because of this identity. As Hegel expresses it:

> God is attainable in pure speculative knowledge alone and *is* only in that knowledge, and is only that knowledge itself, for He is Spirit; and this speculative knowledge is the knowledge of the *revealed* religion.[25]

What is absolute about this shape of consciousness is the identity in it of consciousness and its object. In this identity consciousness itself, with its characteristic bifurcation of spirit into consciousness and object, is implicitly overcome and absolute knowing makes its appearance, but in the guise (*Kleid*)[26] of religion, that is, as a system of representations. Despite this presentation of spirit in a system of re-presentations, this religious consciousness is identical with the absolute that is known in it. This identity is the revealed knowledge that is the absolute being of absolute religion.

3. Greek Religion

a) Art as Greek religion
How do matters stand, by comparison, with the situation and shape of consciousness found in the religion of art? In revealed religion, consciousness knows spirit as a self-consciousness. This knowledge of consciousness is *ipso facto* the identity of consciousness and self-consciousness. Spirit known as self-consciousness is already this identity, for the knowledge of this identity is precisely what this identity is.

Is this identity a part of the religion of art? Is this identity revealed in art in some other way than through knowledge? One could answer for Hegel by saying all religion consists of this identity, but that in natural and aesthetic religion this identity is only implicit. As we saw above, however, the identity in question is the actual, explicit identity of consciousness and self-consciousness. So even by the account just given, other religions lack this identity.

This identity is not found in the religion of art because this identity *is* the revelation of it, and only absolute religion is this revelation. The simple fact is that, in the religion of art, the identity of consciousness and self-consciousness is not disclosed. Undoubtedly this identity is experienced by this religion, but not as something known. Or else, this identity is "known," but only in the sense that spirit has the "know how" to produce it. Aesthetic spirit knows this identity not through a revelation of it, and not through a *noesis* (a thinking) or insight directed toward it, but through the *poiesis* (the making) of it. The identity of consciousness and self-consciousness is known in art only on the condition and to the degree that it is represented.

Hence, the identity of consciousness and self-consciousness at the heart of religion is present in art, too, but not immediately. It is present only through a mediation, only as the result of a *poiesis*, only in the work of art, only as *poiema*. In its religion the Greek spirit knows as the work of its own hands not the substance of spirit but the joining of this substance with the consciousness of this substance.

In religion of art, substance is present to consciousness as the "material cause" of art. Spirit is only "conscious of itself" in art once matter is given the form of a work, a work being something of and for spirit. Substance itself can never become known in art—and therefore consciousness and self-consciousness can never be fully identified—because matter can never be completely joined to the form of spirit. At best, matter desires union with form; that is to say, matter is form *in potentia*. But matter cannot effect this union. Art, the presence of absolute spirit in Greek religion, therefore finds its origin outside itself. Or, the union of consciousness and self-consciousness in art requires an efficient cause, the genius of the artist. For this reason Greek religion is "musical" in the etymological sense. This religion knows not only gods but also muses; it is consciousness not merely of votaries but also of bards.

b) Art as the self-consciousness of the Greek world
In Greek private and public life, there is found a world of norms, laws, obligations, and powers such as Fate, Necessity, Eros, and Death. This world is spirit itself in its presence to the Greeks. But it is spirit only as spiritual substance. Later, in his *Encyclopedia*, Hegel referred to this state of affairs as "objective spirit."[27] In Greek religion, however, this objective world-spirit, this simple spiritual substance that Hegel calls the "beautiful harmony and tranquil equilibrium" of Greek life,[28] acquires a conscious relation-to-self, a self-consciousness. Religion is the self-consciousness of a world. But a world-spirit that knows itself is immediately more than this, for when a consciousness becomes a consciousness-of-self, it is *ipso facto* a new and different consciousness.

The religion of art is the elevation of the Hellenic world-spirit from substance to subject, from world, as the simple correlate of a worldly consciousness, to spirit as a self-conscious and self-contained activity. The consciousness of this now self-conscious spirit, withdrawing purely into itself, has thereby set aside its world-

directedness, its worldliness, its secularity. It is now a consciousness which, as self-consciousness, has set its own worldliness (both
the beauty of its world and its secure possession of it) within brack-
ets and placed it under a different sign, just as the mathematician
might set an algebraic expression (for example, 2x/4) within brack-
ets in order to give the expression as a whole a negative value (such
as -[2x/4]).

In an analogous way, Greek religious self-consciousness is not
its former world-consciousness and so is the simple negation of it.
Greek religion is not a consciousness of the Greek world; rather, it
is a consciousness *of this consciousness*. Hellenic religion is a self-
consciousness, having as its correlate not an object as such, but the
consciousness of an object. With this movement to self-consciousness, Hellenic spirit has withdrawn into itself and drawn away
from its world, a spirit which through its peculiar religiosity has set
its own worldliness into decline (*Untergang*).[29]

This means that religion, as it initially appears among the
Greeks, brings with it an as yet unresolved antithesis between its
own consciousness of spirit (its religious spirit) and its now passed-
by world-consciousness (its objective spirit). This antithesis is not
a simple antithesis, however, since it represents for religion a task,
an obstacle to be overcome in order for religion itself to be what it
is: the concrete apprehension and comprehension of spirit, as spirit,
by spirit. The overcoming of the secular/religious antithesis is a task
that falls to religion itself, a task religion is certainly capable of, according to Hegel, and a goal that is its destiny.

For the reasons just cited, the passed-by and hence declining
world-consciousness of the Greeks is, in its religion, equally
elevated and raised to self-consciousness. This world-spirit—with
its elements, the womanly hearth-religion and cult of the dead, the
public law-religion and the *polis*, the "beautiful totality" of true ethical spirit—is ironically set into decline, precisely as something
beautiful, by the advent of its greatest achievement: its architecture
and statuary, its festivals and games, its lyric, epic, and tragic art.
This art is not an isolated aspect of the Greek spirit; it is this spirit
itself in its actual consciousness-of-self as spirit. In the historical experience of consciousness revealed by the phenomenology of
spirit, what we innocently call "art" is actually the Greek world
knowing itself in a product of its own making, knowing itself as
this product, and embracing this knowing as its religion.

c) Tragedy as the consciousness of a religious conflict in Greek life
The advent of art, the Hellenic spirit in its concreteness, means that
the elements of its world-spirit are revealed as mere aspects, simple
abstractions which in their claim to self-sufficiency (the life of the
beautiful totality is fundamentally this claim) condemn themselves
in advance to destruction. It is not Greek religion which initiates
this decline. The religion of art merely signals this spiritual dishar-
mony because it is the consciousness of it. The self-dissolution of
the beautiful totality has already taken explicit form in the conflict
between the family law and hearth-deities of the netherworld
which govern the actions of blood relations, and the public law and
culture-deities of the city which bind each citizen through reason
and justice.

The aesthetic self-consciousness of the Greek world takes upon
itself the shape of this conflict. But when it takes on this shape it
has already surpassed it, for the Greek spirit is this conflict for itself only in the art in which it is represented, that is, in tragedy.
Tragedy is an art form which, according to Hegel, is a self-presen-
tation of the Hellenic spirit in self-conflict. Hegel alludes in this connection to, among other things, the *Oresteia* of Aeschylus, a form
of the Greek spirit that is not itself the conflict it describes but rather
a consciousness of this conflict, the self-consciousness of the Greek
world in decline.

d) Tragedy itself as a conflict between religion and life
As we saw, Greek religion is really Greek life in its totality and consciousness-of-self. It was necessary that Greek religion give this
self-consciousness the form of the work of art since it could only
join together the consciousness of its world with its consciousness
of this consciousness in a representation. But the identity of consciousness and self-consciousness that constitutes the heart of all
religion is essentially the knowledge of this identity. This
knowledge, however, is actually present only in *revelation*. The
revealed religion, accordingly, is "absolute religion."

Revelation is, of course, absent in the Greek experience of art;
the knowledge that unites consciousness and self-consciousness is
lacking in Greek religion. Therefore, Greek religion has brought
about—has represented—an aesthetic self-awareness of Greek life
which it is unable to unite with this life as such. It belongs to the
nature of Greek religion that it has engendered a conflict between

secular consciousness and religious self-consciousness, a conflict which this religion as art lacks the resources to resolve.

This antithesis is the *fate* of Hellenic life as a whole. It is the fate of the harmonious totality to be out of harmony with the consciousness of it. This totality is condemned to achieve beauty in its art at the expense of beauty in its world. This is why the self-consciousness of this world must be a tragic self-consciousness. When the Greeks come to represent their previously spontaneous (un-self-conscious) relation to the gods, then war breaks out among the gods and between the gods and mortals. Greek art cannot quell these conflicts; it can only depict them. In the end it can only alleviate the conflict for itself by making these gods and the human heroes they envy the objects of derision.

e) The resolution of conflict and perfection of Greek
    religion in comedy

Tragedy must give way to comedy. In this way, says Hegel, the "expulsion of these shadowy, insubstantial picture thoughts," which the early philosophers had demanded, first gets under way in comedy.[30] Comedy is the "sophia" which "philo-sophia" merely desired. Comic self-consciousness thus represents a certain satisfaction; it is a "happy consciousness"[31] which is contented because it has relieved itself of the burden of the gods, the gods whose art religion has put Greek life at odds with itself.

A similar movement takes place in connection with the hero: the sublime and terrifying *pathos* which gripped the hero and governed his actions in the epic has devolved in tragedy into the lowly passions. The hero is not moved by great purpose but by lust. He is not at the mercy of impersonal destiny, but at the mercy of contingent desires.[32]

The artwork in which all of this is represented is not the "drama" or the "play" in the modern sense; it is the comic actor on stage who addresses his audience as both artwork and artist, that is, both with and without his mask.[33] In comedy, the whole of the now declining Greek world gathers itself together and withdraws into this "spiritual work of art."[34] There it finds itself represented—comically, ironically—as nothing more than a moment of an actual spirit, that is, as existing only in the individual self-consciousness of the person who acts. The actor is one with the chorus and spectators; he is their religious self-consciousness. In this self-consciousness the whole community can play with the gods as the latter once played with them, can put on and take off its customs and laws as the actor puts on and takes off his mask.

f) The transition to revealed religion
But comic religion is only relieved of its burden—the broken Hellenic world—by finding amusement in it. Comedy is therefore an ironic self-consciousness, and though it is happy and at rest from its conflict when it has withdrawn into its element—art as show (*Schein*)—it is about to be made unhappy. Happy consciousness is about to become an "unhappy consciousness"[35] that is capable of grieving over the loss, and even death, of God. Unhappy self-consciousness is really the advent or initial shape of revealed religion. Comedy has prepared its way by reducing the gods of art-religion to mere representations. It has also prepared for it by presenting for us on stage the actual, individual self-consciousnes—the actor—who transforms himself by his mask into a representation of the whole of Greek life. The comic actor makes himself into an image into which all elements of the world-spirit withdraw and become conscious of themselves. He makes himself a *Vorstellung* in which the identity of the Greek (secular) consciousness of the world and its (religious) consciousness of self is represented.

The actuality of this union in the comic *persona* is about to be replaced by the revealed awareness of this identity in the incarnate God-man. Comedy is proto-revelation, the comic actor a proto-incarnation.[36] In comedy, the otherness of the statue, of the temple, of the athlete, of the hero, and of the *personae* of tragedy has fallen away. In comedy, spirit is for itself in itself. The actor and all those who behold him are aware that the spiritual substance which ruled the nation is only a property attaching to actual, individual human self-consciousnesses. In this way Greek spirit, although self-consciously decadent, has returned in comedy to a kind of self-certainty that "exhibits itself as an absolute power."[37] Comedy is a happy consciousness, but it is not yet blessed; it is not yet revealed religion. The latter is a blessedness because it can provide what Greek art-religion cannot, namely, the certain knowledge (faith) that it and its god are one.

4. The synthesis of revealed religion

a) The presence of Greek religion in Christianity
The oneness of faith and its object in revealed religion has overcome
the antithesis or conflict between secular consciousness and
religious self-consciousness. The Christian religion *is* this overcoming. But in Hegel's view, the overcoming of the conflict in revealed
religion is given only in principle; the reconciliation between the
religious and the secular must still be worked out. Accordingly, the
overcoming itself is something merely promised and so hoped for,
rather than seen. Faith is an earnest of this reconciliation, but the
reconciliation itself belongs to the future. Religious spirit is only
"present" to itself in absolute religion in some absolute (because
nontemporal) "future." Therefore the religious instinct of consciousness to withdraw from its world—the decisive mark of Greek
religion, an instinct which also left its unmistakable imprint upon
Greek philosophy—is carried over into Christianity as a conflict
between flesh and spirit, church and world, heaven and hell.

b) Christianity as the determinate negation of Greek religion
In terms of Hegel's phenomenological science, Greek religion must
undergo the skepticism and supersession he calls "the experience
of consciousness." In the course of this experience, Greek religion
is negated and its relative place within the life of spirit determined.
But the next shape of spirit, the shape that has negated it (revealed
religion), is therefore its determinate negation.

As the determinate negation of Greek religion, revealed religion
bears the negated religion within itself, just as the logical expression
"non-A" bears the negated "A" within it as part of its logical content. In Hegel's view, it is both logically necessary and historically
the case that Christianity emerged as an organic totality nurtured
on the art religion of ancient Greece.

The self-alienated consciousness of self which is found in this
pre-Christian religion—its deities and the works of art that fill its
cult—is religion in the form of a simple self-negation. In pagan
religion, spirit discovers a sacred self-consciousness (an infinity)
that is everywhere the antithesis of its existence in the world (its
finitude). Absolute religion, Christianity, is the negation of this self-
negation. It is the absolute self-affirmation and self-recovery of

religious spirit; it is religion that has faced the negation of religion and appropriated this negation to itself. The revelation characteristic of revealed religion is simply "Christ crucified," the negation of the negation of spirit. The incarnate Christ is the infinite gone out into finitude; the crucifixion is the negation of this finitude and hence the return of the finite to the infinite. Revealed religion is absolute because it has endured its destruction of itself, a religion therefore that has itself as its own result. Revealed religion is an absolute *synthesis* of spirit.

As a result of this synthesis, revealed religion is now spirit itself; it is the concrete totality and has Greek religion—as the self-alienated religious self-consciousness—within it as one of its moments. Therefore, Christianity too has a task: to overcome the latent conflict in it between religion and world and to overcome what is Greek in its structure and content. Unlike Greek religion, Christianity understands "salvation" precisely as a salvation from this conflict between itself qua religion and its world. Christianity consists in the revelation of this salvation—the gospel announces God's love for the world—and the "working out with fear and trembling" of this salvation in the world itself (Phil. 2:12).

By assigning this task to itself, however, revealed religion has taken over the chief problem of Greek religion. The appropriation of this problem signals what for Hegel is the finitude of Christianity, that is, the limit and deficiency of revealed religion as an appearance of spirit.

5. The presence of the past in actual spirit

a) The *Er-innerung* of science
The finitude of revealed religion consists in the fact that the accomplishment of its task is not merely its *telos* but also its *eschaton*—its final appearance, its end, its cancellation. Furthermore, because revealed religion is the last religion, the absolute and all-encompassing religion, its resolution of the conflict between the secular and the sacred also means the cancellation of religion as such. This cancellation coincides with the advent of "actual spirit"; the actualization of spirit as "science" (*Wissenschaft*) is this accomplishment.

As we have seen, the content of spirit's experience of self-alienation and self-reconciliation has been revealed to faith in absolute religion—that is, delivered over to it from an external source (grace). But this content itself is reconciled with actual spirit in its existing world (nature) and present age (the *saeculum*) as soon as this content can be deduced from the internal, logical source of spirit itself.

The internal source of spirit, the element of spirit's authentic self-relation, is the speculative-logical Concept (*Begriff*). Spirit recovers itself in this element by discovering itself in everything external to it. In this element it is able to make any form of itself it finds on the outside part of its inner life and relation-to-self. Hegel calls the process of converting the exterior to the interior—a process that is identical with actual spirit—"re-collection," or *Er-innerung*.[38]

As we have seen, spirit comes to itself by passing through the experience of religion and, finally, by passing beyond religion into science. Because this passage into science internalizes everything in religion that is still external to spirit, the cancellation of religion through science—or internalizing recollection (*Er-innerung*)—is equally a preservation of religion as spirit's curriculum. By means of this, the pedagogical content of revelation is imported into the interior of spirit. As a result this content is made deducible through the Concept by strictly logical means. At last spirit can derive, recognize, and possess—in a word "conceive" (*begreifen*)—itself through its own essence, that is, through the freedom and necessity of its own nature (the *Begriff*), rather than receive this essence slavishly and contingently in the attitude of religious faith.

The scientific rehearsal of spirit's journey through the whole compass of its experience—this "phenomenology of spirit"—is spirit's recollection and internalization of its past appearances, whether classical-pagan or Christian. This recollection therefore constitutes spirit's final return-into-self, its coming to be for itself what it is implicitly as such, its becoming actual as spirit.

b) The *Er-innerung* of religion
Each stage of this journey is animated by the Concept—the essence, life, and *telos* of spirit which empowers spirit to find its true element. Accordingly, the Concept is implicitly present at every stage of this journey. But spirit becomes aware of itself as a process of internalizing recollection for the first time in religion; religious spirit was already conscious of itself as an internalizing recollec-

tion. This underscores the intensity, the virtual infinity of spirit in religious self-consciousness in Hegel's *Phenomenology*, religion's inherent finitude notwithstanding.

Hence, religion is the self-consciousness of *Er-innerung*; spirit becomes *Er-innerung* to and for itself in religion. Spirit's consciousness of self as a recollection first appears in the Homeric minstrel's "musical" (inspired by the Muses) experience of the divine power of Mnemosyne, or Memory.[39] Later, recollection returns in the unhappy, nostalgic consciousness directed toward the same mnemonic power, but now as a lost and irretrievable world once borne of and now delivered over to Fate.[40]

c) The place of "classicism" in the emergence of science
This negation and submergence of the Muses by Fate means a withdrawal of the gods and a stripping of content from the poetry of Hellenic religion. The now-emptied spirits of Greek religion emerge for nostalgia as the abstractions we call the "classics." These abstractions, these bits of self-alienated spirit, are just those externalities in which spirit must learn to recognize itself, must internalize and make its own in a phenomenological *Er-innerung*.

In a commencement address "On Classical Studies," which he delivered as rector of the Nürnberg Gymnasium in 1809, Hegel reiterated and underscored the spiritual significance of an *Er-innerung* of classical antiquity.

The substance of Nature and Spirit must have confronted us, must have taken the shape of something alien to us, before it can become our *object*. Unhappy he whose immediate world of feelings has been alienated from him—for this means nothing less than the snapping of those bonds of faith, love and trust which unite heart and head with life in a holy friendship. The alienation which is the condition of theoretical erudition does not require this moral pain, or the sufferings of the heart, but only the easier pain and strain of the imagination which is occupied with something not given in immediate experience, something foreign, something pertaining to recollection, to memory and the thinking mind. . . . The demand for this separation, however, is so necessary that everyone knows it as a familiar and common impulse. What is strange, and far away, attracts our interest and lures us to activity and effort:

it seems to be the more desirable the more remote it is and the less we have in common with it. The youth enjoys the prospect of leaving his native country and living like Robinson Crusoe on a distant island. It is a necessary illusion to begin by mistaking distance for profundity; in fact, the depth and strength to which we attain can be measured only by the distance between the point to which we were fleeing and the center in which we were engrossed at first and to which we shall finally return again. . . . This centrifugal force of the soul explains why the soul must always be provided with the means of estranging itself from its natural condition and essence, and why in particular the young mind must be led into a remote and foreign world. Now, the screen best suited to perform this task of estrangement for the sake of education is the world and language of the ancients. This world separates us from ourselves, but at the same time it grants us the cardinal means of returning to ourselves: we reconcile ourselves with it and thereby find ourselves again in it, but the self which we then find is the one which accords with the tone and universal essence of mind."[41].

D. Conclusion

As this makes clear, classicism has nothing to do with the Greek experience of consciousness or with the Greek standpoint as such. Its "revival" of things Greek is not traditionalism, and its "return" to the Greeks is not a going back in time. Indeed classicism is a gesture of preservation, but in the context of an ongoing pedagogical movement toward the *telos* of spirit. Hence, classicism is not really about the old, but about the new; it belongs essentially not to antiquity, but to modernity (*die Neuzeit*). Therefore, both historically and phenomenologically, classicism is not only post-Hellenic, it is post-Christian. Classicism, in fact, is a pedagogical "humanism" (*studia humaniora*). Despite the dissonance and divergence of spirit between classicism and naturalistic science during the Renaissance, the principles of Hegel's treatment allow us to view the classicism of the Renaissance as the first intimation of modern philosophical *Wissenschaft*. If Hegel understands classicism as an "apparent fall back into childhood, but in fact a proper elevation into the Idea,"[42] then classicism is a shape of consciousness that has already moved beyond the problem we call "Christianity and the classics." For us this phrase speaks of the relation between biblical and nonbiblical worldviews. But Hegel's *Wissenschaft* supposes that these two have been fully synthesized and integrated in the experience of consciousness, a marriage whose issue is science as actual spirit, or spirit that possesses a reality equal to its appearance. According to the self-interpretation of Hegel's thought implied by the *Phenomenology*, however, this absolute self-related spirit is more than any synthesis—the historical order of spirit's appearance notwithstanding. Although we see the spirits or standpoints of Greek and Christian religion synthesized in absolute knowing, phenomenology does not present spirit as built up out of these elements. Greek and Christian religions are, on the contrary, abstractions from actual spirit, and their history is the history of their retreat into science as their actual ground. Accordingly, Hegel's philosophy—its standpoint interpreted in light of the *Phenomenology of Spirit*—is not a synthesis of Christian and Hellenic points of view. It is a free-standing, fundamentally self-contained "absolute" standpoint (the Concept) which claims to render these finite perspectives intelligible in their logical and historical necessity.

Notes

1. For example, see Errol E. Harris, "Hegel and Christianity," *The Owl of Minerva* 13, 4 (Summer 1982): 1-5.
2. See Helmut Kuhn, *Die Vollendung der klassischen deutschen Äesthetik durch Hegel* (Berlin: Junker & Dünnhaupt, 1931); Jacques Taminiaux, *La nostalgie de la Grèce à l'aube de l'idéalisme allemand* (The Hague: Martinus Nijhoff, 1967); Dominique Janicaud, *Hegel et le destin de la Grèce* (Paris: J. Vrin, 1975). Other literature on Hegel's relation to the ancients includes Hans-Georg Gadamer, "Hegel and the Dialectic of the Ancient Philosophers," in *Hegel's Dialectic: Five Hermeneutical Studies*, trans. P. Christopher Smith (New Haven: Yale University Press, 1976) and Martin Heidegger, "Hegel und die Griechen," in *Die Gegenwart der Griechen im neueren Denken* (Tübingen: Mohr, 1960).
3. Compare Sander Griffioen, *De roos en het kruis (Assen: Van Gorcum, 1976)*.
4. Hegel, *Werke in zwanzig Bände* vol. 18 (Frankfurt am Main: Suhrkamp Verlag, 1969-79) 320; hereafter cited as *Werke*.
5. Hegel, *Early Theological Writings*, trans. T. M. Knox (Philadelphia: The University of Pennsylvania Press, 1948) 324.
6. Hegel, *Philosophy of History*, trans. J. Sibree (New York: Dover Publications, 1956) 223.
7. Hegel, *Phenomenology of Spirit*, trans. A. V. Miller (Oxford: Oxford University Press, 1977) 413; hereafter cited as *Phenomenology*. Two useful sources on the *Phenomenology* are Jean Hyppolite, *Genesis and Structure of Hegel's "Phenomenology*

of Spirit," trans. Samuel Cherniak and John Heckman, Evanston: Northwestern University Press, 1974, and Werner Marx, *Hegel's "Phenomenology of Spirit,"* trans. Peter Heath, New York: Harper & Row, Publishers, 1978. For a recent survey of Hegel's work see Otto Poggeler, ed., *Hegel,* (Freiburg: Verlag Karl Alber, 1977).

8. Ibid., 493; together, history and phenomenology make up "comprehended history" ["die begriffne Geschichte"].

9. Ibid., 413.

10. This is the actual title of the book we call the *Phenomenology of Spirit,* the latter being its subtitle.

11. *Phenomenology,* 55f.

12. Ibid., 14.

13. Ibid.

14. Ibid., 51.

15. Ibid.

16. Ibid., 493.

17. Ibid., 14.

18. Ibid.

19. Ibid., 10: "Only by being worked out to its end, is it [spirit] actual."

20. See also Ibid., 14ff.

21. The recollection structure of Hegel's *Phenomenology of Spirit* recalls that literary genre of late antiquity to which the *Confessions of Augustine* belongs.

22. Hegel, *Vorlesungen über die Philosophie der Religion,* Werke 17, 188ff and 194ff.

23. *Encyclopedia,* 564; *Werke* 10, 372-78.

24. *Phenomenology,* 460.

25. Ibid., 461.

26. Ibid., 412.

27. *Encyclopedia,* 483-552; *Werke* 10, 303-365.

28. *Phenomenology,* 289.

29. Ibid. This *Untergang* is, from another point of view of course, the *Übergang* into another form of spirit.

30. Ibid., 449.

31. Ibid., 443.

32. Ibid., 449.

33. Ibid., 450.

34. Ibid., 453.

35. Ibid., 130-138.

36. Ibid., 453.

37. Ibid., 452.

38. Ibid., 17 and 492ff.

39. Ibid., 441.

40. Ibid., 456.

41. *Early Theological Writings,* 327ff.

42. "...[E]in erscheinbares Zurückfallen in die Kindheit, aber in der Tat ein eigenes Erheben in die Idee," *Vorlesungen uber die Geschichte der Philosophie,* Werke 20, 11.

Christianity and the Classics: A Typology of Attitudes

Albert M. Wolters

In this paper I will attempt to organize into a single pattern the various types of attitudes traditionally found among Christians with regard to the classics and represented by various figures dealt with in this collection of essays. My proposal is in the nature of a working hypothesis which can serve to highlight fundamental similarities and differences among advocates of a Christian appreciation of classical culture.

A. Definitions
The first issue is that of definition. What precisely do we mean when we speak of "Christianity" and "the classics"? Two preliminary observations are in order by way of introduction to this question. Both of the terms around which our discussion revolves are exceedingly vague and subject to age-old disputes reflecting fundamentally different worldviews and value systems. We cannot hope to formulate a clear definition of either category which will not be seriously disputed by many. Yet, we are condemned to equivocation and muddled thinking if we fail to make the attempt. If we discuss the relation between X and Y without stating clearly what we mean by the poles of that relation, we cannot hope to achieve helpful insight.

1. The classics
A number of different descriptions of the classics have been put forward, some of which are defended in the other papers. The classics have been referred to as a canon of literary works, as a tradition of

philosophy, perhaps specifically the Aristotelian one (compare the notion of *philosophia perennis*) or alternatively as the rhetorical tradition. Others have commented that the idea of classics has shifted from age to age. The classics to which Basil the Great was referring are not necessarily the same classics as those to which Christians in thirteenth-century Europe were referring or those classics appropriated anew in the Italian Renaissance. Prominent components of the classical tradition are ignored or marginalized in some versions but highlighted in others. Clearly the reception of Roman law is an integral part of the classical heritage and is an important part of it for Calvin, but the Romantics tended to downplay it. A similar point holds good for the ancient art of war which was of decisive significance during the Spanish-Dutch Eighty Years War but today is virtually forgotten even by classical scholars. The Roman state functions as part of the classical heritage for Augustine, as Greek religion does for Hegel. The whole concept of the classics, if subjected to a moment's scrutiny, appears so protean and amorphous that no single definition could capture all its shapes and manifestations.

For the purposes of our discussion (and this is a crucial qualifier), we shall cut the Gordian knot by simply defining the classics as "pagan Greco-Roman culture," and by distinguishing two main phases of its relationship to Christianity. The first phase refers to the period when this culture was in fact the ambience of a fledgling church, the cultural atmosphere which it breathed; the second phase refers to the time when an established church had to deal with the remains, chiefly the written remains, of an earlier pagan culture. There is, of course, a continuity between these two phases; it will not do to postulate a sharp break at the time of Constantine. Nevertheless, in addressing the general theme of Christianity and the classics, we must recognize that this issue takes a significantly different shape if the classics are a Christian's own immediate environment, so to speak, or if it is largely a literary tradition perpetuated in schools. In that sense Basil and Aquinas are confronted with quite different situations.

To elaborate on our proposed definition, it is necessary to point out that I mean it include all of what for a century or more we have included in the term "culture." It embraces Greek sculpture (recall the influential work of Winckelmann) and all other branches of the fine arts. It comprehends Roman law, astrology, medicine, mathematics, mythology, and military science. Its range is as vast as the subjects dealt with in Pauly-Wissowa's monumental *Reälen-cyclopaedie*, the great repository of *Altertumswissenschaft*. Classical studies, in other words, is not restricted to literature but quite properly includes archaeology, epigraphy, papyrology, numismatics, and so on. These are not simply auxiliary or secondary disciplines which can justify their existence only inasmuch as they contribute toward the reading, interpretation, and appreciation of Aristophanes or Cicero.

We must also point out that the significant remains of pagan Greco-Roman culture vary not only with each century but also from place to place and person to person. It may be reduced to a literary canon, a philosophical corpus, or an academic tradition. Perhaps, taking our cue from Kristeller, we may say that the rhetorical tradition constitutes the significant remains which defined humanism.[1] Each of these dimensions or components of the classical heritage can be paradigmatic for the classics as a whole. In the case of Aquinas, for example, Aristotle is seen as the exemplar of classical culture. From Aquinas's attitude to Aristotle, we can deduce his general appreciation of the classical inheritance.

A third comment is that the adjective "pagan" (i.e., beyond the pale of biblical religion) is a key qualifier in my description of the classics. It seems clear to me that the relationship of Christianity to *Christian* Greco-Roman culture, that is, the whole patristic heritage, is in principle a different problem. At any rate, for the sake of the general point I want to make, I am somewhat high-handedly excluding the Christian classics from the classics in general. The attitude of any given Christian thinker to pagan classical culture bears no necessary relation to his or her attitude to the culture of the early church. We are here dealing with incommensurate entities. This tallies, I believe, with general usage. The reception of Origen or Jerome in late Christian thought is not usually taken to be an example of the Christian appropriation of the classics or the problem which this involves.

A final remark about my proposed definition is that "Greco-Roman culture" refers to a *synchronic* entity, a complex of contemporaneous phenomena. Historians of art, or science, or medicine may deal with an aspect of classical civilization, but they treat it with a *diachronic* interest, as the antecedent of later, nonclassical phases of this discipline or specialty. To read Plato with a view to writing the history of mathematics is one thing, but to read Plato's works, including his discussion of mathematical questions, as the expression of certain ideal of *paideia*, is quite another. It is only in the second case that we are dealing with classics properly speaking, since we treat mathematics as part of a general cultural matrix situated in a particular period of history.

2. Christianity

The second pole of the relationship we are discussing is almost equally multiform and probably even more debated than the first. How shall we define Christianity? Perhaps we should speak of Christiani*ties* in the plural. It is indeed true that the forms of the religion named after Christ are legion, and it will not do to assume that there is a single steady tradition which relates to the classics in a consistent way. The very talk of a "typology of attitudes" presupposes a wide diversity. If the classics is a shifting concept, then surely Christianity is at least as fluid a notion. Nevertheless, there is an important qualifier to be introduced at this point. The factual diversity of Christendom does not exclude a normative conception of Christianity. On its own terms, Christianity is not to be confused with the empirical religiosity of its adherents. Different traditions of Christian belief and worship have often been competitors, each claiming to be more true to Christianity as it ought to be. Constitutive to the very idea of the Christian religion is some notion of a normative standard, usually closely linked with the person of Jesus Christ and the Christian canon of Scripture. In my judgment it is impossible to avoid some implicit or explicit criterion (whether it be called "biblical religion" or the "gospel" or the "apostolic tradition") by which empirical Christendom must be measured.

B. Classics and the Nature-Grace Paradigm

My main thesis is the following: the problem of Christianity and the classics is one facet of a broader problem, namely, the relationship of "nature" and "grace." These are the terms which have traditionally been used in theology for the problem we are addressing.

This problem of the relationship of nature to grace is fundamental to all Christian thought and experience. It is a confessional problem (in its developed intellectual form we might call it a theological problem) which is unavoidable. At bottom, it deals with two fundamental realities: (1) the new life in Jesus Christ, whether it is called "redemption," "the kingdom of light," "salvation," "the spiritual," "grace," or "Christianity" and (2) the reality of the old life outside of Jesus Christ, whether it is called "bondage," "kingdom of darkness," "death," "the profane," "nature," or "paganism." These terms are not all synonyms, but they all designate one of the two basic poles that we are dealing with here. All Christians have to deal with the primacy of the realities of new life in Jesus Christ and old life outside of Christ. This is a basic issue which all Christians cannot help but confront, to which they cannot help but give some basic answer, whether or not that answer is explicit.

The same issue crops up in many different ways. It can arise in terms of the relation of faith and reason, of church and world, of Christ and culture, of the sacred and the profane, of theology and philosophy, of re-creation and creation, and in many other formulations. All of these, I am suggesting, are manifestations of that one simple fundamental confessional or theological problem.

To return then to our theme, it is my thesis that Christianity and the classics is only one further manifestation of this fundamental problem of the relationship of grace and nature. Like the other versions of the problem, it is intimately connected with the way Christians understand certain key biblical concepts, especially soteriological categories, such as "world," "church," "flesh," and "spirit."

Like many other fundamental problems in the history of thought, the number of basic answers to the problem is limited. Taking my cue from the writings of the Dutch theologian Herman Bavinck and from H. Richard Niebuhr's little classic *Christ and Culture*,[2] I shall distinguish five basic paradigms or models which Christians have used to construe the relationship of nature to grace, and then relate these to the basic variety of Christian responses to the classics. We shall order these basic conceptions according to the degree of appreciation which each accords to nature in contrast to grace—from most negative to most positive.

But first we need to say a word about this slippery word "nature." When used in the present context, it has the precise connotation of natural life, often called the secular or the profane. It refers to created life outside of redemption. For our subsequent argument, it is crucial to note that nature in this sense has a built-in ambiguity or rather two-sidedness: it contains within itself an element of the good creation as well as an element of perversion because of sin. As we shall see this accounts, at least partially, for the divergent attitudes that Christians have adopted toward it.

I shall briefly list the five paradigms, giving a short characterization of each, and then relate them to a few illustrations of the attitude of noteworthy proponents on the issue of Christianity and the classics.

1. Grace opposes nature

The first paradigm is the one in which grace *opposes* nature. Here the natural is antithetical to the spiritual. This is the model Niebuhr calls "Christ against culture."[3] Grace or the new life in Christ is an alternative to the old creation. God, as it were, starts from scratch and begins anew. The old nature is already passing away and is doomed to complete destruction and annihilation. This is an emphasis which puts nature at its farthest extreme from grace. It depreciates nature more than any of the other paradigms. Historically it has been associated both with the radical Reformation and with dialectical theology. It emphasizes, as a matter of principle, the tension between nature and grace.

2. Grace perfects nature

The second paradigm is the one which probably has the most widespread adherence in the tradition of Christian orthodoxy: grace *perfects* nature. It is the model of the mainstream, according to Niebuhr, who labels it "Christ above culture."[4] The natural is basically excellent and good as far as it goes, but it does not go far enough. It cannot come to the point of complete realization of what it strives for. It is "imperfect" in the Latin sense of being incomplete, unfinished. It must be completed or perfected by grace. This view, usually associated with the official teaching of the Roman Catholic church, received its classical formulation in the work of Thomas Aquinas. It is also found in sacramentalist traditions of Protestantism. According to this model, nature is subordinated to grace in a hierarchical order.

3. Grace flanks nature

For the third model, by contrast, grace *flanks* nature.[5] This is the view that the natural stands alongside the spiritual as an independent realm with its own validity. It does not need to be validated or in any sense raised to a higher level by grace. Nature stands next to grace in its own right; it has its own independent significance. Sometimes this perspective has been called "dualism," but that term applies equally well to the first and second paradigms. The so-called "two-realm theory" of classical Lutheranism is the most prominent representative of this model, but it is also found in much of evangelicalism. Characteristic of this view is the juxtaposition of the "religious" and the "secular."

4. *Grace restores nature*
In the fourth place we have the paradigm in which grace *restores* nature. Here grace enters into nature in order to renew it from within, to bring it back to its created purpose. In a sense nature is here the goal of grace—a kind of reversal of the relationship as construed in the second model. The purpose of grace is to reinstate nature, but in order to do this it must oppose the sinful perversion of nature. In Niebuhr's typology this is the perspective called "Christ the transformer of culture."[6] Historically, it has been associated with such thinkers as Augustine and Calvin.

5. *Grace equals nature*
Fifth and finally we have the view that grace *equals* nature.[7] In this paradigm nature is itself salvific. Redemption is a fruit of nature. All sense of contrast, or even distinction between nature and grace, is here eliminated. Grace or salvation is the development of potencies already given in nature. This perspective is characteristic of much of classical liberal theology, including, for example, Ritschl and the social gospel movement.

C. Christianity and the Classics: A Typology
To return now from these rather abstract and theological descriptions to the specific issue we are dealing with, it can be shown that Christian attitudes to the classics parallel these paradigms rather closely.

1. *Overt rejection*
The first paradigm implies the resolute rejection, as a matter of principle, of the classics. The new life in Christ is simply incompatible with classical culture and must avoid it. The most radical and consistent application of this view is found in those Christians (many

monks, for example) who in fact avoided all involvement with classical culture, or rather its remains, and consequently had nothing to say about it. Another class of representatives of this paradigm are of more interest to our present purpose: they are the ones who overtly reject the classics or state their intention to reject everything about the classics but in spite of themselves assimilate significant aspects of them. We see this attitude illustrated in the story of Jerome, who had a dream in which the Lord addressed him accusingly as a Ciceronian. This is the Jerome who is still close to the ascetic ideal of cultural otherworldliness, but who nevertheless cannot help but be fascinated by the beauty of classical literature.

The best known representative of this perspective is Tertullian with his famous exclamation, "What does Athens have to do with Jerusalem!" Ironically the very passage in which this exclamation occurs is patterned after the best models of classical rhetoric. Paradoxically, Tertullian in his violent opposition to the representatives of classical culture interacted a great deal with them and was profoundly shaped by them. In the process of trying to demonstrate (in his *De Anima*) that every Christian heresy could be traced back to a pagan philosopher, he defended an essentially Stoic theory of the soul.

The same paradox recurs again and again. In the sixteenth century Castello self-consciously avoided stories of classical antiquity in the textbook which he wrote for the Protestant schools—but did so in elegant Ciceronian Latin. And his contemporary, Daneau, articulated his negative attitude to the classics by using the categories of Aristotelian logic.[8] This paradoxical feature seems to be a distinguishing mark of the first paradigm.

2. Praeparatio evangelica
The second paradigm sees grace as perfecting nature. As we noted, this has been the most widely used model and it is closely associated with the themes of *praeparatio evangelica* and of grace as *donum superadditum*. The former theme is mentioned by Helleman in connection with Basil the Great and by Verstraete in connection with Erasmus. The latter theme is, of course, the classical formulation of Thomas Aquinas.

According to this construction of the relationship, the culture reflected in the remains of classical antiquity already points forward or paves the way for the advent of Christianity. Under the providence of God, the classics prove to be a step along the way to the Christian religion. Use of the classics is therefore justified in terms of something extraneous to themselves; they are appreciated in an instrumental way.

We find the same pattern in the traditional Roman Catholic conception of a *duplex ordo*. The natural order is imperfect, inadequate, needs fulfillment. The supranatural order completes it, fulfills it, reorganizes it with a view to grace. Nature calls for grace and grace is the answer to the call, but in such a way that it supervenes upon nature as its crown or culmination. Again the relationship is one of hierarchical subordination. In this way natural reason is perfected by revelation, and the cardinal virtues of classical antiquity (justice, temperance, prudence, fortitude) are complemented and relativized by the theological virtues of Christianity (faith, hope, and love). Throughout, the emphasis is on nature's intrinsic goodness, qualified by a decisive "not quite perfect." Ultimate perfection is beyond the reach of the natural order as such. Christianity, therefore, has a basically positive attitude to the classics, yet one which relegates the classics to the position of *praeparatio* and *praeambula*. Against the first paradigm this perspective affirms, in the famous theological phrase, that *gratia non tollit naturam* but then hastens to add *sed perficit*.

3. *Classics as a parallel authority*
The third paradigm, as we saw, construes grace in juxtaposition to nature and has been particularly influential in the Protestant tradition, most clearly in the Lutheran "two-realm theory." In this view the realms of the sacred and the secular coexist alongside each other, each with its proper validity, but with no intrinsic connection between them.

A good example of this perspective is found in Melanchthon, who was, of course, a close associate of Luther. In his first commentary on the biblical book of Proverbs, he gives in the body of the text a translation of the Hebrew original and inserts in the margin equivalent sayings culled from classical authors. For example, in Proverbs 3:28 (*NIV*), where the biblical text has "Do not say to your neighbor, 'Come back later; I'll give it tomorrow,'" Melanchthon adds in the margin *bis dat qui cito dat*, the familiar classical proverb. Again, in Proverbs 30:33, where the Hebrew proverb has "as churning the milk produces butter, and as twisting the nose produces blood, so stirring up anger produces strife," Melanchthon's marginal insertion is the well-known Greek phrase *meden agan*. Finally, alongside Proverbs 29:20, which reads, "Do you see a man who speaks in haste? There is more hope for a fool than for him," Melanchthon supplies the classical parallel *speude bradeos*, the Greek original of *festina lente*, "make haste slowly."

There is something symbolic about the fact that these classical *adagia* are put in the margin parallel to the biblical texts. In the introduction to his commentary, Melanchthon provides a fairly elaborate theological justification for following this procedure of physical juxtaposition. He writes that the pagan sages attained to an ethical truth which is perfectly legitimate in itself, but they were ignorant of the fear of the Lord. It is the latter element which the Bible supplies as its specific contribution to human ethics. Apart from this component there is great congruence between the proverbial wisdom of pagan antiquity and that of the Bible. Melanchthon even adds, in addition to the marginal citations, an appendix to his commentary entitled *Dicta sapientium*, which gives eighty-five short *adagia* or aphorisms that further illustrate various truths found in Proverbs. The wisdom of the pagan sages has its own validity alongside that of Christianity. It needs to be supplemented, to be sure, by biblical teaching but not in a way which subordinates or depreciates the former.

4. *The* spoliatio *motif*
In the fourth paradigm we have the model in which grace restores nature. As we noted, this view has traditionally been associated with Augustine and also has strong ties with Calvinism. It is perhaps best illustrated by Augustine's use of the *spoliatio Aegyptiorum* theme as found in his *De doctrina Christiana* II, 60. In that context Augustine is defending the Christian use of pagan letters and cites the story of the Israelites who were commanded by God to take from the Egyptians all kinds of vessels of gold and silver as well as expensive items of clothing at the time of the Exodus (Exod. 12:35-36). These were later used, says Augustine, in the construction of the tabernacle for the worship of God. Augustine uses this as an analogy or allegory of the Christian appropriation of pagan culture, specifically the Greek intellectual heritage. What is particularly significant about this passage is that he uses the word *convertere* when he comes to the point of his analogy. He writes at the conclusion

of this passage: "[I]t is proper to accept and to have the goods in order to turn (*convertenda*) them to Christian use." A number of commentators on this passage have correctly pointed out that what Augustine means here is not simply transposing an Egyptian object into another context, but that it must be transmuted for the worship of the true God. In a sense it has to undergo a *conversio*, it has to be reformed in order to serve its new purpose. In any case, this interpretation is in line with the general project that we find in Augustine. All the riches of classical antiquity, notably Roman literature and law, are not rejected by him, nor are they put in a place of hierarchical subordination, nor are they simply accepted without qualification, but instead they are drawn into a great project of Christianization.

We find an example of this perspective in the seventeenth-century Calvinist Daneau, who undertook to reform physics on the basis of biblical givens. Aristotle's philosophy was not simply to be taken over but must undergo internal renewal.

5. The classics equated with Christian truth
Finally, we have the perspective in which grace can be said to equal nature. The four paradigms which have been dealt with so far have strong traditions within the overall context of orthodox Christianity. This is not true of the fifth paradigm. With it the newness which Christianity brings is a natural development of what is already given beforehand. Classical culture already contains in germinal form the new reality announced in the gospel.

As an example of this view I would like to adduce Marsilio Ficino, the animating spirit of the Florentine Academy in the fifteenth century. Other members of Ficino's circle, notably Pico della Mirandola, would illustrate the paradigm equally well, but we will restrict ourselves to Ficino himself.

Perhaps the best way to illustrate Ficino's view of the relation of Christianity to the classics is to tell the story of his involvement with pagan Neoplatonism, specifically the writings of Plotinus. During some thirty years of his life, Ficino was engaged in an intensive study of the *Enneads* of Plotinus, which he finally translated into Latin in the period 1484-88. His appreciation of Plotinus was very much shaped by the Neoplatonic conception of intellectual history, which presupposed a primordial golden age from which the religious and philosophical traditions of many nations derived.

One such tradition was that of Greek philosophy, especially
Platonism, another was the Hermetic tradition of late antiquity,
another Zoroastrianism, another the biblical tradition which gave
birth to Christianity, and another was the Jewish Cabbala. In this
conception, to use an often quoted phrase from the third-century
Platonist Numenius, Plato was simply "Moses speaking Attic." All
of these were variations of a single basic truth which was ultimately Christian in character. For Ficino this meant that Plotinus and
Christianity were eminently compatible.

It is telling in this connection that Ficino, during the time that
he was working on his Latin translation of Plotinus, was ordained
a priest and as part of his clerical duties began preaching in one of
the churches of Renaissance Florence, the Santa Maria degl'-
Angelis. It turns out, however, that the content of his preaching
was in fact an exposition of the *Enneads* of Plotinus! Moreover,
when his Latin translation was published in 1492 it contained a
preface which was originally his address to his audience in the
church. In the conclusion of this *Exhortatio Marsilii Ficini*, in which
Plotinus is compared to a second Plato, we find the words: "You
must imagine that Plato himself is calling out to Plotinus as follows:
'This is my beloved son in whom I am well pleased. Hear ye Him.'"
The quoted words are, of course, based on Matthew 3:17, Mark 1:11,
and Luke 3:22 where God the Father addresses Christ in these
terms. The effect in Ficino's preface, originally spoken in a Christian church, is that of virtually equating Platonic and Christian
truth. Plotinus is put in the position of a divinely accredited mouth-
piece of Christian truth. This is a thought which is echoed
throughout Ficino's writings. In his *Theologica Platonica*, for example, the Plotinian theory that the Intellect, or *Nous*, is generated
from the One as the son of Kronos is interpreted in the light of the
Christian dogma of the eternal generation of the Son from the
Father.

In general we can say that for Ficino there is virtually no sense
of a religious or spiritual antithesis, or even discontinuity, between
classical Greek culture and the gospel. The latter does not compete
with the former but is simply its natural product or extension.

This seems also to be the conception governing Hegel's treatment of classical culture in its relation to Christianity. As Rowe
points out, there is for Hegel a kind of necessary progression from
classical antiquity to Christianity. To be sure, this involves a fairly

radical antithesis, but an antithesis which is robbed of its sharpness in the overall scheme of things. Ultimately it is *aufgehoben* and becomes part of the necessary self-unfolding of the cosmic *Geist*. Here, too, grace ultimately equals nature.

D. Conclusion

To conclude this very sketchy overview with a brief comparison and evaluation, let me make the following comments. First of all, any such evaluative comparison must of necessity reflect the position of the evaluator and I shall not pretend to be completely neutral or objective in my analysis and assessment. Having said that, it seems to me fair to say that each of the five paradigms we have outlined can be said to have its own strengths and weaknesses.

The strength of the first paradigm, in my judgment, is that it honors the religious antithesis or spiritual discontinuity between the gospel and Greco-Roman culture. It does this, however, at the cost of completely depreciating or denigrating the cultural achievements of Greek and Roman antiquity. The second paradigm has the virtue that it does allow for an appreciation of classical culture but only within a framework in which that appreciation must always be qualified by the basic adjective *imperfectum*. There is always an implicit "yes, but" in the affirmation of the natural within the *duplex ordo* conception. Moreover, nature receives its validation from something outside of itself. In the third paradigm, the natural can indeed be appreciated fully in its own right but at the expense of standing in complete isolation from the religious or spiritual. There is here no subordination, but neither is there a genuinely *Christian* appreciation of the classics. As for the fourth paradigm, this has the advantage that it fully affirms the validity and legitimacy, in its own terms, of classical culture and at the same time gives a religious critique of its perversion, but it has the drawback of being fuzzy and imprecise when it comes to defining exactly what is creationally valid and what is sinfully distorted in the natural. The fifth paradigm, finally, has the advantage that it honors fully the intrinsic value of classical culture but does so at the expense of blurring the distinction between paganism and Christianity altogether.

For my own part, I take it as essential that we honor both creation and antithesis—that is to say, that we fully recognize and affirm both sides of that key category "nature." On the one hand, natural life (including pagan culture) participates in the goodness of creation and must, therefore, be received with thanksgiving. We ought, therefore, to be positive and appreciative of the cultural achievements of the Greeks and Romans in art, science, philosophy, law, technology, and so on. On the other hand, natural life (including pagan culture) is seriously warped and distorted because of human perversion and, therefore, stands in spiritual opposition to the gospel call to repent and believe. By biblical standards there is much in classical literature that is *to eba*, "abomination," and much in classical philosophy that is *moria*, "foolishness." It seems to me that from an authentically biblical perspective both the positive and the negative dimensions of natural life must be unequivocally affirmed.

Yet I do not mean this in a dialectical or paradoxical sense since creation and antithesis are not mutually exclusive. Properly conceived, these two basic themes are not in competition but reinforce each other. Because human sin, the antithesis of God's holiness, is at bottom perversity, that is, the perversion of the good creation, the negation of sin is at the same time the affirmation of creation and vice versa. A Christian appreciation of Plato's *Symposium* will negate the philosophical autonomy and sexual distortion which it embodies, but in such a way that it affirms the legitimacy, within the created scheme of things, of philosophy and sexuality. Conversely, to advocate *Christian* philosophy and *holy* sexuality will be at the same time to reject the distortions of these good gifts of God.

Thus it is only in the fourth paradigm that both creation and antithesis can be fully honored. By "fully" I mean not only radically and comprehensively but also integrally, one theme reinforcing and supporting the other rather than detracting from it. All the other paradigms, in one way or other, either restrict the full weight and scope of these two fundamental biblical teachings or else play off the one against the other. But the challenge is to conceive of both in their comprehensive integrality.

This is an exceedingly difficult position to maintain since there is always the temptation to simplify matters. It is much easier to reject the *Symposium* out of hand as pagan foolishness, to accept it uncritically as a glorious monument of the human spirit, or else to distinguish neatly between a neutral level of "nature" and a religiously sensitive level which transcends this. The fourth paradigm forces us at every point to struggle to discern between the creationally valid and the sinfully perverse and thus confronts us with a never-ending task which requires not only competence but also spiritual discernment. Yet this is precisely the task which we must assume, even at the risk of being vague on specifics. The alternative is to compromise basic themes of authentic Christianity.

Notes

1. As above in A. Vos's discussion of Calvin in "Calvin: The Theology of a Christian Humanist," 109-118.

2. H. Richard Niebuhr, *Christ and Culture* (New York: Harper & Row, 1951).

3. Niebuhr, op. cit., note 2, 45ff.

4. Ibid., 116ff.

5. Niebuhr calls this "Christ and Culture in Paradox." Op. cit., note 2, 149ff.

6. Ibid., 190ff.

7. Niebuhr refers to this model as "The Christ of Culture." Op. cit., note 2, 83ff.

8. As above in D. Sinnema's discussion of "Aristotle and Early Reformed Orthodoxy," 119-148.

Bibliography

A—General: A selection of books which are of general interest for the topics discussed.

A. H. Armstrong, ed., *The Cambridge History of Later Greek and Early Medieval Philosophy* (Cambridge: At the University Press, 1967).

T. D. Barnes, *Constantine and Eusebius* (Harvard University Press, 1981).

C. Bené, *Érasme et St. Augustin* (Geneva: Librairie Droz, 1969).

M.-D. Chenu, *Toward Understanding St. Thomas*, trans. A.-M. Landry and D. Hughes (Chicago: H. Regnery Co., 1964).

J. Le Clercq, *The Love of Learning and the Desire for God* (Mentor-Omega, 1962).

E. R. Curtius, *European Literature and the Latin Middle Ages*, trans. W. R. Trask (New York: Harper and Row, 1963).

J. P. Dolan, ed., *The Essential Erasmus* (New York: Mentor-Omega, 1964).

H. F. Fullenwider, *Friedrich Christoph Oetinger. Wirkungen auf Literatur und Philosophie seiner Zeit* (Goppingen, 1975).

A. Ganoczy, *La Bibliothèque de l'Académie de Calvin* (Geneva: Droz, 1969).

A. Ganoczy, *Le Jeune Calvin: Genèse et Évolution de sa Vocation Réformatrice* (Wiesbaden: Franz Steiner Verlag, G.N.B.H., 1966).

E. Gilson, *History of Christian Philosophy in the Middle Ages* (New York: Random House, 1955).

J. Huizinga, *Erasmus and the Age of the Reformation* (New York: Harper Torchbooks, 1957).

W. Jaeger, *Early Christianity and Greek Paideia* (Oxford, 1961).

D. Janicaud, *Hegel et la Destin de la Grèce* (Paris: J. Vrin, 1975).

A. H. M. Jones, *Constantine and the Conversion of Europe* (Toronto, 1979 [first edition 1940]).

M. W. Jurriaanse, *The Founding of Leyden University* (Leiden: E. J. Brill, 1965).

P. O. Kristeller, *Renaissance Thought* (New York: Harper, 1961).

H. Kuhn, *Die Vollendung der Klassischen Deutschen Aesthetik durch Hegel* (Berlin: Junker und Dunnhaupt, 1931).

M. L. W. Laistner, *Christianity and Pagan Culture in the Later Roman Empire* (Cornell, 1951).

H. Lehmann, *Pietismus und Weltliche Ordnung in Würrtemburg von 17. bis zum 20. Jahrhundert* (Berlin, 1969).

H. Lloyd-Jones, *Blood for the Ghosts* (London: Duckworth, 1982).

B. Lonergan, *Verbum: Word and Deed in Aquinas* (Notre Dame: University of Notre Dame Press, 1967).

G. Mälzer, *Johann Albrecht Bengel* (Stuttgart: 1970).

H.-I. Marrou, *A History of Education in Antiquity* (Mentor, 1964).

A. Momigliano, ed., *The Conflict Between Paganism and Christianity in the Fourth Century A.D.* (Oxford, 1963).

A. Momigliano, *Studies in Historiography* (London: Weidenfeld and Nicolson, 1966).

H. R. Niebuhr, *Christ and Culture* (New York: Harper & Row, 1951).

J. C. Olin, ed., *Christian Humanism and the Reformation* (New York: Harper Torchbooks, 1965).

M. O'Rourke Boyle, *Christening Pagan Mysteries: Erasmus in Pursuit of Wisdom* (Toronto: University of Toronto Press, 1981).

W. Oschlies, *Die Arbeits- und Beruf-pädagogik August Hermann Francke* (Witten, 1969).

T. H. L. Parker, *John Calvin* (Philadelphia: Westminster, 1975).

J. Pelikan, *From Luther to Kierkegaard* (St. Louis: Concordia, 1963).

R. Pfeiffer, *A History of Classical Scholarship from 1300-1850* (Oxford: Clarendon Press, 1976).

J. Pieper, *A Guide to St. Thomas* (New York: Mentor-Omega, 1962).

J. F. Quinn, *The Historical Constitution of St. Bonaventure's Philosophy* (Toronto: Pontifical Institute of Medieval Studies, 1973).

E. Rummel, *Erasmus as a Translator of the Classics* (Toronto: University of Toronto Press, 1985).

J. E. Sandys, *A History of Classical Scholarship*, (Cambridge: 1903-08) 3 vols.

W. R. Schoedel and R.L. Wilken eds., *Early Christian Literature and the Classical Intellectual Tradition: Essays in Honor of R. M. Grant* (Paris, 1979).

L. Schucan, *Das Nachleben von Basilius Magnus "ad adolescentes"*. *Ein Beitrag zur Geschichte des Christlichen Humanismus* (Geneva, 1973).

F. van Steenberghen, *The Philosophical Movement in the 13th Century* (New York: Thos. Nelson and Sons, 1955).

F. van Steenberghen, *Thomas Aquinas and Radical Aristotelianism* (Washington, D.C.: Catholic University of America Press, 1980).

J. Taminiaux, *La Nostalgie de la Grèce a l'aube de l'idéalisme allemande* (La Hague: Martinus Nyhoff, 1967).

U. von Wilamowitz-Moellendorf, *History of Classical Scholarship*. Intro. by H. Lloyd-Jones (London: Duckworth, 1982).

H. Zimmerman, *Caspar Neumann und die Entstehung der Frühaufklärung* (Witten, 1969).

B—Specific Authors

Basil

F. Boulenger ed., *Saint Basile Aux Jeunes Gens* (Paris, 1935).

M. Harl, *Origène, Philocalie 1-20, Sur les Écritures* (Paris, 1983). In the series: *Sources Chrétiennes*, H. De Lubac dir., no. 302.

W. Metcalfe, *Gregory Thaumaturgus, Address to Origen* (London: S.P.C.K., 1920).

N. G. Wilson, *Saint Basil on the Value of Greek Literature* (Duckworth, 1975).

Augustine

R. H. Barrow, *Introduction to St. Augustine "The City of God"* (London: Faber & Faber, 1951).

H. Bettenson, trans., *Augustine Concerning the City of God against the pagans* (Harmondsworth, England: Penguin Books, 1972). Intro. by D. Knowles.

P. Brown, *Augustine of Hippo* (London: Faber & Faber, 1967).

R. A. Markus, *Saeculum: History and Society in the Theology of St. Augustine* (Cambridge University Press, 1970).

F. J. Sheed, trans., *The Confessions of St. Augustine* (London and New York, 1943).

Aquinas

Thomas Aquinas, *Expositio Super Liberum Boethii De Trinitate.* Ed. D. Decker (Leiden, 1955).

Thomas Aquinas, *Expositio Super Dionysium De divinis nominibus.* Marietti edition (Turin, 1950). No English translation available.

Thomas Aquinas, *On the Unicity of the Intellect, Against the Averroists of Paris.* Trans. Sr. Rose E. Brennan, S.H.N. (St. Louis, Mo.: B. Herder Book Co., 1946).

Thomas Aquinas, *Sententia Super Metaphysicam.* Marietti edition (Turin, 1950). This has been translated by J. P. Rowan, *Commentary on the "Metaphysics" of Aristotle* (Chicago: University of Chicago Press, 1964).

Thomas Aquinas, *Summa Contra Gentiles.* Trans. A. C. Pegis et al., 4 vols. (North Bend, Ind.: University of Notre Dame Press, 1975). This was originally published as *On the Truth of the Catholic Faith* (Doubleday and Co., 1956).

Thomas Aquinas, *Summa Theologiae.* Blackfriars ed., trans. Th. Gilbey, et al. (New York: McGraw-Hill, 1963). In 60 vols.

Erasmus

Erasmus, *Collected Works of Erasmus* (Toronto: University of Toronto Press, 1969 and following years). Abbreviated *CWE.*

Bibliography

209

Erasmus *Opera Omnia* (Amsterdam: North Holland Publishing Co., 1971 and following years). Abbreviated *ASD*.

Calvin

John Calvin, *Institutes of the Christian Religion*. Trans. F. L. Battles (Philadelphia: Westminster Press, 1960). In *The Library of Christian Classics*, vols. XX, XXI.

Early Reformed Orthodoxy

Aristotelis, *De Naturali Auscultatione seu de Principiis*. Cum praefatione Doctoris Zanchi (Strasbourg, 1554).

Theodore Beza, *Correspondance* (Geneva: Librairie Droz, 1978/83).

L. Daneau, *Christianae Isagoges ad Christianorum Theologorum Locos Communes* (Geneva, 1583). With preface by Th. Beza.

L. Daneau, *Opuscula Omnia Theologica* (Geneva, 1583).

L. Daneau, *Physica Christiana, Sive de Rerum Creatarum Cognitione* (Lyon, 1576).

L. Daneau, *Opuscula Omnia Theologica* (Geneva, 1583).

G. Zanchi, *Opera Theologica* (Geneva, 1618).

The Pietists

J. A. Bengel, ed., *Gregorii Thaumaturgi Panegyricus ad Origenem*, Graece et Latine. (Stutgardiae, 1722).

J. A. Bengel, ed., *Johannis Chrysostomi de Sacerdotio Libri Sex*. Graece et Latine. (Stutgardiae, 1727).

J. A. Bengel, ed., *M. Tullii Ciceronis Epistolae ad Diversos Vulgo Familiares* (Stutgardiae, 1719).

F. C. Oetinger, *Biblisches und Emblematisches Wörterbuch* (Stuttgart, 1776).

F. C. Oetinger, *Inquisitio in Sensum Communem et Rationem* (Tübingen, 1753). Reprinted with intro. by H. G. Gadamer (Stuttgart, 1964).

F. C. Oetinger, *Theologia ex Idea Vitae Deducta* (Berlin: K. Ohly, 1979) 2 vols.

G. W. F. Hegel, *Early Theological Writings*. Trans. T. M. Knox (Philadelphia: University of Pennsylvania Press, 1948).

G. W. F. Hegel, *Phenomenology of Spirit*. Trans. A. V. Miller, (Oxford: Oxford University Press, 1977).

G. W. F. Hegel, *The Philosophy of History*. Trans. J. Sibree, (New York: Dover, 1956).

G. W. F. Hegel, *Werke, In Zwanzig Bände* (Frankfurt am Main: Suhrkamp Verlag, 1969-79).

Index

Vulcanius 121
Walaeus, Antonius 123
Wilamowitz-Moellendorff, U. von 12
William of Auvergne 70
William of Moerbeke 69
William of Orange 121
Winckelmann, Johann Joachim 51, 190
wisdom 18, 23, 33-35, 39, 45, 47, 48, 78,
    79, 84, 94, 105, 113, 114, 130, 134, 137-
    40, 147, 148, 155, 157, 198
Wissenschaft 162, 169, 183, 186, 187
Württemburg, state of 150, 153, 154
Wolmar 111
world 186, 190, 193
worldliness (see also otherworldliness)
    177, 178
worldly 177
worldview 16, 19, 28, 49, 85, 91, 100,
    132, 142, 143, 187, 189
Xenophanes 134
Zabarella 120, 144
Zanchi, Girolamo 23, 120-47
Zinzendorf, Count Nicholas Ludwig
    von 150-53
Zoroastrianism 200
Zurich 124, 131, 145
Zwingli 124, 144